331.88

D1251636

331.88
A769w

Aronowitz.

Working class hero.

Easton Area Public Library
6th & Church Sts.
Easton, PA. 18042
1983

NO LONGER PROPERTY
OF EASTON AREA
PUBLIC LIBRARY

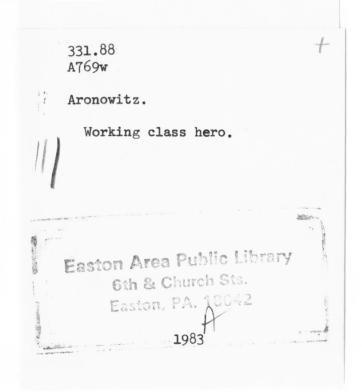

WORKING CLASS HERO

WORKING CLASS
HERO

A New Strategy for Labor

Stanley Aronowitz

The Pilgrim Press
New York

Easton Area Public Library
6th & Church Sts.
Easton, PA. 18042

331.88
A769w

Copyright © 1983 by The Pilgrim Press
All Rights Reserved

No part of this publication may be reproduced, stored in a retrieval system, or
transmitted in any form or by any means, electronic, mechanical, photocopying,
recording, or otherwise (brief quotations used in magazine or newspaper
reviews excepted), without the prior permission of the publisher.

Library of Congress Cataloging in Publication Data

Aronowitz, Stanley.
Working class hero.

Includes index.
1. Trade-unions—United States—History.   I. Title.
HD6508.A756   1983   331.88'0973   83-13120
ISBN 0-8298-0653-9

The Pilgrim Press, 132 West 31 Street, New York, N.Y. 10001

FEB 2 2 1984

CONTENTS

ACKNOWLEDGMENTS

MANY individuals have read the entire manuscript of *Working Class Hero* and have made valuable suggestions for improving it. Colin Greer performed the unenviable task of helping to structure the book as well as editing specific portions. It was his commission to write an essay for another project that began the process that led to writing this book. William Kornblum was a gentle critic who made me look at some of the more problematic formulations; Cornel West, Ellen Willis, Bill De Fazio, and Jon Weiner provided valuable support and critical readings. John Brenkman edited much of Part Two, which was published as an article in Social Text #5.

I wish to thank The Ford Foundation and its project officer for labor, Robert Schrank, for supporting some of the research for this book. Esther Cohen and the staff of The Pilgrim Press have been a source of constant support.

INTRODUCTION

THERE are two dominant theories of the labor movement, the heroic view and the instrumentalist view of the role of workers in society. According to the first, the heroism of workers consists of the task of transforming society—to abolish exploitation and hierarchy and establish a new social order based upon equality. Within this broad historic task, the working class movement is defined as much more than the trade unions fighting for the day to day gains of workers within the context of social and political change; it also comprises the major political parties representative of the working class; informal work and community groups at the base of society; and youth, women, and movements of national and racial minorities that have strong ties to the working classes.

The second theory has implicitly guided the development of American labor. Day to day struggle is accorded primacy in all actions of workers, and political action is merely an extension of the slow fight to win decent living standards and working conditions. Far from addressing history, workers address their own immediate needs. In the United States they discover through their activity as well as reflection that they can dispense with alien ideologies as long as the economic system makes room for meeting their demands. Further, the instrumentalist view more or less ignores the larger workers movement, holding instead that the trade unions are the genuine and most representative movements of the workers and that collective bargaining replaces politics as the major site of labor conflict. According to the instrumentalists, workers are not a class, but a series of groups that are constituted of the industry of craft within which they work. At best, the labor "movement" fights for the interests of its members, especially those recruited in the unions.

Working Class Hero is a commentary on the historical transformation of the labor movement and an argument for the idea that the conditions which produced the victory of the instrumentalist view of labor's social role have been superseded by economic and political developments. For most of my adult life, I was convinced of the heroic perspective and tried to conduct my daily life in its terms; I still find much to commend this view, but not on the grounds of historical inevitability, religious mission, or moral imperative. After thirty years of intellectual and practical activity in and about the workers movements, I have come to a somewhat different position: I believe the triumph of instrumentalism parallels the course

ix

of U.S. capitalist development and remained viable through the Depression, when the labor movement modified its perspectives to include political action, if only within the framework of corporate domination. Second, I argue that the old philosophy and ideology is preventing the workers, their unions, and the labor "movement" from solving their current and future problems. Third, I offer elements of a new agenda for American labor.

Working Class Hero is an outgrowth of ideas and observations begun in my previous book about American workers, *False Promises,* published in 1973. In the course of that work I was forced to break with a number of traditions of American labor studies—the most important being the assumption that the history of workers could be told adequately through the development of the trade unions. For left-wing historians like Philip Foner the struggle for employer recognition of labor unions as the elementary organizations of the working class constituted a reliable measure of working class political development.[1] American employer resistance to labor seemed, in comparison with Western Europe, particularly powerful and effective. Workers who attempted to form unions during the rise of industrial capitalism after the Civil War, not only risked their jobs but frequently lost their lives in the course of organizing and during strikes. Liberal writers focused on institutional history for different reasons: They regarded the idea that workers had a history separate from the institutions that represented them, the leaders who guided them, and the legal and political context in which labor functioned, as little more than the romantic musings of "workerist" intellectuals who refused to face the facts of American labor history. The inchoate worker, lacking education, skills, and other levers of power, simply could not make history without the benefits of organization. Unionism was the form by which workers achieved not only higher wages, job security, and protection of their work conditions, but also a measure of influence on society. For Selig Perlman, an early representative of this view of American trade unions, Samuel Gompers defined the objectives of the working class: labor's horizons were bounded by the search for a larger share of the economic pie.[2] Contrary to radicals for whom trade unions were the necessary first step in labor's inexorable journey to political and social liberation from the shackles of capitalist social relations, Perlman accepted Gompers's view that the labor movement was not constituted by revolutionary philosophies or utopian dreams of workers' autonomous social and cultural life; its task was to pursue the day to day struggle for economic justice—a "goal" eminently practicable within and not against the framework of corporate capitalism.

False Promises was deeply shaped by my effort to overcome the "business" union perspective of traditional labor studies of the left as well as liberal persuasion. I was not enamored of the tendency of the "new" Left to portray the history of American labor from below, as if the larger economic, political, and social landscape had little influence, except as a constraint, on the development of the workers movement. Although the new "social" approach to labor studies, particularly the work of Herbert Gutman, David Montgomery, Staughton and Alice Lynd, and, more recently, James Green, had paid careful attention to the character of workers' culture and community, it virtually ignored the influence of the growing mass culture of the twentieth century as an influence on workers' lives. But I, too, failed to address the relation of labor to politics. For us, politics of the workplace and the political struggles between the rank and file and union leaders constituted the realm of the political. We saw the history of the American working class in terms of the battles against employers for control over the labor process, and the fight of the membership to establish democratic processes within their own unions against an oligarchy that maintained control in an effort to bring unions into junior partnership with capital.

I did not share the optimism of institutional and social historians regarding the fate of the working class because I saw the disintegration of the old working class industrial culture in the wake of the partial eclipse of mechanization and the rise of the new cybernetic technology, which has produced new work relations outside the industrial traditions, such as Taylorism, male dominated shop culture, manual labor as the dominant form of work, and informal work groups. Further, drawing from my own experience as a union activist and full time organizer, I saw the growing bureaucratization of the unions and contended that a new type of union leader had emerged who rendered the formal democratic procedures of most unions archaic. If workers were unable to exercise power in the workplace because they were being displaced by new technologies, and the unions as mirrors of the industrial order were becoming increasingly centralized and dominated by managers and technicians, what chance was there for the rank and file to reclaim their unions? I argued that the only hope resided in the new generation of workers on the assembly lines in offices, and in service jobs. Influenced by the rise of 1960's youth culture, I placed my bet outside the unions, in the expectation that youth culture had penetrated the workplace and transformed working class consciousness.

I was both right and wrong—right because unions had lost much of their original dynamism, wrong for not recognizing that the trade union remained the only institution capable of defending and extending workers' interests, especially in times of rapid and devastating personal and social changes. I also underestimated the extent to which even the modest gains made by organized labor in the 1960's would be challenged by an alliance of employers and conservative politicians in the 1970's and 1980's.

Working Class Hero is in part a critique of my own earlier work as well as an attempt to overcome the one-sidedness of the three major schools of American labor and social research: history from below, the new economic structuralism and conventional institutional studies. My earlier evaluation of the American trade unions was influenced by C. Wright Mills's characterization of labor leaders as "new men of power" who had formed a three-part alliance with giant business and liberal governments since the 1930's. Mills's theory of the evolution of trade unions was oriented by Weber's theory of bureaucracy as well as his elite theory of social and political power. Although descriptively accurate, Mills underestimated, as I had, the fragility of the partnership. Lacking a historical perspective, particularly the extent to which the dramatic gains made by industrial workers and others were dependent on the dominant U.S. position in the world economy, I, like many others, assumed that the high living standards enjoyed by a substantial segment of American workers was irreversible.

In the era of long-term no-strike agreements between employers and large industrial unions, privately financed welfare programs through the union contract, and joint labor-management committees resolving problems such as technological displacement, work rule infractions, and other issues through discussion, Mills's thesis of corporativism seemed entirely plausible. Under these circumstances, unauthorized job actions and strikes, rank and file revolts against entrenched leaders, and other measures that placed distance between the members and their leaders often were the only means of regaining a measure of justice on the job. Some of my colleagues among the emerging generation of labor intellectuals concluded that the other arena of collaboration had been electoral politics, particularly the alliance of the trade union with the fraction of capital and professional machine politicians who dominated the Democratic Party. Even those who, lacking a political alternative, voted for the liberal Democrats in despair or declined to vote at all, thought labor leaders had committed a major sin by abandoning struggles on the shop floor for reform politics.

I shared this antipolitical stance: *False Promises* tacitly considers labor's participation in electoral politics an instance of corporativism for one of the major capitalist parties. This book constitutes a substantial change in my views of the relation of labor to politics. While remaining critical of the course of trade union political participation, particularly the refusal of unions to invent forms of independent political action except in isolated instances, my perspective on the reasons for this turn are no longer moralistic.

Recent labor and social history retains its historical perspective because it has not been able to grapple with the evolution of the working class and labor in the last fifty years. Jeremy Brecher (whose *Strike!* is still the best recent perspective on the actual struggles of workers for social justice[3]) treats the state and politics as constraints to be overcome rather than legitimate arenas for working class action. James Green's *World of the Worker* corrects earlier tendencies to regard politics as evil, but offers no new theoretical or historical tools for understanding workers' struggles.[4] For example, the passage of the historic National Labor Relations Act (1935), which provided legal sanctions for workers' organizations, receives no analysis, and the industrial union upsurge is portrayed as principally a saga of ground-up labor struggles in which trade union leaders play a more or less antagonistic role and the state tries mightily to limit union rights within a predetermined legal framework. According to Green, "the courts allowed unions to engage in collective bargaining over a limited range of issues, but prohibited them from using the kind of militant, direct action that had built the CIO." Rather than bemoan the compromise unions made with the state in the form of the National Labor Relations Act and its ultimate legalization by the courts, we must see it in the context of the actual movement of American workers. John L. Lewis led the organizing of unskilled and semiskilled workers in the most dramatic mass struggles in the history of American workers. But a fraction of capital "helped" the organizing by agreeing to accept a legal framework for collective bargaining. And Roosevelt, who recognized that the great crisis was not only the result of an economic collapse but also the fruit of an archaic political system, finally supported labor's right to form unions of its own choosing as part of broad political reforms that included minimum wages, relief for the unemployed, public housing programs, and a variety of other measures designed to ameliorate the effects of the economic crisis.

Many historians have separated the rank and file upsurge of the 1930's from the New Deal, others have attributed the great organizing drives of the decade to Roosevelt's efforts to forge a political coalition capable of undertaking economic recovery. *False Promises* contains both assessments without adequately linking them. The history of the labor movement demonstrates that the fate of labor struggles are as dependent on the shape of political relations as on the economic climate. It is not merely a question of civil liberties, although this issue is very important for deciding whether, after unions have been formed, the state will impede direct action such as strikes or whether it will employ repressive force to crush workers' efforts to achieve employer recognition of their right to bargain. In the era of advanced capitalism, which in the United States emerged in the late nineteenth century with the enactment of such measures as the Sherman Anti-Trust Act and railroad regulation, the backwardness of labor relations became an anomaly.[5] The New Deal not only provided civil liberties for workers' organizations but assisted them in preventing employers from abrogating these rights by refusing to bargain "in good faith."

The New Deal innovation in labor relations was neither exclusively a revolution from above nor the result of rank and file militancy alone. It represented a partial *defeat* for those capitalists who tried to hold on to an arcane system of labor repression. The alliance of the Democratic Party, the industrial working class, and that fraction of capital which was prepared to "modernize" the interventionist state, was forged primarily by the new surge of worker militancy. In these struggles the central role of old socialists like Sidney Hillman of the Amalgamated Clothing Workers of America (ACWA) and old conservative industrial unionists like John L. Lewis was to have insisted on the political character of the struggle for industrial organization. Those for whom reform is always a betrayal of workers' interests have portrayed this class compromise in pejorative terms, arguing that the self-organization of workers always entails a struggle against the state and its regulatory apparatuses. Others decry the failure of the CIO to form an independent labor party.

The American labor movement has not chosen the path of independent political action for a variety of specific historical reasons. One of the purposes of this book is to explain the reasons why American labor has taken a road markedly different from that of its European counterparts which formed labor and socialist parties. At the same time, contrary to conventional wisdom that holds to the view of the apolitical character of American unionism, I argue that the course of organized labor has been profoundly political. Further, rather than accept the shibboleth that union traditions may be divided between "unionism, pure and simple,"— a phrase uttered by the longtime American Federation of Labor (AFL) president Samuel Gompers—and social or political unionism, I will show that Gompers's indelible stamp on the development of the labor movement combines both tendencies: American unions have accepted the necessity of political action, although not the imperative to form their own political party, but contrary to the main tenets of orthodox socialist political theory, they have recognized the need to form temporary alliances with the state and capital.

Working Class Hero is not a new labor history; it does not attempt to cover the same ground as many other books, but instead is a "reading" of the main tendencies in the development of the American labor movement and an analysis of its contemporary dilemmas. It is also an intervention in the current debates concerning present and future strategies for the trade unions and the fate of the historic alliance that dominated the agenda of domestic politics from the mid-1930's to the late 1960's—organized labor, blacks, a significant section of middle class and professional strata, and a fraction of big business. It offers a new strategy for labor that breaks with some of its traditions as a necessary response to the economic, political, and social crisis facing the labor movement and the whole country, while at the same time disputing the claim that labor needs to abandon all of its past—especially its alliances with other movements and social classes.

The major premise from which I proceed is that labor has lacked a theory adequate to its situation since Perlman and Gompers. Even when the CIO mobilized millions of industrial workers in the 1930's or during the explosion of public sector unionism in the 1960's, labor in general refused to reflect on these changes in new ways and as a result, did not emerge with a new strategy capable of making the most of gains at both the organizational and political levels. And after Gompers defeated the socialists, labor lacked an ideology apart from a vision of his own contract union philosophy.

The elevation of industrial unionism to a doctrine provided the impetus for the split of those like Lewis and Hillman from an apparently hidebound, craft-union-oriented AFL. Leaders like Lewis simply extrapolated the *organizational principle* of industrial unionism—the idea of One Big Union of all workers and occupations in a single industry—from its revolutionary garb, adopting the form without the old revolutionary content and bringing the revolutionaries into the new movement because they understood its principles better than the conservative trade unionists of the AFL. Yet, the old notions invented by the AFL leaders Gompers, Peter McGuire, Adolph Strasser, and William Green remained in force: American unionism was never put into the theoretical and ideological context of social transformation because Gompers, the main theoretician of American labor, understood unions as institutions of *industrial citizenship*—labor's vehicle to achieve a greater share of an expanding capitalism rather than a means for opposing the system as a whole. Contrary to the usual charge that Gompers was, above all, a pragmatic, day to day tactician of craft unionism, I show that he was a self-conscious theorist for whom the constraints of the political and economic order, the real power relations of society, provided the framework within which labor must formulate its objectives.

To this degree, Gompers was eminently anti-utopian in comparison with both socialists and the revolutionary syndicalists of the Industrial Workers of the World who adopted industrial unionism as an ideological linchpin. As Perlman has argued, Gompers's theory of the labor movement was more adequate to the actual conditions under which labor was obliged to function at the turn of the century. The remarkable fact is that what I shall call *social contract unionism*—a theory of the labor movement that combines economic struggle with political action in defense of labor as a particular group within society—survived massive shifts in the occupational composition of trade unions, the entrance of radicals into labor's leadership in significant numbers, and the transformation of unions from a client of organized capitalism to a partner of the system. The tenacity of social contract unionism is explained by its ability to integrate disparate social forces within the working class in the context of America's rise to global economic leadership. As long as the United States economy expanded, Gompers's vision of expanding workers shares could be realized through struggle and compromise at the economic and political levels without placing labor in global opposition to capital. Even the breakdown of the political system in the early decades of the twentieth century, which gave space to an unprecedented and unrepeated radicalism in labor's ranks, was insufficient to displace his doctrine in favor of class struggle.

I recognize that my present position is, in part, constituted by the times in which it was developed, just as *False Promises* resulted from the left critique of the ways of seeing that had become institutionally fixed in the postwar period. 1967–73 seemed to be a period of profound shifts in the history of our country, especially in the character of social movements such as the civil rights struggle, the anti-war movement, feminism, and ecology. My hope had been that the truly radical impulses of some of these movements, combined with the emergence of a new political culture among large strata of youth, would produce a new birth in a labor movement that, for the first time since the early 1930's, appeared in need of profound renovation. I overestimated the attacks in the wake of economic crisis on even the modest gains represented by the coming of age of social contract unionism. Further, liberal democracy is, after all, a fragile achievement in a country that had granted the rudiments of industrial citizenship only a generation earlier, after a century of labor struggle. In this book, I take account of the conservative shift in our polity, the partial disintegration of labor's traditional base, and argue for a new alliance in which unions will play a major role but will have a different political and social complexion than the earlier New Deal Coalition.

Today, for the third time since the modern American labor movement was formed in the early 1880's, American workers, their unions, and their traditional allies face a major turning point that may determine not only the destiny of the labor movement, but of the country and the world as well. The old gains are under attack and with them the social contract upon which they were secured. In this time of crisis labor may elect to negotiate a new social contract in which the working class interest will subordinate itself even further to the interests of dominant fractions of corporate capital, or it may embark on an entirely new direction informed by the vision of the working class hero that is adapted to our own times. In this book, I am addressing the progressive wing of the trade unions and those who are concerned with building a new alliance that can transform American society from one in which the corporate imperatives dominate all other agenda. I intend this book to be a critical but constructive intervention towards revitalizing the labor left and others who are increasingly excluded from political and social power.

Working Class Hero is divided into three parts. *Part 1* is an interpretation of the development of the American labor movement since the Civil War. I focus on Samuel Gompers, the first president of the AFL, because I believe he was the pivotal figure in determining the direction of labor politics into the twentieth century and the specific configuration of trade union practice in the United States. In this section I will argue that, contrary to accepted wisdom, Gompers was the first advocate of social unionism while at the same time being the leading proponent of trade union voluntarism. My thesis is that there never was an articulated alternative to Gompers with a chance of success after the collapse of radical labor perspectives shortly before the First World War.

Part 2 is an analysis of the contemporary crisis of the American labor movement. Its main point is that the trade unions during the New Deal became the core of a new coalition that was able to set the agenda for American politics until the mid-1960's. The recent numerical and political decline of organized labor is a symptom of a profound change in American economic, political, and social life which in turn has deeply affected the shape of American politics for the past fifteen years. I have tried to understand what Walter Dean Burnham has called the "breakup" of the Democratic Party as a function of the growing marginalization of the industrial working class, and more generally manual labor, in the political and economic system.

Part 3 argues that the condition for rebuilding and reconstituting the progressive coalition is to revive the labor movement in new ways. First, I point to organizing directions for the unions, especially the urgent task of meeting the needs of new constituencies, some of which are far from the conventional conception of what the American labor movement really is. Second, I insist that organizing the unorganized is the same issue as the need to link the major social movements of critique and opposition to the dominant corporations—that organizing must address itself to feminism, black liberation, professionalism and the growing concerns of the middle strata with issues of social consumption, particularly ecology. Third, I offer a new political and ideological perspective without which the labor movement and the progressive alliance cannot be expected to revive; my point of departure is class struggle rather than class compromise—in effect, a new social unionism that is able to go into the opposition. In advocating this position my main emphasis is not on the morality of the anti-corporate coalition but on its political necessity and, more saliently, its feasibility in the wake of the decisive rightward turn of the liberal fraction of capital with which labor was traditionally allied. Fourth, I offer a programmatic chapter, not directed to a cookbook version of legislative alternatives but to three levels of actions: the absolute urgency of restoring the social safety net (the welfare state, the social wage, call it what you will); the need to provide concrete steps to shift control over investment and economic steering mechanisms from the private to the public sector without denying the importance of market considerations in economic decision making (a fundamental shift towards worker control, self-management, participation in the labor process); and the crucial significance of labor's participation in the so-called social issues, especially racism, sexism, and environmental destruction.

In short, this book analyzes past and present and advocates a political/ideological approach to a new future for the American labor movement and other forces of potential opposition. It aspires to making an intervention in what I believe must become a lively debate about the revival of the labor movement and the broad left in American politics.

PART

I

THE RISE OF THE AMERICAN LABOR MOVEMENT: AN UNROMANTIC VIEW

CHAPTER 1

GOMPERS AND AMERICAN EXCEPTIONALISM

THE CONFLICT OVER THE LABOR CONTRACT, AS IS WELL KNOWN, HAS PASSED THROUGH THREE STAGES. IN THE FIRST STAGE, THE INDIVIDUAL MANUFACTURER IS OPPOSED BY THE INDIVIDUAL WORKER. IN THE SECOND, THE INDIVIDUAL MANUFACTURER IS ENGAGED IN CONFLICT WITH AN ORGANIZATION OF WORKERS, AND IN THE THIRD, ORGANIZATIONS OF WORKERS ARE LOCKED IN CONFLICT WITH EMPLOYERS' ORGANIZATIONS.

(FINANCE CAPITAL) 1915[1]

THUS Rudolph Hilferding expresses the classical Marxist theory of the evolution of trade unions under capitalism. In Hilferding's view, the transition from the first to the second stage marks a dramatic change in the power relationship. In the first stage, the power is clearly on the employer's side because he can discharge or otherwise undertake disciplinary action against any individual worker who demands higher wages or a change in the work rules. But the founding of trade unions changes that relationship. According to Hilferding, "the function of a trade union is to eliminate competition among workers on the labour market. It tries to achieve a monopoly of the supply of the commodity 'labour power'. Thus it constitutes . . . a quota cartel."

The earliest trade unions were established among workers who were considered "skilled." "Only when it is a question of skilled labour power can a workers' organization succeed in curtailing production by taking appropriate measures." Until the turn of the twentieth century, trade unions had the power to curtail production by using strikes as the basic weapon of workers in their quest for better standards in pay and working conditions only among skilled workers. Even during periods of change, such as the rationalization of tasks that resulted in de-skilling labor, the unions retained their ability to disrupt production by controlling the supply of skilled labor power still required by employers.

The third stage of the conflict over the labor contract witnesses the formation of employers' organizations; now, the combined power of capital ceases to be merely a metaphor for expressing the economic and political orientation of the state on the side of the employer. It is not merely a question of an individual employer gaining a court injunction against mass picketing or enlisting the support of the police to protect non-union labor entering or leaving a plant during a strike. Combined capital has the ability to support the individual employer with such mechanisms as "strike insurance" guaranteeing employers their average rate of profit during strikes; the formation of large corporations' political action committees to finance political campaigns of anti-labor candidates; the lobbying on behalf of anti-labor legislation; the thwarting of union organizing by controlling the technical processes that govern labor relations, such as the enforcement of laws prohibiting unfair labor practices by employers.

Hilferding describes the third stage in the conflict over the labor contract as a point in time where employers regain the upper hand by means of a syndical combination not unlike that which defines labor organizations. But employers' organizations are not merely replicas of trade unions; they invest in changes in the labor process that reduce the power of skilled workers, or circulate a blacklist to prevent union militants from finding other employment when they lose their jobs because of economic conditions or trade union activity. Finally, in order to forestall workers' organizations from controlling the production process and winning their economic demands, capital has become highly mobile. International cartels of capital disregard national boundaries and make agreements to control patents, regulate prices, limit the supply of goods, and direct investment. While plants are decentralized across national boundaries, there is increasing centralization of control among fewer corporations. The prime example of this development is the advent of the "international" automobile. The number of car manufacturers has diminished considerably in the past twenty years, but joint ventures among former competitors located in different countries have become commonplace. The German firm Volkswagen produces some of its cars in the United States; so does the "French" state-owned company, Renault; Ford and GM, American corporations, produce in Britain, Germany, and Japan; Fiat, an Italian company, has important assembly facilities in Yugoslavia and has a licensing agreement with the Soviet Union.

Labor has been weakened considerably because of the globalization of production corresponding to the world character of capital. This weakness may not become apparent during periods of rapid expansion of the production and consumption when the national framework of conflict over the labor contract seems adequate for adjudicating disputes between employers anxious to maintain high levels of production and sales, and unions armed with considerable control over the continuity of production. However, during the long periods of economic crisis with which capitalism has been plagued since the First World War, the collectivization of capital on a global scale has forced the labor movement into a defensive posture at the bargaining table. Unlike the 1950's and 1960's, when wage increases were progressive and virtually taken for granted as one of the inevitable gains resulting from strikes and contract bargaining, the issue now is whether unions may win the *same* wage as the previous year or whether they will be forced to make concessions in order to protect jobs.

This represents a fundamental change in the bargaining environment, altering the terms of "conflict over the labor contract." The capacity of unions to represent workers' interests is seriously undermined by the degree of collective organization of their adversary—international capital. In many countries of Europe this new situation has led to new arrangements between employers and trade unions. In France, Germany, and Italy, trade unions, regardless of their ideological persuasion, have enlisted the state to redress the imbalance between capital and labor. Perceiving that economic inequality may be vitiated by the exercise of labor's political power, trade unions affiliated with worker and socialist parties and gained considerable power both in parliament and within the administrative apparatuses of the state. Consequently, in contrast to the first decade of the twentieth century, when Hilferding wrote his monumental *Finance Capital,* unions have found ways to gain power in the labor contract through such innovations as government mediation of labor disputes, the German "co-determination" giving unions some authority over corporate investment and marketing decisions, and tripartite industry boards such as those in France where the law has forced employers in certain industries to bargain with unions.

In the United States unions have pressed equally hard for legal remedies to the growing inequality in labor relations. Once hated by some trade unionists as an impediment to a free workers' movement, the last two generations of American workers have regarded the state as their salvation—not only against the ability of large corporations to mobilize government repression against labor organizing but also in a positive sense, as a provider of work and/or income during times when the capitalist economic system failed to provide jobs. The evolution of the workers' social and political perception of the state as an ally may be traced precisely to the historical moment when finance capital (the economic and political merger of industrial and banking capital) produced collective capital whose consciousness was now that of a *class* with broad interests, rather than a collection of firms competing in the marketplace on the basis of individual interests. The rise of the trade union, then, was more than an expression of the collective laborer, to use Marx's felicitous phrase. It was the signal for the self-organization of capital beyond the marketplace. In the era of competitive capitalism, bourgeois class consciousness was deposited in the ideology of its intellectuals—those who administered the repressive apparatuses of the state such as courts, prisons, and the political parties, as well as those who functioned in the ideological apparatuses such as the press, religion, and education. Thus, in order to demonstrate the allegiance of the state to capitalist interests, critics were obliged to claim that its "neutral" appearance was a mask for its deeper integration with capital by means of ideology. The socialists tried to show that legislatures, courts, and other instruments of bourgeois justice were structurally linked to property. The concepts of equal rights, welfare, and social justice were delimited by the motto that what was good for private property was good for the nation.

THE IDEOLOGY OF AMERICAN LABOR

At the end of the nineteenth century it was already becoming apparent that with the rise of the labor movement and its challenge not only to the profit rate but to the legitimacy of the capitalist system, the ordinary wheels of domination no longer sufficed to assure capital's hegemony over society. Workers were forming political parties which, however reformist their programs, were placing restrictions on capital's mobility as well as on the authority of its personification, the employers. To be sure, a measure of reform legislation was accepted by enlightened capitalists as a necessary corrective to the excesses of the industrialization period. Long working hours and low pay were reducing a large section of the working class to pauperism, a condition that threatened the reproduction of the worker as such. The employment of women and children, which employers had deemed necessary during the early accumulation of capital, was no longer needed in an age when mechanization was reducing the proportion of labor to fixed capital. Further the agricultural crises in Europe, as in the United States, combined with the pull of industrialism and urbanism to produce a surplus labor force that became available for immigration to the new technology which required vast amounts of unskilled labor. Labor reform was seen by some as a rationalizing instrument to contain the most "anarchic" tendencies of capitalism, just as state regulation of trade and commerce, public subsidies of roads and communications systems, and direct state investment in development activities were understood as innovations which, contrary to public perception, served capital's interests. But the formation of the Labour Party in Britain, the Social Democratic parties of Germany and Scandinavia, and the radical movements based upon immigrants and native migrant labor in the United States had a different significance. This new stage in labor's development, abetted, in part, by the process of monopolization of capital, further spurred capital's own organizations at the political as well as economic level.

Following the basic outlines of Hilferding's theory, labor formed its own political parties in Scandinavia and Great Britain, but only after a protracted effort to reform the parties of the liberal capitalists. In Germany trade unions affiliated with the social democratic movement; the party here was not an organic development of the labor movement as such, but a fusion of intellectuals and workers whose social origins as well as types of political experience were diverse. To understand better the socialist or communist "fusion model," a contemporary example might be the history of the recent Polish Solidarity union, with an autonomous workers movement making an alliance with intellectuals against the Communist Party and the Polish state dominated by it. Italy, Spain, and France followed a model closer to the German development: the ideological orientation of the labor movement roughly corresponded to the overtly repressive character of the state, but, more importantly, to the small scale character of production prevalent in these countries until well into the twentieth century.

The acceptance by the European labor movement of social democratic party formations corresponds to the emergence of collective capital. Labor forms, or affiliates with, a political party with a specific class-based ideology and program only when capital itself becomes centralized and begins to form alliances with the political directorate.

The United States had a course of capitalist development that appears classical from the perspective of Hilferding's theory. To be more precise, the period of competitive capitalism, or primitive accumulation of capital, combines with rapid industrialization. The American Civil War is a convenient event marking this combined development, although the industrialization process began in the 1830's with the founding of a modern textile industry and the invention of the steam engine. From a vast agricultural nation marked by small-scale production performed by artisans, the United States had, by 1900, become a major industrial power, its labor force fueled by a vast migration from northern, eastern, and southern Europe. By 1900, as agricultural production became rapidly mechanized, half the burgeoning American population lived in cities and smaller urban areas.

The modern American labor movement, which owes its ideology and growth to the small group of skilled trade unionists around the imposing figure of Samuel Gompers, faced exactly the same conditions as its European counterparts. Having swept away the last remaining obstacle to rapid capital accumulation, northern industrialists extended their wartime alliance with the Republican Party and constituted a virtual dictatorship of capital that lasted until 1910. The new power bloc of state and capital maintained free rein to develop transportation and communications systems with state subsidies, driving small farmers from the land; it instituted a free trade policy that not only insured the immigration of unskilled workers from depressed agrarian regions of Europe, but placed the United States army behind imperial adventures to secure raw materials from Indian lands at home and mineral rich Latin American countries abroad.

Perhaps the best way to illustrate the quality of unionism and union leadership before the AFL is to look at Samuel Gompers's own autobiography.[2] Gompers, who led the Federation from its inception in 1881 to his death in 1924, is the characteristic leader of this era, not only because he stood at the pinnacle of the union hierarchy, but also because he embodied the values of the artisans and craft workers, many of which linger to our own time in such trades as construction, toolmaking, and among mechanics of all kinds. Gompers was an immigrant like many others in the trades, but as an English Jew he had the advantages of both feeling comfortable in the language of his adopted country and being literate. Like others in the cigarmaking craft he was also an intellectual. Although formal education was sparse, the factory was, in the years immediately following the Civil War, a better university than those institutions that claimed the imprimatur of learning. As Gompers tells us:

> Life in the factory is one of my most pleasant memories. I had real joy in living. I took artistic joy in work and loved the daily intercourse with fellow-workmen. Shop talk was generally on serious subjects, but often it ran the whole gamut of personal interests.

In this passage Gompers reveals the differences between the small shop in the 1870's inhabited mainly by craftspersons and the modern factory housing thousands of workers. Whereas work gave him "artistic joy," the assembly line could hardly be described in those terms. Gompers and his mates produced the whole product; the semiskilled workers in the typical modern factory are confined to a single operation or, at best, a few simple tasks. The factory in Gompers's era was more than a site of convivial conversation and joyful work:

> In the shop there was also reading. It was the custom of cigarmakers to chip in to create a fund for purchasing papers, magazines and books. Then while the rest worked one of our members would read to us perhaps for an hour at a time, sometimes longer. In order that the reader might not be the loser financially, each of the other men in the shop gave him a definite number of cigars. . . .
> We subscribed to several labor papers in the shop. . . . There were at that time many pamphlet publications of interest to labor, and cheap paper covered editions of books. Henry George's *Progress and Poverty* was first published in pamphlet form. If my memory serves me, the George articles read in our shop were published in the *Irish World*. Whatever we read served as a basis for discussion.

Gompers studied the works of Karl Marx, Ferdinand Lasalle, and other leading figures in the International Socialist and Workers movement. As he makes clear in the Marx-Lasalle debates, he was sympathetic to Marx's position that workers needed trade unions to fight for their immediate economic interests as well as political action to prepare them for power over the state, whereas Lasalle argued that political action was the only valid tactic for the labor movement and considered trade unions aimed at winning economic concessions from employers futile. But Gompers never became a "Marxist." Rather, he found himself opposed to those who tried to impose socialist doctrines on the labor movement in the name of either Marx or the anarchist leader, Mikhail Bakunin. Gompers was among the earliest advocates of trade unionism as a self-sufficient doctrine. While not opposed to political action aimed at "rewarding labor's friends or punishing its enemies," he felt obliged to oppose those for whom the goal was everything, the movement nothing.

In the aftermath of the industrial union movement of the 1930's, historians sympathetic to the concept of social unionism as opposed to trade unionism "pure and simple," tended to put Gompers down for his opposition to the new industrial unionism. A careful reading of his autobiography reveals little antipathy to organizing the unorganized, whether skilled or unskilled. However, Gompers did oppose radicals within the AFL and, although the United Mineworkers, an AFL affiliate, had adopted an industrial form of organization, generally favored dividing workers by craft rather than uniting them in One Big Union, even within a single industry.

Moreover, Gompers's *social* unionism reveals itself as early as the struggle for the eight-hour day, the issue which established the AFL as America's most important trade union federation. The AFL campaigned for a national eight-hour law for federal employees, but "in private industry we undertook to establish [the eight-hour day] by direct negotiations" with employers. Gompers's reasons for opposing legislation for workers in private industry are worth reviewing because they shed light on his trade union philosophy:

> Several times the plain question has been put to me by members of the Senate Committee on the Judiciary: Mr. Gompers, what can we do to allay the causes of strikes that bring discomfort and financial suffering to all alike? I have had to answer "nothing." My answer has been interpreted as advocating a policy of drift. Quite the contrary to real thought. Foremost in my mind is to tell the politicians to keep their hands off and thus to preserve voluntary institutions and opportunity for individuals and group initiative and leave the way open to deal with problems as the experience and facts of industry shall dictate. I have with equal emphasis opposed submitting determination of industrial policies to courts.

Thus, Gompers's trade union philosophy is more akin to the doctrine historically called syndicalism than to either social unionism (the combination of economic and political action by trade unions to achieve incremental reform) or socialism. Gompers remained suspicious of reliance upon the state to achieve the goals of organized labor, yet circumstances conspired to compromise his resolve to maintain the voluntary character of the trade union movement.

The first event that was decisive in modifying AFL practices, was the fight to secure the exclusion of labor unions from those provisions of the Sherman and Clayton antitrust laws[3] that attempted to regulate the monopoly tendencies of modern business in order to maintain free competition in the production, distribution, and marketing of goods. In the second volume of his autobiography Gompers describes his intervention in the legislative battles to enact these laws as a measure designed to preserve labor's autonomy, not to signal a new era of labor political action.[4] Nevertheless, Gompers also gives details of the AFL's growing involvement in various legislative struggles of concern to labor. By the First World War, unions were deeply engaged in the legislative process at both local and national levels. When America entered the war, Gompers led the AFL into full cooperative relationships with the Wilson government's efforts to increase production and, as part of that process, to maintain labor peace. Gompers exacted a price from Wilson for cooperation—government assistance in establishing the basis for collective bargaining in some of America's basic industries, notably packing and steel. The AFL succeeded in organizing among packinghouse workers and entering collective bargaining agreements with employers. In steel, the AFL was forced into a losing strike in 1919, a strike that Gompers claimed could have been avoided if the organizing committee headed by John Fitzpatrick, the radical head of the Chicago Federation of Labor, and William Z. Foster, later to become the Communist Party leader, had heeded President Wilson's appeal to delay the strike in order to give his administration time to persuade the U.S. Steel Company to deal with the union(s).

Gompers entered upon the dangerous terrain of social unionism even as he remained philosophically committed to the principle of voluntarism, because by the turn of the century he had become persuaded that the price of abstinence from the political process would be gradual domination of trade unions by the state on the one hand, and by socialists and pacifists within the labor movement on the other. Thus, Gompers became an unwilling advocate of labor's new course—collaboration between employers, workers, and the state in order to further the national interest against threats posed by both the Left and the Right. Where in his early years in the labor movement Gompers showed, by the evidence in his autobiography, an uncommon respect for Marx's concept that workers must organize themselves into unions that can effectively lead the fight for economic justice for all, the later Gompers was to become a patriot and therefore a strong advocate of class partnership. Where in his earlier life he reveals a strong suspicion of intellectuals who seek to lead the workers down a path strewn with thorns—mostly ideological politics—the later Gompers became an open admirer of the most striking figure of the scholar in politics that America has ever produced, the Princeton historian, Woodrow Wilson.

Reading the autobiography, one is struck by the degree to which Gompers remained unaware of the changes in his own trade union philosophy. Although his career spanned the transformation of production from small-scale, artisan-dominated trades to large-scale industry dominated by a handful of huge corporations, the AFL leader remained a voluntarist. I suspect that the changes he pioneered in AFL policies towards state and corporate cooperation were imposed upon him by changing circumstances rather than ideological debate. For Gompers, the goals and program of the AFL remained constant, but the means to their achievement had to adjust to changing times. In the process he gave birth to industrial unionism within the AFL, adopting the IWW program (with some modifications to be sure); as I have already argued, it was Gompers who was the founder of social unionism, not the leaders of the CIO who tied its precepts more explicitly to the interventionist state. However, Gompers is also the leading figure in the development of what has been termed "business" unionism. Opposing positive legislation in behalf of workers in private industry, the AFL under both his leadership and that of his successor William Green, stood firmly on the side of bilateralism. That is, both were opposed to compulsory arbitration, factory laws protecting the health and safety of workers, and such protections against economic crisis as state-sponsored jobless benefits and social security. According to Gompers, winning these measures was the province of collective bargaining. Workers could gain them only by self-organization using the traditional tools of labor struggle such as strikes, job actions, and intelligent negotiations. For Gompers, the union combined the principles of fraternal organizations (an injury to one is the concern of all) with business organizations (the task of the unions is to secure the highest possible wages that the market will bear). Together with his cronies Adolph Strasser (leader of the Cigarmakers Union), P. J. McGuire (leader of the Carpenters and later the first secretary of the AFL), and Mathew Woll (a bookbinder who became Gompers's assistant during World War I), Gompers forged the radical idea that labor could only be successful if it relied on its own resources and that ideals which went beyond the immediate demands of workers were not only irrelevant to the workers' struggle, but detrimental to their interests. To this day, few union leaders have adopted unionism "pure and simple" in its pristine form, but remain anti-ideological much in the manner of Gompers.

THE TRANSFORMATION OF THE LABOR PROCESS

When capital launches its assault upon the artisanal mode of production, it first assumes the function of design of the product, thereby usurping the primacy of the craftsman in the labor process by stages. The transformation from craft to industrial production is one in which the power to determine how the commodity is to be produced is transferred to capital and its agents. Skill becomes subordinate to the machine. While in the first stage capital's power was confined to deciding *what* is made, it now is extended to *how* commodities are made. In the first stage, labor loses control over ownership of the means of production, which gives rise to a unionism that nevertheless observes the continuity of status. Just as the hierarchy was observed in the artisanal mode of production, signifying the power of master over journeyman, of journeyman over laborer, of adult over child, the early unions were organized in a manner analogous to the hierarchical productive organization. The masters and the adults dominated union organizations; consequently the demands of laborers (workers possessing no formal training in a specific craft) were excluded from the discourse of unionism, and the apprentice was not a person within the meaning of the term "unionist" because, as in the patriarchal family, children had no citizenship. But the apprentice and the journeyman were part of a system of domination in which honor of status was bestowed on all; laborers, on the other hand, were not part of the system of discourses of unionism or the labor process—they took orders but possessed no status because they did not "own" a recognized craft.

When Gompers and his associates formed the American Federation of Labor in the 1880's, collective capital had already evolved. Alongside an embattled competitive market for labor, and commodities based upon manual labor skills, a new monopolistic corporate sector had emerged whose fundamental technological practice was based upon natural science and the new pseudo-science of management and engineering devised by Frederick Winslow Taylor and others working to rationalize the labor process into simple units of repetitive operations. Taylor aimed at wresting power over the labor process from skilled workers who dominated in most industries until the 1890's. In contrast to British labor, whose traditions were powerful since they had survived the transition from feudalism to capitalism and had to be factored into the industrialization process, U.S. capital was abetted by the weakness of the native craft traditions. Still, as late as 1890 many skilled workers were recent immigrants from countries of northern Europe, especially Scotland and Germany. Their work culture remained relatively strong in such industries as iron making, machine production, and textiles. These were precisely the industries that were undergoing mechanization—in part because of the shortage of skilled labor but also because capital aimed to compete with the technologically advanced British textile and metal manufacturing for world markets.

The turning point in the struggle to make American capitalism a "world class" competitor was the Homestead Steel Strike of 1892. The strike was triggered by the Carnegie Steel Company's unilateral abrogation of its agreement with the craft-bound Amalgamated Association of Iron and Steel Workers. Carnegie did not object to the union, but to its claim to wage scales and job control based upon certain industrial conditions that he argued had become irrelevant in the wake of the introduction of new steelworking technologies. Therefore, Carnegie asked for a reduction of wages for steelworkers. When the union refused, it was forced tó strike. The Homestead struggle has several significant dimensions. It was the first major instance of an attempt by a craft union to retain its power in the face of technological change. After the union's defeat, its membership, which was 24,068 in 1891, or about four fifths of its jurisdiction, declined to 11,050 by 1900. Following a brief revival in the upsurge of labor organizing in the early 1900's, the Amalgamated claimed less than 8000 members just before the United States entered the First World War in 1917.[5] Second, the Amalgamated was obliged to reach out to other crafts, and, more important, to ask for the support of the unskilled and semi-skilled workers who comprised the overwhelming majority of the labor force in the mill. Third, capital had flexed its muscle against an entrenched labor union and won. The Carnegie corporation enjoyed the support of both its competitors and the state government which gladly supplied armed forces to aid in breaking the strike. To the leaders of the AFL, the Homestead case presented an object lesson: "This strike marked the decline of the steel workers' organization," remarked Gompers. "Probably one of the most injurious handicaps of the organization of the iron and steel workers was that the men who had grown up in the industry and the organization, and had developed a masterful knowledge of all its intricacies, matters of production, markets, prices, national and international had one by one withdrawn from the organization by offers of political position or to the employ of the companies and their representatives. It was not that they were corrupted, but they were weaned away." Gompers believed the strike to be the result of the rise to power of Henry Clay Frick as head of Homestead. Unlike Andrew Carnegie who had grown up in the industry, Frick exemplified the new breed of corporate manager whose origins could have been in sales, finance, or another industry, but who in any case lacked respect for the indigenous craft traditions. Writing at the end of his life, Gompers remembered the strike as a signal that the labor movement had a major problem "holding the lines" unless it undertook to organize among "groups that had been called unskilled workers. We inaugurated the period in which the field of organization was extended and developed the labor philosophy that there is no such thing as unskilled work *per se.*" Unfortunately, Gompers did not conclude from the Homestead defeat the necessity for industrial union-ism—an organizational form that united workers in a single industry re-gardless of craft; he concluded that "unskilled" workers could be recruited into existing craft unions which were organized along horizontal lines regardless of industry. With the major exception of the United Mine Workers, unions chartered by the AFL were required to conform to craft forms despite the obvious fact that the pattern of industrialization re-vealed the fragility of the old crafts in comparison to the new army of dequalified workers in the mills. For Gompers, "paralleling in the labor movement the centralization that was taking place within industrial (i.e., business) organization" meant forming departments of the Federation that brought together different crafts in a single consultative organization, the first example of which was the Building Trades Department. He suc-ceeded in persuading some groups of different crafts to voluntarily merge into a single union, but these efforts maintained the craft distinctions.

However, the AFL leaders did not draw Hilferding's lesson from the third stage of the labor contract. Gompers retained his hostility to the advance to independent political action by labor and he remained op-posed to the fusion of trade unions and socialist parties. His argument that such ideological alliances would reduce the flexibility of unions in the face of changing circumstances, ignored the fact that the old artisan mode of production had already changed. Gompers's meditation on the formation of the power bloc by the trusts and the capitalist state, is notable for its silence on the burning issue of labor's initiative in the field of politics. Although Gompers remained a *practical* trade unionist and pursued labor's goals by participating in the legislative and electoral process, the pragmatic, ad hoc character of these interventions constituted a tacit recognition that the power of capital could not be effectively contested. Thus, notwithstanding Gompers's references to the need to reject the notion of unskilled labor "per se" and the need for a centralized trade union response to the large corporations, the absence of a political strat-egy marks the fundamental difference between American trade unionism and its European counterparts.

Gompers took account of the formation of institutions of collective capital but defined labor's response primarily in terms of innovations in its own forms of industrial organization. Where European labor determined that economic organizations were necessary but not sufficient to maintain and extend the social power of the working class because of the intimate relation capital had forged with the state, the AFL, by refusing to accord primacy to the political in the era of advanced capitalism, moved in two alternate directions. First, it became committed to the bilateral contract in which the state was held at a distance, at least until the New Deal. This strategy was undoubtedly conditioned by the defeats suffered by various

AFL affiliates in the industrial field, but it also expresses the deep ideological suspicions craft unionists harbored of the state. Second, Gomperism is not the assertion of trade unionism pure and simple, if by that one means exclusive reliance on labor's own power in the form of the labor agreement with employers, but it does signal a mutation from the primacy of the political that marked European labor's evolution in the latter half of the nineteenth century. The American form of adaptation to the era of large-scale collective capital was a novel form of what I shall call *corporativism*—the assertion of the identity of global interests between capital and labor even if the conflict model of labor contracts remains in force locally.

AMERICAN LABOR AND CORPORATIVISM

Corporativism is a term that was mostly used to describe the relations between capital, the state, and labor under authoritarian regimes. Historically it was as the *ideology* of the identity of class interests, but a closer examination of the experiences of American and many Western European democracies shows its broader application. In Germany, Italy, and prewar Japan the formation by the state and the fascist parties of new unions to replace the older socialist and communist-led organizations did not, contrary to conventional belief, mean the end of strikes and other types of industrial conflict. Tim Mason has documented many instances of *authorized* strikes in Nazi Germany, just as Victoria de Grazia and others have shown that the fascist unions in Italy were not obliged to crush workers' grievances at every turn.[6] In fact, the regimes of both countries encouraged a measure of union independence within the broad framework of fascist leadership; the fascists frequently used labor strife to put pressure on capital to accelerate investment or to fall in line behind the regime. Fascism was a kind of command state where the "primacy" of politics over other spheres meant that the political directorate had to use persuasion as well as force to maintain control. Moreover, the overwhelming electoral support the Social Democrats and Communists enjoyed among workers in the fateful 1932 elections reminded the Nazis of the importance of winning the hearts and minds of the working class, and semi-autonomous trade unions were a means to achieve this objective.

In the United States, following the defeat of the coal and steel strikes of the early 1920's, some large corporations inaugurated a policy of "company" unions, employee representation plans, and profit sharing schemes in order to thwart worker disaffection which might result in declining productivity and mass unionism. These measures constituted an overt experiment in corporativism without state intervention and trade union cooperation. The National Labor Relations Act in the following decade outlawed company unions and provided legal sanction only to labor or-

ganizations that were organizationally independent from the companies
with which they dealt. However, to this day such giant corporations as
DuPont deal with "independent" unions of their own employees, despite
the efforts, at various times, of three national unions in the chemical
industry to secure affiliation of the DuPont unions. Although the DuPont
unions are nominally autonomous from corporate control, the paternalism
that has historically prevailed in this corporation towards its employees
makes genuine independence difficult to achieve.

Corporativism does not, however, entail the presumption of company
domination of unions at the formal level. It is the ideological and practical
alternative to the formation of a politically and socially independent labor
movement, and so a logical step that accompanies the inability of workers
and their unions to separate their interests from those of capital. Independent political parties are the major sign of labor autonomy in advanced
capitalist societies where parliamentary systems prevail, although adherence by the majority of workers to socialist and labor parties, the pattern
for all Western European countries, does not of course guarantee genuine
independence of the workers movement. Anarchists and other left-wing
libertarians have argued that the age of the interventionist stage, which
opens with the triumph of financial capital at the turn of the century,
vitiates the political and social independence of labor-backed parties, and
that true independence can only be forged on the shop floor. As is well
known, the forms of state intervention in the economy have multiplied
since the 1930's Depression. Not only does the state act as a capitalist
through steering investment according to planning imperatives, but in
response to pressure from the labor movement and other social movements among the underclasses, it is forced to become a mechanism for
income redistribution by increasing social consumption of such goods as
health, joblessness benefits, and old age pensions. The irony of the development of the welfare state is that its origins are deeply enmeshed
with the growing power and influence of the labor movement, but once
established, it tends to buttress the power of capital because welfare
payments of all kinds stabilize some of the system's most volatile elements. Further, the state becomes a mediator between capital and labor,
bringing both sides into line in accordance with the "national interest."
Since the Depression this "interest" is not only invoked during shooting
wars, it has also become the rhetoric of class compromise. The three-part
alliance of the state, trade unions, and capital is held to be the necessary
condition for economic recovery and the maintenance of prosperity.
Thus, despite the existence of mass labor and socialist parties among
Western European working classes, the system of parliamentary and collective bargaining compromises constitute a kind of corporativism in that
workers have accumulated a stake in the survival of capitalism.

This tendency has become exacerbated since the Second World War.

Socialists have assumed the reins of government without undertaking socialist measures, except to increase social consumption at the expense of private investment and to nationalize some industries, particularly those on the brink of bankruptcy. These are not small accomplishments, but they have raised serious questions about the classical theories of the labor movement that equate the formation of independent working class parties with genuine ideological or political independence.

Two Parties, Not Three

In the United States, there has never been a serious question about the possibility of organizing an independent labor party or a party in which labor would play a prominent role. Although there are clear parallels between the United States and European political development (the triumph of welfare capitalism after 1933, the key role played by the unions in the New Deal coalition and its successors within the Democratic Party), the tendency of most students of the labor movement since Werner Sombart's 1906 monograph, "Why No Socialism in the United States," has been to focus on the differences between the two. Sombart argued that the monopoly of the two major parties over political debate and choices was determined by the peculiarities of the American political system, chiefly the United States Constitution that embodied "radical-democratic principles" in which the will of the majority is the most important. To this basic ideological influence Sombart attributes the effective urban political machines, the large corporate contributions to both parties, and the willingness of the party in power to offer office and prestige in councils of state to labor leaders. Finally, Sombart asks the reader to abandon European conceptions of political parties as class representatives when analyzing the United States, arguing that the two major American parties are coalitions of various classes and groups which, in principle as well as practice, can incorporate disparate, even opposing elements.

However prescient Sombart's observations, they did not seem so obvious to trade unionists and socialists, nor did employers and politicians share his confidence that third parties were doomed by structurally determined factors in American history. In the first decade of the twentieth century the question of class struggle unionism was high on the agenda of the AFL; a coalition of socialists and populist unions opposed Gompers at the 1908 and 1911 conventions. A major issue was the need for a labor party to meet capital on its most powerful ground—in the electoral arena. Another concerned the membership of Gompers, John Mitchell of the Miners, and fourteen other labor representatives on the executive committee of the National Civic Federation, an organization founded by Andrew Carnegie and other big employers to find a better path to labor peace. Prompted by the renewed surge of labor militancy at the turn of the century, notably the Miners strike of 1902 and the rail and steel strikes of the 1890's the Civic Federation was a tripartite organization in which civic and social reformers, employers and union leaders comprised the leadership. Since American ideology had not admitted the reality of the intimate involvement of the state with the economy—the watchman image of government still held sway in the popular imagination—the concept of the "public" substituted for the state as the third partner. Labor radicals opposed Gompers and his associates' membership in this blatant effort to find grounds for labor-management cooperation and especially objected to the Civic Federation's self-proclaimed role as a mediator in labor disputes. Gompers was sensitive to the criticism made by socialists who, he said, "were so ardent to take the world by storm at the ballot box that they preached without cessation the doctrine of irreconcilable interests to secure betterment under the existing industrial order." The 1911 Atlanta convention rejected a socialist-sponsored resolution to force officers and members of the AFL to withdraw from the Civic Federation, but this action did not quell the growing conflict between Gompers and the Left.

Gompers had concluded that an independent labor or socialist party was out of the question for the trade union movement, but was aware that class conflict was on the rise. His associate Adolph Strasser's program of day to day struggle and Gompers's own formulae for labor's goals, "more," were clearly inadequate to the new situation. Although Gompers held tenaciously to his doctrine of voluntarism until his death in 1924, the final twenty years of his rule over the AFL were marked by a sharp turn towards corporativism. Joining the NCF, offering full cooperation to President Wilson's call for labor participation in the war effort to boost production, and his growing attacks on socialism and socialists revealed a different Gompers from the image projected by his epigones as well as by his detractors. By 1900 Gompers was well on the way to social unionism. Contract union principles were not abandoned; the bilateral agreement between labor and capital was still the chief vehicle through which labor's economic needs should be met and its demand for social justice realized. But Gompers now perceived the labor movement in the context of industrial progress in which enlightened employers played an important part.

Gompers's social unionism did not evolve in a political vacuum. First, in 1905 the IWW was founded as an explicitly revolutionary union, an alliance of some members of the Socialist Party, dissident trade unionists (particularly the Western Federation of Miners), and radical intellectuals such as Daniel De Leon. Many outstanding socialists in the AFL were no less hostile to the new union than Gompers himself, but the movement within the AFL for a policy of class struggle, a labor party, and industrial unionism enjoyed the support of perhaps a third of the affiliates of the

Federation. Gompers retained control but faced a mounting challenge both to his personal leadership of the AFL and his policies of class compromise.

Second, the Socialist Party had been founded in 1901 as a broad coalition of various groups which had become disenchanted with the sectarian policies of Daniel De Leon's Socialist Labor Party. After an inauspicious start, its electoral successes, especially at the local level, became more menacing to the two major parties after 1908. Between 1908 and 1912, the party elected hundreds of local officials, including mayors, in medium-sized cities such as Bridgeport, Connecticut; Schenectady, New York; and dozens of smaller communities in the Midwest and Southwest, especially Oklahoma where it elected over 300 local officials. It dominated Milwaukee politics until well into the 1950's and Eugene Debs gathered 900,000 votes or 6% of the ballot in the four-way presidential election of 1912 which Wilson won.

Gompers's turn to corporativism, which by the First World War entailed an open and close alliance with the Wilson administration, was influenced by the pressure exerted by radicals within the Federation and the growing weight of the Socialist Party as well as the visible and dramatic industrial organizing of the IWW. By the war, the concept of the "general interest" had been elevated to the level of doctrine and guided the labor movement, although labor retained its independent class organizations. Gompers was no longer the outspoken proponent of labor parochialism, nor did voluntarism actually guide his everyday actions as AFL president. He recognized that unions had a major role in shaping the national destiny; its concerns were first to protect the interests of union members, but since capitalism was being challenged at home and abroad, workers were obliged to choose between class war and class compromise.

Thus, Gompers was an architect of a new labor philosophy that tacitly recognized the unique position of American capitalism in the world market and tied labor's fate to its growing hegemony. The phrase "if you can't fight 'em, join 'em" best describes what Gompers learned from the two decades of turbulent labor struggles at the turn of the century. The old program of the AFL founders, which tried to establish a monopoly on the supply of labor in order to raise its price, was now placed in larger framework. If the AFL did not aggressively organize the masses of unskilled industrial workers, others would occupy that space and threaten the chance for industrial stability—and the entire social order. If business leaders were unwilling to compromise to achieve needed social reforms such as the abolition of child labor, immigration restrictions to protect "native" labor, and control over factory health conditions, the radicals would be correct in their "ardent" advocacy of class warfare. Moreover, capital would have to swallow a harder pill: employers must abandon their irreconcilable opposition to trade unions, especially in large-scale industry. Employees would have to sacrifice the time-tested doctrine of the free market for labor in the interest of industrial stability.

The NCF was the representative of a fraction of capital that was prepared to enter the social process as intellectuals and social reformers rather than permit the entire system to degenerate in unceasing industrial strife. It was a visible indication that capital had begun to create its own intellectuals beyond the formation of a stratum of managers who were structurally separated from ownership of the enterprise. Surely, managerial expertise may be considered the earliest form of specifically capitalist knowledge—the ideas of Frederick Winslow Taylor for reorganizing the labor process were a kind of intellectual labor; similarly, the appearance of a specifically administrative model for the coordination of production and distribution, the achievement of the railroad industry in the nineteenth century, entailed the development of a layer of knowledgeable employees whose profession was the coordination of people and things.

The NCF had a different intellectual form from that in industrial enterprises. It embodied a proposed reorganization of social relations on the basis of cooperation. It was a movement of ideas generated from above, a development completely unanticipated by conventional social and political theory which could account for labor unions, employer associations, and social reform movements, but not for their mutual integration. Equally important, the idea that a proto-state could be established without the active participation of government was beyond the experience of the previous centuries of capitalist development. Moreover, the new intellectuals were recruited from among corporate managers like Gerard Swope of General Electric, traditional intellectuals such as Herbert Croly, religionists such as Walter Rauchenbush whose socialism was tempered by his advocacy of social peace, and above all the legions of women social reformers (of which Jane Addams was a representative figure), many of whom were born of the ruling classes and devoted their lives to ameliorating the conditions of both working people and women. In the tripartite relationship established by the NCF, labor was no longer viewed as the bipolar interest in society opposing capital at the other pole. The "public" was created as a third party with its own consumer interests, since the syndicate of labor and capital, if left to itself, would surely result in a new form of injustice against those with weak levers of economic power—the *old* middle class of farmers, small shopkeepers, and professions; the *new* middle class of salaried professional and technical employees; and workers outside the unions. Later, the state was invested with the mantle of the public interest, a distinction that signified the integration of economic and military security issues, but in the early 1900's a "private" public interest acted as a surrogate for the mediating

role of the state. The "public" became the active overseer of social, political, and economic life, and a myriad of "citizens" commissions dealing
with various aspects of social policy sprung up around the country. At the
local level, these organizations became vehicles for municipal reform;
charter commissions rewrote state and city constitutions to provide a
countervailing legal framework against the urban machines. The contrast
with Europe is quite startling. Even in the relatively conservative British
environment, the capital-labor conflict extended to the parliamentary
level. By 1900, it was clear that the Liberals, the party of the old middle
class, were no longer able to represent worker interests, but had been
subsumed by the main capitalist party, the Conservatives. No such
clarification was possible in the United States, in part because a fraction of
capital sought grounds for a class compromise. In addition, the Gompers
strategy of seeking a share in a noticeably expanding pie seemed eminently more reasonable than the ardent pursuit of class war in an environment in which fragmented immigrant labor increasingly dominated the
new industrial workplaces, while the liberal middle-class activists and
intellectuals tended to side with labor's program of economic and social
justice and provided leverage for substantial victories in state legislatures,
if not Congress. Even though not yet in a position to organize the unorganized in basic industries, Gompers achieved hegemony within the
labor movement. He convinced industry and middle-class activists that
labor was an important economic and social group in society, but not a
separate class with its own ideology and political party that constituted
the basic binary of the social structure. Labor leadership became oriented
to forging a new partnership between trade unions and those sections of
the political directorate and capitalist class able to envision a society based
upon social justice within the framework of the prevailing order, although
this strategy of class partnership and social compromise by no means
precluded intense economic struggles of a traditional kind.

The labor movement moved closer to capital after 1910. As a broad
generalization, the "conflict" model of labor and industrial relations has
not predominated in struggles over the labor contract in this country
since the early 1920's. Even during the industrial union upsurge in the
1930's, union militancy was focused on gaining recognition from employers to be permitted to wage the struggle for social justice for unskilled
and semiskilled workers within the framework of the prevailing social
order. The most farsighted union leaders were less interested in "class
struggle," however much they were obliged to employ its codes, than in
the new codes of cooperation and compromise. As C. Wright Mills per-
ceptively noted, labor leaders became the "new men of power" within an
emerging industrial relations order in which they took their places as
junior partners of the state and the largest corporations. "The labor leader
who has gained the heights becomes a labor spokesman; like other

spokesmen, following the principle of expediency and searching for the main change, he needs a language for his contracts. . . . The language he speaks is the language of liberalism." He went on:

> Co-operative relations between business and labor are rooted in the desire for peace and stability on the part of businessmen, labor leaders and political officials. Such desires, with their monopolistic consequences, were back of the citywide labor-business cartel. Now, on a much larger scale, with consequences that go beyond pure and simple monopoly, a tacit sort of plan to stabilize the political economy of the U.S. is back of many current demands of the spokesmen of the three powerful bureaucracies in the U.S. political economy.[7]

CHAPTER 2

WHAT LABOR LEADERS DO

THE craft union tradition from which most of the major leaders of American unions emanated has frequently been represented exclusively as a conservative brake on the development of a militant working class movement. Indeed, in the era when industrial unionism as an ideology contested the common sense that only workers possessing skills could effectively form strong unions capable of resisting employers, the major debate was whether unskilled workers could achieve power in the workplace on their own. Of course, the AFL leadership was also ensconced in racist doubts as to the capacities of black and immigrant workers to form viable organizations and opposed the entrance of women into the wage labor force as a threat to male workers. Although Gompers himself did not share the egregious opinions of many of his colleagues, he offered unionism to the unskilled only on terms consistent with craft traditions. He believed the culture of skill remained the best hope for strong trade unions and this faith was rooted in a long history of labor struggle. Craft workers were able to exercise power to the extent that they could control the supply of labor available to employers by means of an apprenticeship system that certified which workers were to be considered truly part of the craft. Apprenticeship was a system through which a historical culture was transmitted even more than a means by which specific procedures for performing certain kinds of work were taught. In this way union power became identified with education as the heart of craft union philosophy.

Rarely, if ever, is the story of the labor movement told in terms of the degree to which workers have successfully wielded social power—power over their own labor, their wages, or within society as a whole. Nor do historians and sociologists generally concern themselves with the ways these types of external power are linked to the problem of internal union power.

In the history of American workers unions have presented themselves as "innocent" representatives of workers' interests. The refrain "the union makes us strong" expresses the value that strength (in our discourse, power) is needed to "win." We can only understand power within unions if we abandon the presumption of innocence, although we do not, of course, deny that unions were constituted originally out of necessity.

Workers needed a means of defense against the frequent efforts of their employer adversaries to weaken and even destroy their power in the labor process, a power that originally derived from the inherited crafts which capital appropriated from the earlier "artisanal mode of production" when machinery was subordinate to labor. The early production process was a "task continuous status organization." Each product was made by a series of crafts which through cooperation produced goods, but maintained a "hierarchical productive organization characterized by the relationship between the master craftsman and journeyman (the primary relationship) and between apprentice and adult workers (the secondary relationship)."[1] In the artisanal mode, leadership in the labor process accrues to those who possess status according to their skill. The craftsmen who organized unions in the early stages of capitalism were well aware of their status at the workplace. Although the employer usually owned the workshop and whatever equipment was needed for production, the craftsmen not only owned their own tools but determined the division of labor among themselves as well as laborers and apprentices. Accordingly, the crafts within a workshop did not negotiate individual contracts covering wages and other "benefits," but instead agreed to produce a certain quantity of the commodit(ies) in return for a collective wage. In effect, they sold the commodity to the employer who, in turn, determined its price to the consumer. The combined crafts divided the wage among themselves, distributing it according to the status hierarchy previously established by them.[2]

Thus, the union was not exclusively a bargaining agent between workers and employers, it was also a combination of workers against other workers—the cooperating/competing crafts might claim a larger share of that portion of the value of the product accruing to labor in general, as well as deciding how much they produced and how. Employers had no voice over technique, unless they themselves worked alongside the journeymen, unless they were of the crafts. Management was a clerical/administrative function responsible for keeping books, transporting raw materials into the shop, and moving the finished product to the market. The union, therefore, had a deep stake in preserving this artisanal mode of production and maintaining the status hierarchy. Marx, completely out of sympathy with the artisanal mode, characterized craft consciousness as "idiocy," an enemy of progress which he identified with all the evils of industrialization. The crafts tried to limit the supply of labor through the apprenticeship system, opposed the introduction of machinery that increased productivity and degraded skills, and refused a new division of labor that would make possible the creation of a new labor force recruited from the agricultural regions of Europe and America.

The virtue of the work of Montgomery, Gutman, and others who have reexamined the history of American unions before and during the transition from artisanal modes of production to industrialism is to remind us of the inadequacy of left-wing characterizations of craft unions as merely reactionary. This biased view of craft unions perpetrates a historical injustice because it ignores the genuine contributions of these unions to the worker cause at the dawn of the American industrial revolution.[3]

Later historians have tended to identify craft unionism *exclusively* with policies of exclusion—of racial and national minorities, of women and the unskilled. The new social history has dispelled some of these harsh judgments by showing that the idea of self-management, especially of the labor process, has its earliest forms in the craft tradition, yet the lack of a genuinely critical view of the contradictory character of the craft unions mars the credibility of much of the work of cultural reclamation currently underway. The new social history often appears merely to be a reaction against historians like Foner who, influenced by the romance of revolutionary industrial unionism, dismissed the entire craft union tradition. Of course, both historiographic schools have forgotten that syndicalism and craft unionism opposed the attempt of the first great labor federation, the Knights of Labor, to focus on political action as the best chance for working class emancipation. The Knights became the great antagonists of the AFL in the 1880's and were soundly defeated precisely because they called for combat at the political level and grossly underestimated the interests of craft and industrial workers for whom collective bargaining seemed a shorter route to achieving their immediate goals.

The Knights have been so maligned by historians for their insistence that labor assemblies admit non-working-class members and their failures in the economic sphere, that not a single comprehensive historical work, nor a thorough biography of its leading figure, Terence Powerderly, has been produced in the ninety years since its demise. This omission bears eloquent witness to the antipolitical traditions of American labor historiography and especially the degree to which its focus corresponds to and reflects the real influence still exercised by Gomperism. Gompers's account of the Knights during the early years of the fledgling AFL is instructive as the conventional view of this organization.

The Knights supported strikes but opposed formation of *trade* assemblies; in their opinion, trade unions divided workers, made them craft and industry conscious, and undermined the goal of class unity. Their idea of uniting all workers, regardless of craft or industry, in one union prefigured future efforts, such as the IWW and the CIO councils of the 1940's and 1950's, to place labor as such on the American political and social agenda.

Of course, Gompers had reason to oppose the Knights of Labor. His entire philosophy was based on the preeminence of the most skilled workers in the labor force and he believed that the interests of trade unions and the broad labor movement envisioned by the Knights were irreconcilable:

> Trade unions endeavored to organize for collective responsibility persons with common trade problems. They sought economic betterment in order to place in the hands of wage-earners the means to wider opportunities. The Knights of Labor was a social or fraternal organization. It was based upon a principle of cooperation and its purpose was reform. The Knights of Labor prided itself upon being something higher and grander than a trade union or political party.[4]

Gompers deplored the failure of the Knights of Labor to deny membership to employers, but his most vehement attack was reserved for the "two anti-trade union factions" within the Knights of Labor—"one that wanted a super-labor movement and regarded trade unions as not respectable; and the other, the radical group that wanted one big union for revolutionary purposes." In these passages Gompers reveals more than a strong conviction that the "economic betterment" of workers required organizations able to unite around trade problems, although this objection to the Knights was, of course, the valid and unifying principle around which the AFL was founded. Following Marx's attack on the followers of Ferdinand Lasalle who tried to organize the German workers in political rather than chiefly trade union action, Gompers's reputation for "economistic" trade union ideas rests on these early struggles. Gompers's early philosophy, forged in the heat of the struggle against the Knights' political action and communitarian contingents, was to change in the wake of the devastating defeats suffered in the 1890's by industrial unions such as Eugene Debs's American Railway Union, the Miners, and the Amalgamated. But his trade union position outlived his change of mind. Gompers successfully defined the everyday practice of trade unions in a more or less sophisticated and global theory of the labor movement. The Knights defined labor as a movement of social transformation and the CIO appropriated elements of the ideology of Anarcho-syndicalism for reformist ends.

Gompers prepared the soil for the later developments, even as he constantly reiterated his early philosophy. But with the coming of the machine, the status of the crafts was eroded if not surpassed within the production process. They formed unions to reverse or arrest the process by which they lost their primacy in production, recruiting leadership from among them charged with preserving the task-continuous status organization of the labor process in which the old hierarchy flourished. The irony of the history of American labor was that even when mechanization brought task discontinuity, that is, tasks divided among a large number of unskilled workers as dictated by capital, the hierarchical structure of both the labor process and the labor movement was retained. A portion of craft labor was degraded into a series of operations which changed with changing products, although the essential elements remained the same: repetition, minute division of labor, simplification of tasks, etc. But the agreements with employers, as well as constitutional provisions within unions themselves, retained the power of the craftsman to hire a helper free of the interference of management, even if that "helper" was no longer an apprentice whose temporary subordination to the craftsman was a preparation for future craft status. The helper might never become a craftsman, either because he was not admitted into approved apprenticeship programs and thus condemned to semiskilled labor as long as he remained in the industry, or because he was excluded from the union whose members had the power to select their successors from among their own progeny.

Thus, even when the craft itself was reduced in function within the labor process, craft unions were constituted to make possible the retention of status continuity in which craftsmen stood at the apex of the working class. Although craftsmen eventually lost their power to hire and fire helpers, they retained, through union control over apprenticeship, the power to select those who would reproduce the "trade." Further, the designation "craft" signified higher wages, more job security, and a certain autonomy in the labor process. Craft unions were also able to keep the question of the organization of laborers off the agenda of the labor movement for many years after the Civil War. Industrial unionism simply became a non-decision for the labor leadership except in rare cases, such as the world wars, when the decision was forced upon them by circumstances.

Power in trade unions has accrued to those whose position in the labor process makes them indispensable. While the coming of industrialization eroded the power of the crafts to control their own labor, it did not entirely surpass their indispensability. Knowledge being an inextricable element of power in the new mechanized labor process, power, in turn, constitutes through discourses about the past and the present what counts for knowledge in a particular society or sector.

The unions formed by "knowledgeable workers" had created a leadership that served their interests by imposing their power to set the agenda, that is, set the boundaries of trade union discussion and action. My description of the power of the craft unions differs from accounts by traditional labor historians and sociologists, who maintain that craft unions were constituted to sell the labor power of their members at the highest possible price by controlling the supply of labor. Supply control was achieved through rigorous limits on the number of persons who could qualify as journeymen after completing a more or less formal apprenticeship system supervised by the union; establishing hiring halls that obliged employers under union contract to seek labor exclusively or first among those sent by the union dispatcher at the hiring hall; and instituting union sanctions on those from outside a specific geographic area to work in the labor market controlled by the craft. Thus, even if an individual held a union-approved journeyman card, his ability to work was circumscribed by the union local which threatened employers with strikes if they employed union members from another local without prior approval.

Of course, I do not mean to deny the importance of these *economic* functions of craft unionism. What needs to be added is this: craft union leadership preserved status continuity as the condition of these economic mechanisms by producing knowledge, discourses, and agenda which defined the union itself. The leadership of the early craft unions which formed the AFL after 1886 was more than a purveyor of labor power, it was also a powerful factor in American life. As the certified "representative" of all American workers, the official voice of labor, such figures as Samuel Gompers were able to define what could be decided by unions, what constituted common sense about American labor, and what place unions would occupy in the configuration of national power. It might be argued that Gompers was merely an ideological conservative when he opposed three points of the left-wing agenda for unions: organizing unskilled and semiskilled workers; forming a labor party in which workers' interests would have a political expression; and introducing social doctrines, particularly socialist ideas, into the labor movement. If the concept of power employed here is to be followed, dismissing Gompers as a dyed-in-the-wool conservative will not suffice. Gompers defined leadership. The tasks of labor leadership were to produce a new "common sense" of labor.

Certainly, this new common sense had wide implications for defining the role of workers and their unions in relation to American politics and industrial life. At the turn of the century, the mechanized and rationalized labor process had reduced and marginalized craft to a function of industrial production. Craft workers had become maintenance mechanics, producers of tools of industrial labor who performed the function of setting up the machines upon which unskilled and semiskilled labor worked. As the *independent* journeyman disappeared from all but the margins of economic life, a place was made for the redefined crafts as a dependent variable of the labor process.

In the new industrial environment, Gompers, ever the pragmatist, produced a new common sense about the relation of skilled to unskilled. Craft was still the core of the organizable work force, but the AFL now insisted that the new industrial skilled worker whose "craft" had been considerably degraded by the Taylor system, which broke down the old skills into a series of operations able to be performed by a worker with little or no prior training, should organize according to the old division of labor among the skilled. That is, skilled workers employed within industrial plants should form locals consisting exclusively of members of a particular craft. At first, the semiskilled and unskilled were defined by the AFL leaders as comparable to the crafts. Even when this position became untenable in the industrial union upsurge of the late 1930's, the AFL, following Gompers's common sense, maintained its position that the unskilled could only join established craft unions, but in separate locals. As the CIO under John L. Lewis was forming unions in which all workers in a plant were united in a single local and bargained together with the employer, the old AFL doctrine still imposed itself on those AFL unions that were obliged to compete with the CIO for the same labor force.

The apparent absurdity of this position was an object of considerable derision among the radicals and trade union militants who organized the CIO unions. William Green, a former Lewis associate in the United Mine Workers who retained his presidency of the AFL after his former mentor bolted to form the new federation, followed the Gompers craft union tradition into the 1940's. In all but a few cases the journeymen of the electrical trades, the machinists, the ladies' garment and men's clothing workers, and iron and sheet metal crafts retained their autonomous locals within a broader effort to organize among the unskilled. For the CIO progressives, this fealty to tradition was both venal (it relegated the unskilled to second-class citizenship within the labor movement) and impractical because the transformation of the labor process rendered these old crafts obsolete.

Gompers was to have the last laugh, however. After the Second World War, such paragons of industrial unionism as the United Auto Workers (UAW) began to experience considerable internal tension between their skilled trades members and workers on the assembly line. Among the most cherished of UAW collective bargaining objectives had been the reduction, if not the elimination, of pay differentials between the skilled and the unskilled in the auto industry. A way to achieve this was to insist upon cents per hour, across-the-board wage increases, a measure that would narrow the gap among auto workers. This policy required a different "common sense" among workers. Instead of holding fast to the privileges accorded to craft as a basis for union organization, skilled trades workers would have to accept the goal of labor solidarity through reduced wage differentials as their best means to social and economic advancement. The socialists and militants among the UAW leaders argued that the unskilled constituted the majority of the auto labor force and gaining their support was essential, not only with respect to winning skilled workers' demands for wages, but also for better working conditions, especially greater autonomy in the workplace. Since many of the early UAW leaders like Walter Reuther were themselves recruited from the ranks of the skilled trades, he was among many who became persuaded that the gen-

eral advancement of auto workers depended on the progressive relin-
quishing of craft privileges.

For a decade after the unionization of auto workers the ideology of
solidarity almost became a new common sense. First, the CIO demonstrated that the old common sense about the unskilled was false by bringing millions of assembly line and other unskilled workers into labor's
ranks. Second, the CIO invented a form of union organization that included all workers within a given plant within the same local, even if the
unions were often obliged to bargain for each job category separately.
They accomplished this feat by proposing a formal system of job
classification in which different levels of skill, responsibility, danger, and
training were awarded differential wage rates. But this compromise with
the existing common sense was understood by the new unionists as a
transitional concession needed to win support among the skilled workers
for their program of industrial democracy. By introducing "across the
board" wage demands that reduced the gap between skilled and unskilled
they hoped to forge the solidarity needed to overcome the awesome
power of the giant auto companies.

But the old common sense proved more powerful than expected. In the
mid-1950's the skilled trades in the UAW began to contest the leadership's
effort to reduce pay differentials. They threatened to leave the UAW for
an old craft union—the Mechanics Education Society of America
(MESA)—unless Reuther and other leaders agreed to maintain the differentials, give the skilled trades veto power over any contract to assure that
this position was upheld, and establish a separate department of the union
that would protect the autonomy of the crafts from the rest of the labor
force. After a protracted struggle, Reuther relented and the "new" common sense was dead. Henceforth, wage agreements would provide differentials based on job classification and percentage wage increases, and a
separate department was set up to promote the particular interest of the
skilled trades within the union. The defeat of the progressives' program
for class or industrial solidarity in the UAW was duplicated in other unions
as well. In steel, the union had never gone so far as to advocate the
gradual elimination of differentials. In fact, it always maintained a separate job classification system for the unskilled and semiskilled on one
hand, and for the crafts on the other. Together with the UAW, the Steelworkers became the leading examples of bargaining based on percentage
wage increases in the late 1960's. When combined with differentials
based upon classification, the percentage across-the-board formula has
resulted in widening the gap once again. In the overwhelming majority of
cases the skilled workers have retained their power—not only over their
own privileges, but within the unions as well. For most of the years after
the Second World War, when virtually uninterrupted economic expansion rendered the basic industrial labor force highly ambulatory, the

skilled workers established themselves at the core of the union leader-ship. For example, on auto assembly lines in the 1960's the turnover rate was one hundred percent every five years and other industries faced similar problems. This led to the widespread perception that skilled workers were likely to be the most devoted union members since their desire for lateral mobility was limited by their ability to control their own working conditions. For the companies, effective maintenance me-chanics, skilled installers of machines and good set up workers were infinitely more difficult to find than those charged with setting windshield wipers on a car, stamping fenders, or working a production machine in a parts plant. By the 1960's, industrial unions became the virtual property of the crafts and the historic distinction between the old AFL unions and the new unions disappeared.

What I want to suggest is that the American working class was defined by Gomperism as a leadership style, if we accept the notion that classes are formed both by their place in the structure of ownership and control of the means of production *and* their practices. While it was not within the power of the AFL leaders to change the place of skilled workers in the class structure (they could not be invested with ownership of productive means), they placed skilled labor at the head of the entire labor move-ment for decades after the rise of industrial unions. These workers cum union leaders—George Meany is a prime example—spoke for all working people in public forums. Since the AFL leaders were the voice of labor as a whole, they were able to define its aspirations even though their actual social base was relatively narrow. Although craftsmen constituted an in-creasingly diminished fraction of the working class, their power to gener-ate a discourse of labor by both limiting its scope and specifying what is to be understood by "labor," was to have an indelible effect on the labor movement and its position in national life.

In the large canvas of American labor history Gompers was victorious in producing the knowledge about labor and labor's knowledge of itself. During Gompers's long tenure as president of the AFL, the leadership successfully promulgated and delineated criteria for appropriate member-ship in the labor movement, the aims of organized labor, and, by defining these aims in relation to those objectives which they excluded, labor "outsiders" as well. As I have shown, perhaps the most important element of leadership during the 1880–1930 period was to have plainly separated the American labor movement from the progressive and socialist move-ments. Unlike Europe where socialists and social progressives had as-sisted in one formation of unions as well as other organizations that included the propertyless, Gompers refused to denounce the notion of property when applied to labor. As Seymour Martin Lipset and James Coleman have argued in their study of printers and their unions, Ameri-can craftsmen appropriated the concept of property for their jobs. The training afforded by apprenticeship not only insured a relatively high wage for journeymen, the union contract gave them a *job property right* as well. Thus, training, as distinct from a broad liberal education, became the rite of passage to union citizenship. The skilled worker in particular was held capable of participating in the rituals of democracy, especially its concomitant of participation and self-organization. Thus, according to Gompers's doctrine of the labor movement, craftsmen could ill afford to remain socialists, at least in their trade union practice. As property owners—of their own jobs albeit not of the means of production—their social interest was not always antagonistic to capital for which private property was the sacred possession. As with Hegel's identification of property with citizenship, many AFL leaders could not conceive of common labor within the definition of industrial citizenship. Common labor was defined as an absence—the absence of training which often subsumed reading and writing. Just as Thomas Jefferson had argued that only an educated citizenry could constitute the basis of any democracy, so the leadership of the craft unions imposed their version of this doctrine in the workplace.

It would be easy to take these views as merely the reflection of the privileges of craft—legitimating ideology of power. Unfortunately, this way of seeing the function of leadership in the formation of the labor movement does not take a wide enough perspective. It was not merely for the purposes of excluding the unskilled, or securing the dominance of skilled labor within the labor force that this common sense was disseminated, it also produced a culture of craft of which the union was the major repository. As I have already argued, early craft unions during the period of industrialization (1865–1910) were fraternities as much as bargaining agents. Craftsmen found the sinews of solidarity in their shared skills more than their shared nationality or ethnicity. They constituted local unions as communities of equals, replete with rituals of initiation, secret passwords reminiscent of masons and other fraternal societies (although Gompers opposed these), and a rich social life that embraced both the individual and his family around the union hall. Labor historians have traced some of these cultural practices to the illegality suffered by trade unions during the "gilded age" of American capitalism, but have failed to discuss the degree to which they were generated as elements of a conception of trade unions as a *form of life*. It was not until much later that the businesslike character of the unions took firm hold and workers came to relate to them as a bureaucratic institution.

Unskilled workers, lacking union organization, exercised their cultural needs through immigrant and ethnic clubs and the barrooms of the working class neighborhoods, rather than the union hall except in the largest industrial centers. But the main crafts associated with the artisanal mode of production (cigarmaking, tailoring, leather trades, carpentry, bricklaying, and the early mechanical trades) constructed their culture around the shop and the union local. It was precisely the subcultural character of these locals that made their rituals and knowledge powerful instruments for dominating others at the workplace. Later, when industrial unions finally broke through the wall of hostility proffered by the dominant craft organizations, the craft subculture permitted these unions to organize the unskilled but hold them in bondage. Unskilled workers and skilled workers lacking an accredited journeyman's card might join unions, but not on an equal footing with the crafts. Thus the AFL chartered separate locals of industrial workers, not in order to grant these groups autonomy to deal effectively with their employers, but to protect the status of the crafts within the labor movement and their domination over the unskilled.

LABOR'S NEW CONSTITUENTS

The craft unions required an outside force, the Congress of Industrial Organizations (CIO), formed as a breakaway by a handful of leaders of old AFL unions, to persuade them that they could no longer ignore the unskilled workers or exclude them from trade unionism.

The CIO forged a new principle of trade union organization and a new style of leadership. *Industrial* unionism signified the organization of workers regardless of skill or occupation within a single industry. Thus, workers were recruited in the rubber, auto, steel, women's and men's clothing, and other industries in locals affiliated to an "international" union for the industry. In some cases, notably the electrical industry, workers in several closely related branches were brought together in a single organization. The United Electrical, Radio and Machine Workers organized among all workers engaged in allied industries, but the inclusion of "machine" in the title led inevitably to battles with the Steelworkers, the Machinists, and other international unions that claimed the same jurisdiction. These conflicts were resolved during the early days of the CIO because the veritable vacuum that had been created by AFL dereliction in organizing the unorganized, opened enough opportunities for all aggressive unions. The industrial union organization principle entailed a different style of leadership. As I have noted, the organizers of the new unions were obliged to constitute a new common sense to replace the status foundations of craft unionism.

Industrial unionism found an equivalent set of practices or power to replace craft. Most important in the early stages was an ideology of organizing—how to persuade mass production workers that they could win against powerful corporations despite their ethnic and racial fragmentation and lack of craft. In this regard, the CIO leaders drew heavily, albeit with modifications, on the One Big Union concept of the now moribund Industrial Workers of the World, with *solidarity* being the power equivalent of craft. When workers, regardless of sex, race, national origin, or occupation, banded together in a factory or workplace and were able to prevent employers from recruiting strike breakers either by force or by persuasion, industrial unionism could make gains believed, hitherto, to be the exclusive capacity of skilled workers. Unlike the xenophobic AFL, the CIO validated the industrial citizenship of immigrant workers and declared its opposition to discrimination based on race, sex, or national origin in employment, public accommodations, and voting. It may be claimed that the progressive positions of industrial union leaders were simply a response to the necessities dictated by the composition of the labor force in mass production industries, many of which had consciously recruited immigrants and blacks. This point is especially important for mining, steel, and rubber industries where the ethnic and racial minorities constituted the overwhelming majority of production workers until the Second World War. Nevertheless, opportunism aside, there can be no doubt that the decision to organize among these workers implied leaders possessing a new union common sense, who had broken with the prejudices of the craft traditions.[5]

Unskilled and semiskilled immigrant labor flocked to the CIO in the 1930's, responding chiefly to the syndicalist component of industrial unionism, its emphasis on economic struggle at the workplace and its slogans of industrial democracy. But the political side of social unionism never sank deep roots among these workers. Democratic political machines in cities such as Chicago, New York, Detroit, Boston, and Pittsburgh were more attractive to many precisely because they retained the patriarchal character of their old rural social relationships. The party bosses offered assistance to the unemployed who needed relief, jobs in city government or recommendations to private employers, housing relocation following evictions and fires, and many other services that the fledgling trade unions could not yet offer. Moreover, the social unions were convinced that their capacity to offer a political challenge to conservative, business-minded public officials depended on their ability to build a mass working class based on the shop floor. The limits of industrial unions were that, with few exceptions, they stayed there. Although the communists, socialists, and liberal labor leaders formed the short-lived American Labor Party in the 1930's in New York State, the labor movement in general capitulated to the historic separation of economics and politics that has marked the American labor movement since the founding of the AFL. To be sure, the ideological left formed a mass neighborhood-based organization of the jobless called the Workers Alliance during the Depression, which was able to compete with the Democratic machine for the hearts and minds of immigrant and ethnic workers in a few places. In the late 1930's and throughout the 1940's the militant housing and pro-welfare activities of the Workers Alliance translated into the establishment of left-wing political machines in East Harlem, New York, around the charismatic personality of Representative Vito Marcantonio (in 1948 the already split American Labor Party briefly won a seat in Congress in a traditionally Democratic district in the Bronx); and in San Francisco left-wing Democrats were elected to public office with the backing of the left-wing Longshoremen's Union. Labor and the Left established other toeholds in mainstream politics, especially in Seattle, Detroit, and Chicago. But these political efforts, while closely tied to the labor movement, especially the Auto Workers and Steelworkers, were much more oriented towards building a liberal wing within the Democratic Party than an independent labor party.

In the main, labor organizations had been fully transmuted into the social unionism and were ensconced in an alliance with the New Deal; many political action committees replaced the formal Democratic Party organization as the leading wedge in electoral campaigns. At the national level, especially after 1936, labor's financial and mobilizing support became essential to any Democratic victory. In fact, until 1968 endorsement by the AFL-CIO leadership was a necessary condition for a successful candidate's nomination for President of the United States.

CHAPTER 3

THE NEW SOCIAL UNIONISM

SOCIAL unionism, built on the trade union base forged by Gompers and the political orientation of the socialists, took its significant steps to maturity under the leadership of John L. Lewis. After his elevation to the presidency of the United Mine Workers in 1919, Lewis spent the 1920's perfecting a strategy of class compromise with employers in order to preserve the embattled union. He was accused by his socialist and militant opponents of having abandoned the miners more than once to the arbitrary authority of employers seeking to transfer the burden of the crisis in the coal industry onto workers' backs. He tried to run the union on two principles: the primacy of organizational survival and autocracy as a leadership style. Lewis, never a passionate champion of union democracy, was a labor intellectual who held no brief for social radicalism. Yet it was Lewis who inaugurated Labor's Nonpartisan League, to reelect Roosevelt in 1936.

Lewis became the chief spokesperson for the old dream of One Big Union of workers regardless of race, sex, or creed. During the Second World War he was the singular figure within organized labor willing to call a national strike in wartime and he went to jail for his effort. Lewis also recognized the talent of socialists and communists during the organizing phase of the industrial union movement, insisting against right-wing criticism that they be integrated into the campaign. After the Second World War, when the mining industry was once again plunged into crisis because of the rising use of oil as a home heating fuel, Lewis promptly negotiated a series of agreements with the coal operators that provided a fund, extracted from the price of a ton of coal, for the establishment of miners hospitals and a substantial pension program. In return, the union permitted the operators to introduce labor saving technologies which, together with the declining market for coal, resulted in mass unemployment among miners in the Pennsylvania and Illinois fields, as well as widespread mining outside the union jurisdiction that eventually produced shutdowns and the near loss of the hospitals.

Thus Lewis was hardly the epitome of the new social unionism. At the bargaining table he was capable of the most egregious compromises with employers to save the union and the jobs of a minority of miners, even if these agreements resulted in mass layoffs for the majority. On the political and social level he was an architect of labor's historic compromise with the Democratic Party which produced a viable national coalition that set the agenda for American politics for thirty years, especially the struggle for legislative and social equality; this helped labor become a major force in many state and local governments. Lewis himself virtually abandoned his own strategy after 1940. His subsequent reversion to business unionism is, of course, of little consequence from an historical perspective. Just as Gompers, who was early attracted to socialism, became its implacable enemy on voluntarist and political grounds only to become Wilson's most enthusiastic supporter during the First World War, so Lewis became the leading figure of social unionism, although his last years were spent as the best ally the coal companies ever had in their struggle for survival.

Unlike Gompers who ruled the Federation with something less than an iron hand because he was constrained by the federated principle that maintained trade autonomy, Lewis brandished a leadership style that brooked no opposition from within the ranks. Lewis's successors, from Phillip Murray and Reuther to Jimmy Hoffa, were similarly suspicious of the fraternal principles of voluntarist unionism. The leaders of the CIO lost little time before expelling their left-wing opponents. Further, in contrast to the voluntarist idea the union dues should be collected, by hand, from each member, the CIO was joined by some AFL unions in seeking the checkoff which relegated dues collection to a bureaucratic procedure removed from the shop floor. Automatic checkoff deprived the steward, the primary shop floor leader, of some of his or her power and responsibility. Finally, the CIO unions were, in many cases, highly centralized organizations where full-time officials held undisputed reins of authority over contract enforcement, union policies, and political affiliations.

As Gompers understood, the tendency towards centralizing power is produced in part by the highly centralized nature of the basic manufacturing industries with which the industrial unions were obliged to do battle. On the other side, with important exceptions, the AFL unions were based in highly competitive local industries such as construction, retailing (especially of food), and manufacturing of consumer goods such as garments, cigars and cigarettes, and plastics. AFL unions adopted the industrial form of organization, as in transportation, meat packing, and aircraft, only if this move was dictated by strong competition from CIO unions.

Historical conditions are not, however, sufficient to account for the centralism of industrial unions. Another important reason was the military model of union organization and national strikes within which these unions developed. Lewis was above all a generalissimo, a leader who followed the basic precept that labor, in order to win, required strict discipline—not only on the picket line but in the conduct of everyday union affairs. The CIO built its political organization along industrial organization lines. The fundamental goal was not greater *democratic* control by workers over the political and economic life of the country. The CIO was a movement for social justice defined as the achievement of more equality for workers in the distribution of economic resources. If we conceive democracy to consist of *more equality*, the CIO was, in this sense, a democratic movement. Similarly, the CIO attempted to get workers to vote, an advance dictated by the fact that Democratic candidates for national office before Roosevelt had suffered notoriously from relative apathy among unskilled and semiskilled workers who would have voted for them if they had seen a reason to vote at all. But the CIO was primarily a movement to improve the standard of living for those union members who had been rendered "ill housed, ill clothed and ill fed" by the ruthless drive of capital to accumulate at their expense.[1]

For Arthur Goldberg, General Counsel of the Steelworkers and later a Supreme Court Justice, the military model was all the more appropriate since unions were constituted to serve the economic interests of their members; they were not "class" organizations dedicated to broad social goals, especially strengthening democratic society. The struggle for economic and social justice implied by measures to guarantee a good job at decent pay regardless of race, sex or national origin did not require the union to become a debating society. On the contrary, according to Goldberg, unions should adopt a command structure in which leaders held centralized power. This arrangement corresponds, he said, to the centralization of decision making in large corporations. Unions were obliged to match the ability of these corporations, to organize themselves to achieve the maximum maneuverability. If unions allowed themselves to bog down in endless debates, constant turnover of union leadership and rapid shifts in trade union policy, the whole, carefully constructed, structure of collective bargaining would break down. This disruption was certain to produce chaos, instability, and ultimately would hurt the common interests of business and labor.

Here I wish to enter a caveat. For many workers and union leaders the CIO did offer the chance for transforming America into a new economic and political democracy, in which the internal life of the unions was considered prefigurative of the future society. Many locals cherished their newly-won ability to manage union affairs afforded by such democratic, decentralized organizations as the United Auto Workers, the Oil Workers, and the Electrical Workers. They supported the objective of national agreements with multiplant employers such as GE and US Steel, but they also held to the idea of *local autonomy*—especially the right of workers not only to elect their own leadership without interference from the national organization, but also to negotiate with employers on local conditions before the conclusion of any national wage and benefits settlement. Local leaders disagreed with the tendency of some national unions to remove officers of locals who opposed central policies. They also waged a determined struggle to amend the constitutions of many national unions so that wage agreements were subject to membership approval rather than the decision of delegated bodies such as wage policy committees. The idea of a membership referendum to elect national leaders became, in the 1950's and 1960's one of the major issues within the trade unions, especially in the Miners and Steelworkers, which were, ironically, the two unions that Lewis built.

The old leadership was often bewildered by the passion of the rank and file rebellion against their perceived high-handed authoritarian style. Critics of union bureaucracy have often attributed venal motives to the leaders. Of course, in the Miners case, Lewis's successor Tony Boyle, corresponded to this charge. But in other cases, the charge of venality was, at best, a fragment of the truth that often concealed more than it revealed about leadership in the industrial unions. If we are clear that the democratic ethos has never dominated the American labor movement but that the old slogan of economic justice prevails, the virulent response by labor's industrial union leaders to struggles to democratize the unions becomes easier to comprehend. Mass unionism may bring a better standard of living to unskilled and semiskilled workers, but some leaders asked: Is this goal compatible with turning the movement over to the unskilled and semiskilled, most of whom are uneducated and are literally incapable of seeing the big picture or even managing the union which in modern times is a business as well as a movement?

To the end of preparing workers to run their own local organizations, many CIO unions ran education programs, but never elevated these activities to an important place within union life. Education was often considered marginal rather than important work within the union. Too often, even in those unions which maintained full-time education staffs, the person was selected as a reward for union loyalty rather than for possessing a specific talent for the job. Today, education remains marginal in older trade unions but is rising among service and public employee organizations. In industrial unions education has become skills rather than concept oriented, reflecting the need to train a limited number of shopleaders to handle grievances, transmit labor's political goals, and negotiate some aspects of local contracts. In most unions, however, many of these functions have become the territory of full-time representatives appointed by the top leaders or, if elected, part of the political machine that rules many local and national unions.

LABOR AND POLITICS

The legend of Gomper's attitude toward trade union political involvement has outlived the facts. As early as 1886, Gompers joined with the rest of New York's labor movement in providing vigorous support for the candidacy of Henry George for Mayor against the two entrenched Democratic machines. While Gompers was head of the speakers bureau of labor's political effort in that campaign, he disagreed with others such as John Swinton on the question of whether labor's intervention in the mayoral campaign signaled the formation of an independent labor party. Gompers favored ad hoc endorsements of candidates for public office, and campaigns to support pro-labor legislation, but was firmly opposed to labor forming its own permanent political vehicle that presented itself as an alternative to established political power.

Prior to the industrial union drives of the 1930's, some major AFL leaders such as Dan Tobin of the Teamsters were important in the high councils of the Democratic Party, while John L. Lewis of the Miners had been a well-known Republican, although he was never identified with partisan politics. The AFL's policy regarding partisan politics remained "reward labor's friends and punish its enemies," a pragmatic position which committed the Federation to neither major party, but which at the ideological level implicitly accepted the framework of capitalism as the proper basis for any political action deemed appropriate by the union leadership. With the single exception of the 1924 election when the leadership felt constrained to support the Progressive Party candidate, Robert LaFollette, because both major political parties had nominated Presidential candidates identified as enemies, labor's overt political moves were confined to endorsing its friends at the local and state level. But there was no question of extensive political education efforts, either on the major issues or on the nature of electoral politics.

The early AFL represented a third type of unionism—business unionism. This did not mean that it was apolitical. As we have seen, Gompers joined the top circles of the National Civil Federation, an organization dominated by a fraction of big business searching for the elements of a new social policy to replace anti-laborism and antiquated laissez faire ideologies. During the First World War, he openly aligned labor with the war effort and played a prominent role in the War Labor Board, Woodrow Wilson's attempt to create a mechanism for government intervention in labor relations at a time when labor unrest threatened to disrupt his plans for war mobilization. What characterized business unionism was that it renounced social goals. Its vision was the welfare of its own members, not of a class of workers regardless of skill, industry, or nationality. In short, business unionism regarded the negotiation and administration of the labor contract as the far horizon of the labor movement, for it was in the multiple relationships with employers that the interests of workers could be served.

Now, nearly fifty years after the beginning of industrial unionism, we can take a measure of the degree to which industrial and business unionism have merged into a single new form—social contract unionism, which Gompers anticipated in his last years. Today's labor unions are solidly involved with the political and legislative process; AFL-CIO legislative representatives and political operatives play an active role in legislative action at the national and at the state levels, participating in the nominating process within the Democratic Party as well as enjoying formal power in its institutions at all levels. They are actively engaged in the regulatory process—not only in matters affecting labor organizing and collective bargaining, but in such issues as social welfare, energy, defense, and the environment. The president of the AFL-CIO is a major spokesperson on national and international affairs. Recently, a labor sponsored project, the American Institute for Free Labor Development (AIFLD), has played a prominent role in promoting land reform in El Salvador, actively cooperating with the now deposed Duarte government in its campaign to defeat the guerilla opposition as well as the extreme right wing. Similarly, since the Second World War, U.S. labor representatives have worked to strengthen anti-communist unions in Europe and Third World countries and have provided labor attachés for U.S. embassies abroad from among its ranks. In sum, there is not a single major concern of the United States government at home and abroad on which organized labor does not take a position and for which it does not provide political and administrative cadre for carrying out U.S. foreign and domestic policy. This deepening involvement in the affairs of state represents the permanent defeat of Gompers's early slogan, "unionism, pure and simple," advanced to oppose the socialists' attempt to politicize the AFL. However, it is important not to overemphasize the difference between Gomperism and the new social contract unionism of today's Federation.

Gompers led the Federation to close collaboration with the government in the First World War for reasons not so distant from those that motivated the AFL to adopt a social union stance after the Second World War—the threat of radicalism. Recall that the IWW had achieved its most stunning advances in the years immediately prior to the outbreak of the war, when Debs's Socialist campaign captured nearly one million votes on a left-wing platform, or about six percent of the popular vote.

Of course, Gompers's political activism was partially eclipsed after his death in 1924 by the perception of AFL leaders that the strategy of independent political action which they reluctantly adopted that year had failed. Actually LaFollette did well for a new third party candidacy that year: he gained more than four million votes on a populist/labor platform that prefigured most of the social welfare programs of the "second" new deal, including labor's rights. But the advance in labor's political program represented by the independent party could not be sustained ideologically by a leadership deeply committed to meeting its needs within the framework of the two party system. Further, and perhaps more important, the period of the late 1920's and early 1930's was one of precipitous decline for the AFL unions. Even before the Depression weakened labor's power, some key unions in the Federation suffered defeats at the picket line that reduced them to a shell of their former selves. Two examples will suffice: By 1925 the Communists had gained control of the large Dress Joint Board of the New York Ladies' Garment Workers Union. Reacting to employer demands for severe wage and benefit concessions, the union leaders called a general dress strike in 1926. The outcome of the strike was disastrous and the garment workers returned to work without having achieved their objectives. After 1926 the employers dictated terms to most workers in the dress industry. By 1929, having driven the Communists from leadership, David Dubinsky, Charles Zimmerman, Luigi Antonini, and other socialist labor leaders found themselves presiding over the virtual corpse of a once proud union. Similarly, after John L. Lewis took the reins of the powerful United Mine Workers in 1919, he spent most of the 1920's trying to pick up the pieces of lost strikes. By the mid-1920's he was making compromises with the coal operators in order to retain some semblance of a union. Besides the attacks of the employers on the hard won gains of the miners, he faced a determined campaign from the Left. Powers Hapgood, John Brophy, and other militants—socialists who did not have Communist Party support for their insurgency—were challenging Lewis's leadership and came close to unseating him. Lewis learned the lesson of his near defeat. When political and economic conditions became favorable to industrial organization in the 1930's he wasted no time hiring Brophy as organizational director of the newly formed CIO. In 1933 both Dubinsky and Lewis were able to rebuild their unions to mass proportions. But by the time the new surge began, the memory of independent labor action had already faded into history. Mine Workers and Garment Workers organizers scoured the Pennsylvania coal fields and the Eastern seaboard dress shops carrying the message of section 7A of Franklin Roosevelt's National Recovery code: labor's right to organize without coercion was approved (although not enforced) by the Act. "The President wants you to join the union" became the organizing slogan of the early industrial union drive. The New Deal appeared firmly implanted in the collective consciousness of labor's most aggressive and progressive leaders. Even if, in the subsequent decades, various labor leaders (including Lewis himself) were to raise the specter of a labor party, this approach was never taken seriously, either by Democratic Party politicos or by the rank and file union members.

THE EVERYDAY LIFE OF UNIONS

My account of the apparent victory of social unionism over its arch business union rival applies chiefly to national politics. When we examine the day to day conduct of union affairs, the reverse is largely the case. Local union activities are mostly confined to the task of administering the contract, including in many locals the social benefits that labor has been unable to negotiate through political action with the legislative and executive branches of the national government. I want to discuss the form of business union leadership at the local level in three dimensions: (1) the administration of issues of wages, working conditions, and job security—the policing of the contract between employer and union; (2) the "welfare," "security," or "health" plan run by the international or local union; (3) the internal life of unions—what happens at union meetings, the union's educational and political actions programs, and the daily life of the union as an institution.

The contract and the union that administers it tend to inscribe the past. One of the union leadership's main tasks is to persuade workers that their interests are served by strict observance of the contract's provisions. In many cases this is a correct position from the point of view of workers. But since the contract is nothing but a formalization of the relationship between worker and employer at the time it is negotiated and becomes a constraint upon the new relationship as it emerges in the labor process, neither employer nor worker feels bound by its provisions.

Of course, when capital requires changes in the work process in order to respond to changing market conditions, the contract becomes a protection for workers. To the extent union leaders enforce it, contract unionism is perforce opposed to the logic of capital which, as Marx has argued, requires the constant revolutionizing of the labor process through new forms of organization, introduction of labor-saving machines, and the relocation of capital investment. During the period of expansion experienced by the United States after the Second World War, the union leadership insisted workers respect the past in the face of new opportunities presented by relatively full employment. Leaders were also advocates of workers rights to the extent that the contract prevents employers from unilaterally altering its terms in order to procure advantages against competitors for new markets.

We can see this contradictory role of union leadership in the case of the steel industry. For most of the post-war period the most important provision of the basic steel agreement prohibited corporations from introducing new labor processes, including machinery, without the prior agreement of the union. At a time of relative prosperity for the industry employers had little incentive to challenge this contract provision, preferring to maintain long-term labor peace rather than provoke militant action. The unintended consequence of the economic conditions enjoyed by U.S. steel producers in a world market hungry for its product until about 1955 was that technological "progress" was relatively slow. However, when European and Japanese steel mills were rebuilt (in part by U.S.

capital) on the basis of the most modern technologies of industrial organization and machines, the United States industry found itself in a poor competitive position. Consequently, it chose to provoke a nationwide strike in 1959 to recover its position by reducing the contract's ability to stall technological change. The outcome of the strike was a pyrrhic victory for the union. It retained the provision, but as the position of U.S. steel in world markets declined in the 1960's and early 1970's, the union leadership became convinced that this restraint on management's prerogatives had to be removed; strikes as an instrument of collective bargaining were abandoned and a new cooperative spirit was introduced in steel labor relations. The result was massive reductions in the labor force over a long period, shutdowns of the old plants, and union cooperation in company efforts to reorganize the labor process. As a result of the leaders removing themselves from the workers' side, many rank and file members considered them an arm of the employers.

The case of the needle trades unions may exemplify the dilemma of even social unions with a broad vision of the role of the labor movement in society. Both the ILGWU and the Amalgamated Clothing and Textile Workers Union are former socialist-led unions which remain committed to the ideology of social unionism. The Amalgamated has traditionally been among labor's progressive wing, especially on foreign policy issues. It has opposed the virulent anti-communism of the AFL-CIO by advocating disarmament, it opposed U.S. intervention in Vietnam and other countries and supports organizations and programs for world peace and a warming of the cold war. In contrast, the ILGWU's international affairs department has been the cadre organization for the AFL-CIO's foreign policy apparatus which has traditionally stood to the right of the State Department. On the other hand, both unions are actively engaged in defending and extending the institutions of the welfare state through legislative and political action. They both pioneered union sponsored cooperative housing, health programs, and worker education.

Despite the will to social unionism, insofar as both unions are involved in industries whose employers are chronically faced with international competition, low technology, and highly diverse market conditions, the terms under which contract enforcement occurs are extremely ambiguous. What does it mean to insist upon rigorous enforcement of a contract when militancy might drive employers out of business or worse, tempt them to flee to areas such as the American Southeast or overseas where unions do not exist? Since the end of the Second World War the needle trades have faced a virtually permanent crisis in contrast to a historic period of prosperity in other industries. The internationalization of U.S. capital has produced a torrent of foreign-made garments from Taiwan, Korea, Italy, Spain, and the newest competitor, Roumania. Needless to say, these goods are produced by cheap labor, often under industrial regimes that are more advanced technologically than the United States. The progressive diminution of the U.S. garment industry, traditionally among the most highly unionized and socially and economically militant American workers, is a parable for the story of contemporary American labor. Even the most socially progressive unions in the sense defined in this essay become conservative on the shop floor. In order to secure the survival of the union as a force in the industry as well as in society, it may no longer administer the contract in a way that threatens the survival of the employers. Thus, the contract's provisions regarding the rights of workers, and the objective of securing a progressively higher standard of living for union members are subordinated to the survival of the industry. The limit to regarding the contract as a sacred instrument of workers' shop floor interests (the religion of contract unionism), is the degree to which it constrains the ability of the industry to adjust to changing conditions.

During the long prosperity of the postwar years, the grievance-based leadership style became entrenched in the everyday life of the trade unions. American mass production industries had for the most part been inured from the global market, and wage increases became a routine aspect of bargaining. But how well did the union handle major complaints regarding working conditions? Was the seniority rule protected in matters of upgrading, temporary layoffs and other issues of job security? Did the union fight hard to prevent the arbitrary authority of management from unfairly discharging workers? Did the union succeed in regulating the pace of technological innovation?

These activities became the principal work of full-time union representatives. In large locals of major industrial unions such as rubber, oil, steel, auto, and electrical workers, the task was delegated to an elected official who normally was recruited from the shop. In a large General Electric or Ford plant, the chief griever was usually a full-time official paid by the company. In smaller units or in competitive industries such as the garment, textile, or chemical industries, the union paid a business agent or international representative to handle all but the local issues. By 1950, the key operative in the industrial unions was a professional union leader rather than a rank and file steward. At the most elementary level of trade union practice, the AFL model won out. The fundamental battle for recognition having been essentially won except in the South, industrial unions settled down to orchestrating with the companies the terms of a new social contract.

The new social contract consisted of the agreement by workers and their union leaders to renounce the objective of control over the labor process except in regard to a few key issues concerning job security, in return for progressively higher wages and (something unique among advanced industrial societies) the provision of the social wage through the mechanism of collective bargaining. Under these conditions, the rank and file had to be regulated by the union leadership. After the 1946 strike wave during which virtually every major industrial union struck under the slogan "18¢ or 18%" [an hour increase], employers discovered that compromise with this new power bloc was the line of least resistance. In the 1946–49 period unions established themselves as a major force in American industrial relations and came to be regarded by the state as well as the large corporations as a vital link in the expansion of the economy. This new alliance replacing the New Deal was composed of the largest corporations in the major industries, the political directorate of both major political parties (although conservative Republicans like Robert Taft of Ohio were not initially sympathetic to the deal), and the major union leaders. Union leaders gave complete support to the Marshall Plan, the Truman Doctrine, and the other major elements of the bi-partisan foreign policy that named the Soviet Union as the major threat to achieving democracy in Europe and the Third World; they followed the urging of the political directorate to clean house of communists since these trade unionists opposed the cold war; they agreed to disagree with business leaders on the questions of expanding the social welfare state.

Taft and his conservative coterie became persuaded that the lesson of the 1946 strikes was that labor had become too strong and required new restraints through legislation. The Taft-Hartley Act was passed by a bi-partisan coalition in Congress, some of whom feared the unions more than the giant corporations. Others voted for the bill in order to forestall a worse alternative. The unions fought back and President Truman vetoed the measure, but Congress overrode the President's veto. Yet it took three more years for the leaders to learn the lesson of losing the fight against repressive labor legislation. In 1949 the unions were beaten again. Armed with Truman's reelection, a modest expansion of union membership, and their fulfilled promise to clean house of the reds, the social unionists went to Capitol Hill to persuade Congress to enact programs of national health care and major housing for working people. Both fights were lost despite the Democratic Congress that had turned the Republicans out of power in the 1948 election.

"A STATE WITHIN A STATE"

The defeats in 1946 and 1949 set the stage for the displacement of the struggle for welfare reforms to the collective bargaining arena for organized workers. After 1949, nearly all major unions negotiated substantial health care plans and pensions through the union contract. In their early years these benefits were far less costly to employers than money wages because the labor force, most of which was recruited in the 1930's and 1940's, was fairly young. At the same time, the contracts represented delivery on the leaders' promise to win more economic security in return for an abatement of shop floor militancy. Even though money wages rose at the same time, the "fringe benefits" package became the real innovation in collective bargaining in the 1950's—the safety net against sickness, old age, and even temporary protection against capital flight that might have left workers completely destitute in earlier times.

The strategy ... corporate-paid welfare programs pro-... ...dership. In Europe, ...dministered by the ...orkplace and in the ...or official, while still ...andoned most polit-...tuency. Many of the ...gaining table. For all ...ufacturing industries ...istrator as well. ...ements of opposition ...al process punctuated ...were in a position to ...the monopoly sector ...authority over these ...not contest this policy. ...W, James Carey of the ...nd Chemical Workers ...and health funds. They ...onal political programs ...sponsive to labor's de-...efits through the union ...of necessity ...n by design. The labor ... ...l to pass up the chance to deliver economic security at a time when a conservative president occupied the White House and Congress responded to his popularity by placing brakes on social programs.

But it was different to negotiate welfare plans in competitive industries such as the garment, shoe, retail, and wholesale trades, and later public employment. In sectors dominated by small employers the union was both financially and organizationally more suited to administering the programs than any single employer. This was also true of industries at the local level where employers had established associations to conduct joint bargaining with unions. In many cases, particularly in the needle trades and locally based retailing, the union was the main instrument for organizing the employers and took care to limit the association's capacities. Thus, union-administered welfare plans flourished in the 1950's and 1960's, adding a whole new dimension to labor leadership.

The president or manager of a union local, say in the garment industry or among municipal employees, is co-chair of a pension or health and welfare fund that covers thousands of union members and their families. He is also the chief executive officer of the fund, and plays the decisive role in making policy for the program since its funds are in part a product of the contract negotiations; he sets investment policy, hires the lawyers and key administrators. In such circumstances, the term "business" unionism was no longer a metaphor for a political contract unionism. It now assumed the status of a more or less accurate representation of the actual functions of the union leader who in many cases spent less time and attention on contract enforcement than on his new business enterprises.

LABOR STATESMANSHIP

We have come a long way from the era when the dominant debates within trade union circles focused on the distinction between social and radical unions. Since all unions have, to a large extent, become social unions as well as contract or business unions, and the possibility of radical or revolutionary unions has become historically surpassed at least for the present, the new union leader eschews ideological considerations entirely. For one thing, the earlier internal trade union struggles were predicated upon a more or less coherent challenge to the social/business union philosophy of Gompers and his successors by socialists and communists. For all practical purposes, the organized Left has disappeared from the trade union movement. What remains are a significant number of socialist-minded leaders and rank and file members who function as the more left wing of the social unionists, confining their activities to pressing the trade union hierarchy to take anti-war positions, fighting cutbacks in public services, and admonishing the labor movement to aggressively pursue the task of organizing the unorganized.

In historical perspective these are unremarkable issues for the formation of a left wing within the labor movement.

Many of these leaders, such as James Matles of the Electrical Workers and Ralph Helstein of the Packinghouse Workers, have disappeared from active public life. Their local unions are today often indistinguishable from others led by officials with little or no political background. However, a substantial minority of unionists from various ideological backgrounds today constitute the heart of the progressive wing of the trade unions: they emerged in the late 1960's as opponents of the Vietnam War and other aspects of U.S. foreign policy; they have generally supported the Kennedy wing of the Democratic Party against its moderate "neo-liberal" mainstream; some have actively attempted to form a progressive "public sphere" within their local unions by introducing political and economic education among shop leaders; and they have made aggressive efforts to organize the unorganized, especially in public and private service sectors.

The northeast district of the Oil, Chemical and Atomic Workers (OCAW), a union of production workers, and District 65 UAW, a "general workers" union, are two outstanding examples of unions trying to preserve a concept of the labor movement that goes beyond day to day grievance handling and collective bargaining. OCAW has conducted classes for rank and file leaders and union members in economic issues, has developed strong health and safety committees in many plants and has run educational programs on labor's long-term political perspectives. District 65 is among the few unions in the private sectors of New York and New Jersey that have collaborated with the colleges and universities to offer degree programs, largely paid for by the employer. These programs have traditionally made their headquarters into a cultural center, not only for union members but for other social and political groups. Other innovations in cultural and political education have been made by the Amalgamated Clothing and Textile Workers and District 1199 of the National Hospital Union, who began the *Bread and Roses* project, a federally-funded traveling art and union history show. Following the expulsions in the late 1940's, the remnants of the Left chose to integrate themselves into the dominant practices of social and contract unionism so that today many who were literally trained by the Left, function as ordinary union leaders without any philosophy except that of organizational maintenance.

To illustrate this point, it may be useful to draw a composite portrait of the new type of union leader. Since the decline of manufacturing in the late 1960's and the progressive decline of the old industrial unions, public employee unions have emerged as the most dynamic sector of the trade union movement. Most of their members have been recruited since the early 1960's when, through a series of legislative reforms and executive orders by President Kennedy and governors and mayors, public unions gained the right to bargain collectively with employers. In many cases unions recruited workers at the worksite through the benevolent offices of public officials. The sudden spurt in public employee organization was in large measure a tribute to the weight of the trade union political influence in the late 1950's and 1960's within the Democratic Party and among selected segments of the Republican Party.

As a result of this political clout, public employee unions grew rapidly at all levels of government, particularly at the state and local levels where employment expansion, corresponding to the growth of social services and administration within the public sector, was most dramatic. Although not all of the new unions were established from the "top down" many have not to this day succeeded in forming strong, militant rank and file bases, and their general tendency has been to assume the character of associations or insurance companies where members draw benefits. The exceptions are, however, notable. The earliest mass public employee organizations were formed in New York in the late 1950's and early 1960's among teachers, municipal workers, and in voluntary non-profit hospitals under conditions of virtual social war, with dramatic strikes among hospital workers and teachers for union recognition highlighting the strong opposition the trade unions faced in New York in this period. However, such strikes were more the exception than the rule. In many other instances around the country, public employee unions were formed by legislative or administrative fiat. It is no accident then that New York public employee unions have earned the reputation of being among the toughest and most militant in the nation, especially given the state law prohibiting strikes in the public sector.

However, in recent years even the most militant unions have been obliged to make wage and benefits concessions to beleaguered local governments suffering substantial budget cuts. The fiscal crisis of the cities and state governments which has dominated local politics since the mid-1970's has only highlighted the main feature of public employee unionism: since virtually all wages are paid out of public tax levy funds, the process of bargaining is not only engaged in by management and labor but also at the political level between unions and the legislatures and the executive branch of government. All public employee unions devote substantial resources to political and legislative action and the typical leader spends as much time at city hall and in the state capital as on internal union affairs or various aspects of collective bargaining.

The new union leader must be a persuasive lobbyist, an effective manager of substantial pension funds, and someone who gradually learns the "big picture" surrounding collective bargaining. Unlike the old leader who had politically conservative ideas and a style of leadership that more resembled the old Tammany politician, the new public employees leader is smooth, adept at bureaucratic procedures, "progressive in political views," and above all a statesman. Perhaps it would be useful to amplify the concept of labor statesman at this point since it is usually employed by union militants to connote an old fashioned sell-out or at least one who has grown soft in the job—in his soft attitudes towards employers, in his professional upper middle class life style, and most important, in his reluctance to fight for members' interests.

I do not mean to use the term "statesman" to signify betrayal, but rather as a description of the new leadership that has emerged with public employees unionism. Here statesmanship comes to mean that leaders take the point of view of the public interest, especially the economic directorate, rather than remain loyal to their particular constituents—the workers in the agency, department, or other unit they represent. This larger vision may have been acquired in the process of adjusting to the new conditions of fiscal crisis after 1975, but given the conditions of American trade unionism created by Gompers (unions without labor or socialist parties to provide the ideological and political outlook upon which policy is based), the evolution of the union leader into a labor statesman became nearly inevitable. Whereas Gompers acquired this stance in the context of the rapid industrialization of American industry during the early years of the twentieth century, the new leaders have become "responsible" for the whole society during the long wave of economic crisis through which the United States is passing in the 1980's.[3]

At the most elementary level industrial and public employee unions have shared the problem of rapid deterioration in their respective sectors. Capital flight in intermediate technology industries resulting from sharpened international competition, the growing problem of imports, and the labor saving results of the technological development of key sectors such as the auto and steel industry have convinced many union leaders that wage and benefits concessions are necessary to preserve the jobs of the bulk of their members. In recent negotiations with the four leading auto corporations United Auto Workers members voted, sometimes with narrow majorities, to accept wage freezes or cuts as the best assurance of job security. Companies have returned some of these assurances by providing income for long-time employees put out of work and by restricting the production of parts to unionized plants. While public employee unions have returned some wages and benefits for similar considerations, they have further embarked on an extraordinary experiment in "social responsibility"—they have permitted their pension funds to be used to prevent several cities, notably New York, from defaulting on debt service. This use of pension funds is symbolic of the new style of union leadership, an example of the power inherent in their financial control over billions of dollars that have accrued from union administration of negotiated welfare and pension funds. In the process of acquiring this function union leaders have become an indispensable partner in the new coalition of public officials and banks that have taken over the reins of municipal government in many of America's largest cities, particularly those on the Eastern seaboard. The reasons for the corporations' entrance into city and state government and their establishment of almost total power both over finances and many government policies are too complex to be fully expounded here. Suffice it to say that most American cities in the post-war era experienced considerable decline in their ratable tax base owing to capital flight, the decline of residential real estate values, and the urban renewal policies of federal and local governments that provided substantial tax concessions to large commercial corporations as an incentive to remain within the inner cities. Under these circumstances, many cities averted financial ruin by drawing on the expanded federal funds to help them provide social services, highways, and streets, and pay for their basic administration. The rapid growth of public employee unionism after 1955 helped increase the costs of government at all levels dramatically, but most of all it added to the fiscal crisis of the cities that had been produced by urban deindustrialization and labor migration from rural areas around the world to America's urban centers. The union leaders were called upon in 1975 to help save New York City by "give backs" of some of the major gains they had made in the previous ten years. In the process the banks which held most of the municipal bonds that provided the ready cash to pay salaries to city employees and maintain city services, invited the unions to join in the coalition that was entering the administration of and partially displacing the city government. The price for obtaining a seat at the table of social and political power was the unions' willingness to surrender the traditional adversarial relationship that had marked collective bargaining during the period of upsurge. The corporations, having decided to become visible actors in the public arena, also demanded that the price of municipal fiscal solvency was the transformation of the state in the image of a corporation. Consequently, unionism in the new era would enter a social contract which would be based on its recognition that what was good for Chase Manhattan Bank was good for public employees. The deal was this: the large banks would refrain from demanding full payment from the city, would restructure its debt and thereby save the city from default on payment of its notes, in return for which public officials would turn over the central mechanism of city administration—the budget—for scrutiny and approval by a "financial control board" that would certify its parsimony and once again render municipal bonds attractive to investors. To make the agreement, the unions would have to become partners in this new arrangement. They would take responsibility for the integrity of the budget no less than investors and public officials charged with administering it. This responsibility would entail wage and benefit moderation based upon a strict accounting of the effects of such requests on the budget which could no longer be expected to run a deficit.[4]

Now the stage was set for the emergence of the new labor leaders. In addition to spending much of their time trying to pry more money from various legislative bodies, they would spend an increasing portion of their time on matters of budget and finance—collective bargaining became a year-long process. Union pension funds were no longer sacrosanct; they became an element not only in determining the cost of labor but also a major safety net backing up the city budget. When the federal government, faced with increased demands for higher military spending and powerful new conservative attacks against health, education, and social welfare expenditures, began reducing its share of local financing, most union leaders chose to become part of the solution rather than remain part of the problem. They abandoned their position as outsiders, adversaries of the banks and the administrators, and joined the new municipal oligarchy that ruled the cities. The labor leader socializes with the investment banker, joins organizations that proclaim the new partnership, and consolidates the role of the union as a quasi public agency. In New York, the Municipal Labor coalition, an organization that coordinates labor's bargaining policies with the city administration, is dominated by three large unions—the AFSCME district council 37 whose 90,000 members occupy a wide variety of city civil service titles, particularly clerical, social work, municipal hospital workers and professionals; the American Federation of Teachers, organized after a series of hard-fought strikes in the early 1960's and now the largest local of teachers in the United States with some 60,000 members; and local 237 of the Teamsters, a 20,000 member organization that lost the fight to be the major union of public employees in the city to district council 37 but retained strength in the Housing Authority, among the skilled manual trades, and among security officers. The Teamster's leader is also the major figure in this union's group of municipal unions which together number about 35,000 workers. These unions are often in conflict with the political authorities of the city—its mayor and city council. Such battles as are waged against elected officials help preserve some elements of their political independence from the dominant powers that rule New York City government. The most powerful union leaders are consulted constantly by the *real* power in the city— the financial corporations which hold most of its bonds and the heads of major city agencies who run its day to day affairs.

The public employee unions represent members on matters concerning job security, wage issues, and working conditions and conduct a wide range of educational activities, particularly helping members qualify for promotion examinations and other civil service opportunities. These unions have increasingly become involved in assisting individual members in legal problems, retaining a full-time staff to provide such services; they have a fairly extensive counseling service for members with health and personal problems and have recently cosponsored degree granting programs for their members in collaboration with various colleges and universities.

Although the unions are generally democratic in the formal sense and members often contest local union offices and the policies of the top leadership at meetings, the new partnership has necessitated considerable restriction of democratic procedures within the unions. To be sure, local meetings are held regularly but the range of decisions debated and adjudicated by these meetings is pressed into ever narrower boundaries. Union leaders regard the momentous decisions of city and state policy as too complex and important to be left to democratic decision making by members. The union leader is not merely the chief executive of a service and collective bargaining agency representing a finite group of members who pay dues; the leader is a public figure, a financial manager, a statesman.

This does not mean that the union leader would not insist that the broader functions of management into which he has been pressed are not consistent with member interests. But he might make the distinction between immediate, short-term-interest issues of wages and job control and the long-term question of job security or, indeed, the stability of the government. The militancy that might lead to job actions and strikes are always mediated by the leader's recognition that times have changed and these traditional trade union functions may no longer be appropriate to the new partnership. Therefore, the new leader—who rode on a wave of public employees' discontent and militancy in the 1960's, who became one of labor's foremost champions of civil rights, and who in many cases pioneered in the labor movement in opposing the Vietnam War—is now middle-aged, not only chronologically but ideologically and socially as well.

I want to emphasize that although the new style of leadership requires special characteristics which not all union officials possess, the whole managerial aura that now surrounds union leaders makes them figures corresponding to Max Weber's concept of bureaucratic rather than charismatic authority. In the case of industrial unions where, more often than not, the individual plant is also a local union, the larger bureaucratization is only imperfectly reproduced at the local level. The UAW, the Electrical Workers, and other industrial unions still retain some of the features of the old industrial unionism at the rank and file level: local union meetings are often tumultuous; there are frequent contests for leadership for shop as well as local union posts; the steward, traditionally the leader most attuned to the needs of the membership, may still be militant, fighting daily for ventilation, better safety measures, against speed up and against the arbitrary authority of management to discipline the work force.

However, the situation in public unions is much more ambiguous. Since many of these unions were formed from the top with little or no membership participation in organizing and gaining recognition, they have remained weak in their day to day defense of members interests. In some cases, notably district councils of AFSME and the Service Employees, the transition from an employees association to a legitimate trade union was both a prolonged and generally successful process. Many public employees organizations now have effective stewards systems, grievances are handled more or less swiftly, and members participate in many union functions, including the internal business of the local. But these are still the exceptions rather than the rule. Most state and federal level public unions are increasingly like citizens lobbies and service organizations. Members are not the real "owners" of the union but are regarded as *clients* of trained professionals who handle grievances, legal problems, and other individual issues faced by members. The experience of collective action, never strong among this stratum of union members, has become considerably eroded during the period of the fiscal crisis of city and state governments. As a result, the leader is now a remote figure, preoccupied with matters of state while the tasks of day to day representation are increasingly relegated to professionals who head divisions, departments, and other rationalized sub-institutions.

The situation is different for unions in declining industries. For unions in the competitive sector the steady deterioration of textiles and apparel industries, for example, was somewhat accelerated after the Second World War by a variety of broad economic trends, particularly the smaller share wearing apparel commanded of the consumer's disposable income; the dramatically lower level of technological development that resulted in chronically high labor costs; the appearance of significant foreign competition at least fifteen years earlier than in other industries. For union leaders as well as employers, the fringe benefits package provided an alternative to economically meagre wage settlements. From a sector that historically boasted of high wages in comparison to other industries, the apparel trades became one of the lowest paid. But the unions pioneered in the social wage even before the long slide. As early as the First World War, the Amalgamated Clothing Workers was providing a union-sponsored insurance program that included jobless benefits and burial plots; in the 1920's it added cooperative housing and formed a "workers" bank to finance residential cooperatives and small loans to union members.

For socialist-minded unions like the Amalgamated these programs were needed to maintain a measure of economic security for members at a time when the political climate was unfavorable for legislative remedies and a way to organize the unorganized. Even when workers were doubtful of the union's ability to deliver dramatic gains in money wages through bargaining, the union health and welfare plan remained an incentive to join. Similarly, in the 1950's this strategy became generalized throughout the labor movement. Leaders discovered the positive virtues of running their own health and welfare plans beyond the need to respond to relatively adverse political conditions. The health and welfare plan was a way to finance some union functions that could not be financed with relatively inelastic union dues. Pension funds could be used for organizing, legislative lobbying, and in a few cases political patronage. Although, after 1959, the Landrum-Griffin Act placed further restrictions of the use of union funds, including pensions, union leaders as adroit managers were able to manipulate the law to fulfill their ends.

Of course, the press has always delighted in labelling extramural uses of union pension and welfare funds as "corruption." If one sticks to technical conceptions of misappropriation this charge may have merit, but these

are no more corrupt than tax-free corporate expenditures for "entertain-
ment" that are thinly disguised payoffs to politicians or purchasing agents,
or the use of corporate funds for "political action" on behalf of pro-
business politicians. The business of running a modern labor union often
resembles ordinary corporate practices because the unions, having failed
to win such fringe benefits through the legislative process, were obliged
to resort to private plans that were often administered internally. Since
these plans are subject to public scrutiny and legal sanctions, unions have
sought to influence the regulatory procedures just as large corporations
have dominated federal and state agencies designed to regulate their
practices. Further, since unions within large cities often negotiate with
small, peripatetic employers, the importance of organizing in order to
stay abreast of rapid shifts within the industry cannot be overestimated.

Nevertheless, apart from the uses of pensions and other welfare funds
for union business, the most important effect of the privatization of the
social wage has been to generate a "state within a state." As unions relin-
quish their advocacy function because of the complexity of self-insured
health and pension plans, the administration of these funds is only a
logical extension of this new managerial posture into which labor leaders
are increasingly pushed. It is not so much that the union leader wishes to
emulate his counterpart in large corporate and state management, although this psychological dimension may be an unintended consequence
of the evolution of unions into business organizations in their own right.
Nor would I place the onus on what Marxist and other radical critics have
called "class collaboration" as an ideological tendency. In America class
collaboration is an effect of the web of economic and bureaucratic relations of trade unionism. To be sure, labor leaders of socially progressive
persuasion often attempt to segregate their business functions from their
role as part of the liberal wing of the Democratic Party or the progressive
wing of the AFL-CIO. While the leaders are forced to make decisions
concerning the distribution of welfare funds among investment options,
compromises with employers threatening to go out of business if wages
are not cut or frozen, and the disciplining of a group of workers who have
violated not only the contract but the law by walking out of their jobs, the
leaders as likely as not believe that all of these actions are expedients
dictated by economic, juridical, and political relations largely beyond
their control. The question posed by the advent of these new union
functions in the past thirty years is whether the union can remain a
democratic, voluntary association of members, much less retain a different ideological perspective and maintain its capacity to translate this
world view into programs and practices.

Today, the dominant mode of trade union practice and leadership consists of a series of variants of business and social unionism. Union leaders
at the national level rarely function as unionists pure and simple, at least

in the terms Gompers framed that style in the early twentieth century. Especially among the major labor organizations such as the large industrial unions and the public employee groups, the national union leader is deeply enmeshed in legislative and party politics, usually, but not exclusively, within or on the periphery of the Democratic Party. (A small number of national unions, particularly the Teamsters and the maritime unions, have drawn closer to the Republican Party in recent years, joining the building trades who have historically favored conservative politics.[5])

State and city union leaders are also part of the apparatus of party politics and legislative decision making. Unions are not only involved in lobbying for pro-labor bills or supporting sympathetic candidates for public office, they are also part of the constituency for state and local regulatory agencies such as the labor relations boards as well as the banking, commerce, and public utilities committees that supervise their pension funds or set rates and conditions on such services as freight, gas and electricity, and rail lines. The unions are also part of the liberal lobby in the broad areas of social welfare administration, particularly pressing for higher unemployment compensation and improved workers' compensation provisions. Many individual unions maintain their own lobbyists in state capitals as well as in Washington, even though state federations of labor and the AFL-CIO have extensive lobbying staff. The unions represent particular interests in their legislative offices. For example, the Teamsters Union has been vitally concerned with the regulation of freight rates by the Interstate Commerce Commission. Recently, it led the unsuccessful fight against deregulation of truck transportation, perceiving correctly as it turned out that this move would have a devastating impact on members' jobs and wages. Since the deregulation of the trucking industry by the Carter administration many small firms have been forced out of business and the union was required to renegotiate its master freight agreements with long-haul companies. The new contract provides for significant concessions that will freeze wages for years.

Many trade union legislative functions fit into their image as business organizations, although a number of labor's political and lobbying practices are a far cry from socially-conscious unionism. Union pressures to influence executive branch regulatory functions are typically undertaken in concert with the industry trade associations with whom they bargain. The most "progressive" unions no less than the conservative wing of the labor movement have taken their partnership with employers seriously by presenting a common front in matters of federal policy affecting their particular sector. Thus, it was no surprise when needle trades and textile unions supported their "own" employers in seeking import quotas, even though these unions have been traditionally in the forefront of the fight for social legislation and have often espoused free trade policies in the past. Similarly, in the 1980's, the Auto Workers Union has (no doubt to its own amazement) sounded like a protectionist organization after foreign car imports succeeded in capturing about twenty-five percent of a shrinking market. To those accustomed to images of class conflict in labor relations, the coalition between unions and the employers in specific industries facing substantial foreign competition destroys the stereotypical view propagated by the popular press. To its credit, the Auto Workers have joined other unions in metalworking industries which have proposed "domestic content" legislation rather than import duties or quotas to reduce foreign competition. Although the new approach is a departure from the traditional free trade posture of the unions, it is no more protectionist than similar legislation in thirty-one other countries. Moreover, by requiring employers to produce a substantial portion of products in the United States, the effect of the law would be to control capital flight, a major reason for the distressed situation of workers in many industries. The strong trade union support for the domestic content bill is contrary to the interests of the large multinational corporations which have become the leading proponents of free trade. In the coming years unions will find themselves allied with only the smaller employers for whom international production is not a genuine option, and will be obliged to fight against their "own" larger employers.

Collaboration between labor and employers is far more characteristic than antagonism since World War II. For this reason alone recent widespread renegotiation of labor contracts responding to the adverse economic climate should come as no surprise. Trade union leaders have accepted the doctrine that to be committed to the interests of the industry is consonant with if not identical to their members' interests. C. Wright Mills argued thirty-five years ago that unions have become a vital if subordinate part of the triumvirate of power forces—government, large employers, and the "big" unions—that controls the destiny of the U.S. economy and the country's relations with the rest of the world. As we shall see, this judgment must now be severely modified since the U.S. economy is no longer able to determine the balance of world economic forces, and the labor movement is no longer in the same favorable position. Nevertheless, unions still act on the *ideology* of collaboration even though the benefits derived from the strategy have considerably diminished.

THE SOCIAL CONTRACT

The labor movement offers no political alternative to the programs of capital except in the unorganized sectors of the economy. Although these are numerically larger than those that operate within the collective bargaining system, they were not until recently important in the processes of economic reproduction. Just as union leaders played a vital role in ex-

tending the power of U.S. capital after the Second World War by col-
laborating at the political and economic levels, they are now working
within the machinery of readjustment to the new world economic order
that has reduced capital's options for growth within the old production
sectors. As the managers of labor contract, union leaders are being asked
to lead their members into sacrifices in order to protect the viability of
many U.S. corporations which have been weakened since the world economic crisis that matured after 1970. There are virtually no unions, including those with reputations for militancy, that have consistently
refused to play this role.

There are few politically viable alternatives to the concept of wage and
benefits sacrifice to protect the market position of "their" employers.
Such remedies as nationalization are precluded from consideration at a
bargaining table at which employers, unions, and the state iron out their
differences within the social contract. Nor has the alternative of worker-
owned and managed companies been proposed except in a few cases,
notably the Rath Packing plant in Waterloo, Iowa; the General Motors
Hyatt Roller Bearing plant in Clark Township, New Jersey; National Steel
in Weirton, West Virginia; and a number of small firms in the needle
trades. These alternatives would not, to be sure, preclude sacrifices, since
in almost every case where workers assume ownership or control over
near-bankrupt or technologically backward firms they are required to
make concessions in order to keep the plant afloat. Union leaders in the
private sector, accustomed to the formal rules that leave the control of the
workplace to management, prefer to maintain the adversary posture because it relieves them of direct responsibility for failure and obliges them
to step out of the traditional role of contract unionism. Worker ownership
and management or nationalization implies bringing the power of the
union out in the open and challenges the historically evolved division of
power at the workplace in which management retains the right to control
the labor process. Thus, the discourse of trade unionism is still "pure and
simple" and even the social unions are reluctant to upset this arrangement, preferring to treat the crisis within the framework of management's
right to direct the adjustment, subject to limits involving assurances of job
security for the most senior workers.[6]

In recent years intellectuals, managers, rank and file workers, and
some trade union leaders themselves have begun to question the old
social contract. Union leaders have become the most important defenders
of many of its aspects, especially the framework of collective bargaining
within which wages and benefits are determined. Collective bargaining in
turn has suffered considerably from the current crisis because its social
weight depended on the concept of more or less regular wage increases,
an assumption that no longer may be made, at least for the foreseeable
future. Consequently, in a recent special feature the pro-business maga-

zine *Business Week* advocated a new social contract.[7] This contract purports not merely to entail wage concessions by unions, it would also require considerable concessions by corporations regarding their unilateral right to manage the labor process. The proposal asks for a new partnership between labor and capital that would renounce the adversarial relationship of conventional collective bargaining. Unions would no longer regard wage increases as an automatic gain at each contract; employers would be obliged to consult with union leaders on issues of technological change and marketing arrangements.

Since the question of a new social contract has been raised, union leaders have shown themselves more than willing to entertain its major premise. This is because the considerable membership losses sustained by unions in the past three years have considerably weakened labor's bargaining power, and the will to conflict among the remaining employed rank and file is undermined by layoffs and capital flight. Perhaps the most important reason for the relatively pliant posture of union leaders is that the old contract was a partnership as much as a culmination of union victories against management. As responsible officers of the contract as well as their own labor organizations, contemporary labor leaders are caught in the agonies of dual loyalties. On the one hand, they must respond to members' militancy (as in the case of the 1982 strike by Canadian UAW members against the Chrysler corporation after the leadership had negotiated concessions). On the other hand, union leaders are inclined to see the company's point of view, because structurally they are both representatives of and authorities over the workers on the shop floor.

Although the British labor movement evinces similar features (historically, the shop stewards organized their own movement, separate from the national trade union officers), what is specifically *American* about the labor movement is its nearly universal renunciation of ideological class interest in favor of a conception of loyalty that links the union to its particular constituents—the shop floor worker, the company and the industry.

PART

II

CRACKS IN THE BLOC: AMERICAN LABOR'S HISTORIC COMPROMISE AND THE PRESENT CRISIS

CHAPTER 4

THE DEVOLUTION OF THE LABOR MOVEMENT

THE evolution of American unionism defies any attempt to neatly categorize the movement as a whole. Although socialism (as both ideology and practical perspective) was decisively defeated within the labor movement after the First World War, a significant fraction of trade union leaders retain fragments of its visions. These leaders may simultaneously accept the need to enter a partnership with a liberal fraction of capital in order to save both the union and the jobs of its members, and firmly believe in a democratic socialist vision of a new society. The most aggressive and militant rank and file dissidents may criticize the leaders for being too soft at the bargaining table, yet abhor the political role of the labor movement. Some rank and file leaders and a few at the middle and top levels of the labor movement are prone to intransigence against an individual employer while at the same time holding fast to a deeply conservative social and political philosophy. In short, the "movement" surpasses and trails the institution.

The New Deal was a partial exception to this general rule. Apart from some AFL craft unions, the insurgent CIO possessed both a larger social vision and considerable shop floor militancy. To be sure, the social vision was essentially democratic not millenarian; its aim was to widen industrial and political citizenship by following Lewis's prescription that a new partnership with progressive capital and elements of the political directorate could bring about a new birth of the labor movement. Of course, he was right and those to his left had no alternative but to join in the upsurge on terms that fell far short of their own radical goals. Yet it is an error to speak only of the integration of the unions into corporate capitalism in the 1930's or to limit the historical assessment to showing that the union contract facilitated the rationalization of the labor process by insuring management rights. Nor is it sufficient to point out that the Democrats were the second party of capital. These truisms are not a *critique* unless one assumes that a different outcome was possible during the Depression. Given the decimated state of the labor movement at the beginning of the Depression, the successful recruitment of seven million workers into industrial and craft unions in the decade after 1933 could only have been achieved under conditions of coalition. The CIO leadership more or less consciously elected to join hands with the New Deal as labor's best hope for social justice. The stunning victories in the auto, steel, and rubber industries in 1936–37 had been preceded by successful efforts led primarily by radicals on the West Coast waterfront and in the Minneapolis trucking industry. Moreover, the radicals and militants had formed small unions under communist, socialist, or independent craft association leadership in the early 1930's. For example, Lewis's reorganization of the United Mine Workers built on the successes of the communists in forming the National Miners Union, and the Textile Workers' efforts had been grounded in the more or less spontaneous strikes against speedup and wage cuts in which socialists participated in Marion, North Carolina, and communists in Gastonia, North Carolina. Similarly, the sudden agreement between Lewis and Myron C. Taylor of US Steel had been prepared by years of trench warfare among rollers and other skilled workers, and intensive independent organizing in Pittsburgh, Gary, and Buffalo.

The Trotskyists in Minneapolis and the communists on the West Coast joined the CIO for one simple reason: it was the only alternative to building mass unions. By 1938, the entire labor left was folded into the industrial union movement, which by this time had penetrated the AFL as well. Radicals kept their own political counsel and were central in modifying the instrumentalism of the old line leaders like Lewis and Philip Murray. To the radicals belongs the credit for introducing some of the elements of the larger vision that differentiated the CIO from its craft union adversaries.

The New Deal partnership was more than corporatism with a human face; it represented labor's growing political power. Indeed, the second welfare state phase of Roosevelt's administration was instituted as a rationalizing apparatus of social control, although the principal concessions to working people and the poor were undoubtedly linked to this objective. They were also promises to a young power that might have moved leftward if the corporations and the state had behaved like their British counterparts at the turn of the century. Although organized labor failed to constitute an independent political vehicle through which it might have extended its social weight, labor's concerns dominated the domestic program of the Democratic Party for the first time in history and workers regarded the Democratic Party as their own, however limited the truth of this perception might be.

The New Deal effectively limited the influence of voluntarism in labor's ranks. From the late thirties to the present day, unions became more and less than a social movement; they were also a "state within a state" and partners in the late capitalist state's intervention into the economy. The crisis in American labor today can be traced to the successes of this transformation. Part II of this book will discuss the nature of the change that occurred in the past forty years and its effect on the contemporary labor movement.

The American trade unions joined together with other class fractions and castes to dominate the discourse of American politics for over 30 years. The Democratic Party, after 1936, was a grand coalition of forces whose leading precept was support for various elements of the welfare state as much as a rationale for securing the global domination of U.S. capital.

The devolution of the labor movement was, as I will argue in this section, the key element in the decline of the grand coalition. While the sources of the New Right's power and the ideology of neo-conservatism are complex, the conservatives' ability to set the terms for American political discourse are to be explained in large measure by the decline of the New Deal coalition, particularly the working class and its trade union organizations, and the ideological weakness of labor and progressive forces in America today. The conditions for the weakening of labor's political mobilization—which I will trace first with reference to the recent air controllers' strike, then historically, and finally theoretically—are essential to understanding the decisive turn to the right that has brought Ronald Reagan to power.

THE CRISIS OF TRADE UNIONS

American ideology in the period of U.S. industrialization succeeded in framing the discourse of labor relations in purely economic terms. The National Labor Relations Act of 1935 established a pattern of labor-management relations that differed radically from European traditions. Collective bargaining became a privilege that workers gained as a result of a government-administered election among a group designated as an appropriate unit by the Labor Board. Unions were invited to compete for representation on the basis of a show of membership cards. Only one union could represent the unit of workers, and its competitors were rendered irrelevant for that particular unit. In many European countries union membership has been separated from the question of representation. For example, French law provides for the bargaining committee elected by workers in a given enterprise to be selected from among lists supplied by competing labor unions. The unions, more or less ideologically aligned, win delegates on the basis of a system of proportional representation.

The American tradition of trade unionism renounces ideological politics in favor of contract unionism. The business of gaining higher wages, better working conditions, and social benefits for union members through contract bargaining, has become identical with what we mean by the labor movement. Because the labor union is not structurally required to compete with other unions except on the initial question concerning who will be certified bargaining agent, American unionism is depoliticized.

There are two exceptions to this rule. The first is the prohibition of strikes during "national emergencies," whether during wartime or in industries essential to economic stability, i.e., growth. The second, which has become more significant since the rise of public sector unionism in the 1960's, is the legal prohibition of strikes among federal employees and the public employees who are not only barred from striking, but often do not have recourse to compulsory arbitration to settle outstanding issues of the contract, even if individual grievances may be submitted to arbitration.

The no-strike provisions of public labor relations law tend to force most public employees unions into being little more than company unions, except in those states and localities where the labor movement plays a strong role in politics. Since John Kennedy signed the executive order in 1961 recognizing the right of federal employees to bargain collectively, several large unions have formed from the small labor organizations that had previously been confined to lobbying Congress and various agencies. The most important of these are the American Federation of Government Employees (AFGE) and two unions among postal employees, the American Postal Union and the Letter Carriers. In 1970, hundreds of thousands of postal workers struck against the advice of their union leaders. The national wildcat strike was met by President Nixon's attempt to move the mail with the National Guard. There was no threat of permanent firing despite the law's provision that this was a possible consequence of the strike action. For the most part, federal unions have observed the no-strike law and, as a result, have negotiated relatively weak agreements with federal agencies.

The small Professional Air Traffic Controllers Organization (PATCO) had been no exception to the general rule of compromise and observance of the law. Its 15,000 members, who controlled the air space at all major U.S. airports, are mainly white males from families in the small and medium-sized cities that have formed the foundation of the neo-conservative penetration of organized labor. PATCO, although affiliated with the AFL-CIO, supported Ronald Reagan's 1980 Presidential campaign because he represented the socially conservative views of many of America's airline employees. He was their kind of parsimonious, middle-American figure. He embodied patriotic values, particularly the idea that America should be the economic and political leader of the world.

The controllers, however, faced problems in the performance of their jobs that made many of their conservative ideological precepts anachronistic. Like other members of the technical intelligentsia whose occupations are marked by high levels of technology, their everyday working levels required enlarged responsibility without the concomitant power to control their working conditions. The distinction between the two has created a new occupational hazard—burn-out or stress. *Stress has become the black lung of the technical classes.* When technical employees are subjected to rigid time boundaries, penalties for lateness and absenteeism, a power hierarchy in which their autonomy on the job is limited by rules imposed by managers, and increasing segmentation of job duties, their professional status is threatened. The expectation, shared by many employees in categories of knowledge production and control, that skill should entail a qualitatively different relation to the labor process than that suffered by manual workers is increasingly called into question by managerial rationality.[1]

The demands which brought the air controllers to the picket lines in 1981 arose from this experience of a loss of autonomy in the workplace and a degradation of the labor process. However, their formulation of those demands did not aim at altering working conditions but only at alleviating their effects. The controllers went on strike when the federal government and the Federal Aviation Administration (FAA) refused to negotiate a shorter work week and earlier retirement, insisting that bargaining gains be limited to salaries. Even though the proposed salary settlement did not meet controllers' goals, it was clear from the outset that the real dispute concerned working conditions. Faced with the serious job hazards of responsibility over human life without genuine self-management, the workers sought an "unwork" solution rather than demanding more power over their labor process.[2]

Why did the controllers choose the "unwork" solution over self-management? Like other technical employees they do in fact "love their work," recognizing its intrinsic importance not only with respect to the product but also with respect to the process of production. These workers are prevented from grappling with the issues associated with management's arbitrary authority because their critique of management prerogatives remains an action-critique rather than an ideological and theoretical, that is, political critique. A contradiction infuses workers' struggles in America: intellectual and manual labor accepts the fundamental structure of production relations while at the same time refusing the experience of these relations. This contradiction between workers' experience of the production relations and their cognitive grasp of these same relations provides a more precise formulation of the proposition that the genius of the U.S. social formation lies in its continual separation of economic from political relations. The consequence is exemplified by PATCO itself, where the most stubborn resistance by workers to the power of capital appears entirely consistent with their ideological adherence to the main conservative forces in American politics and the framework within which power is exercised.

The air controllers were forced to strike not only because of the absence of a substitute mechanism to adjudicate labor disputes among public employees, but also because the Reagan administration followed a line of "take it or leave it" bargaining. What must be explained therefore is what produced this stance, which contrasts so dramatically with the attitude of prior administrations, including Nixon and Ford. In the decade since Nixon faced the postal strike, the economic and political climate had changed sufficiently to embolden the Reagan administration and its conservative base. Further, while the postal workers in 1971 sought a wage increase that was aimed at establishing parity with the income of manual workers in highly unionized industries, the PATCO demands threatened to plow new ground in collective bargaining. And there is little doubt that the new administration was anxious to show a new tough stance towards federal unions. The Postal Union, the most militant and effective federal employees organization, was making noises that it would not accept a "normal" settlement in 1981. Other impending negotiations, particularly those with the Treasury employees' union and the AFGE, the largest union among federal departments, were slated to open.

Had PATCO confined its demands to a substantial wage increase and some improvements in the fringe benefits package, there would have been a basis for compromise. As Reagan supporters during the 1980 campaign, the union's leadership was confident that the administration would be willing to grant some economic concessions. But the rank and file had different ideas. Instead of following the ritual in such cases of dropping its more innovative demands (a shorter work week and earlier retirement) in return for a higher money wage, the membership greeted the compromises that its leadership was prepared to make with swift disapproval, forcing the FAA and the union leaders back to the bargaining table.

The FAA stood firm behind its last offer of a fairly liberal wage settlement that amounted to about 10%, slightly higher than the average increase in the unionized sector in 1980. The FAA was constrained by several factors, chiefly the administration's austere wage policy that corresponds to its program of reducing the federal budget except for the military and its resolve to hold the line on any offensive demands by labor. These "offensive" demands would constitute a qualitative change insofar as they explicitly offer a critique of working conditions, particularly the labor process. The PATCO membership did not advance its retirement and shorter hours claims on the basis of more leisure, but because it argued that the quality of work life had become intolerable. The air controllers were choosing the only option available within the discursive limits of American labor relations: *less work.*

Beyond its resolve to refuse the new demands in the strike, the Reagan administration made an accurate assessment of its adversaries. The AFL-CIO did little more than support the strike with money and some moral support. Pilots, mechanics, other maintenance employees, and flight attendants were unwilling to test the legal and political consequences of a secondary boycott. Whatever their economic power to stop the flights, the unions retreated to their legal obligation not to strike. The constraints of contract unionism held sway. Moreover, there was a real fear among union leaders to call a war to which nobody would come. The Reagan administration felt able, for the first time since Roosevelt and Truman took on unions under wartime conditions, to use repressive state powers to defeat them. Reagan's historic hubris, carried to the extreme of refusing to back down when it became apparent that neither firings nor union decertification would daunt the overwhelming majority of the strikers, is a stark symptom of the political and moral disrepair of the American labor movement. For the unions had been out of power long before Reagan's electoral victory. Their failure during the Carter administration to win the long struggle for a labor reform law that would have eased the way to organizing the unorganized was a stunning lesson for those who harbored illusions that the old New Deal coalition was intact. Labor's power in the political sphere and the economy has withered in the context of the sharp drop in union membership, the pervasive loss of social vision within labor's ranks, and the long-term economic slide of the 1970's.

PATCO did prove that, even without work stoppages or slowdowns by other airline employees, it could inflict deep economic losses on the airline industry. There is no reason to underestimate the strike's economic effects, as industry experts initially tried to do by claiming that the strike aided the rationalization of the chaotic industry by forcing smaller carriers out of business, hastening mergers among competitors, and reducing the number of half-filled flights. Employer and financial sources estimated losses of some $25 million a day in the early weeks of the strike. After three months, allowing some recovery through rationalization, the industry might still lose as much as $10 billion in sales and $1 billion dollars in profits. Nonstriking air unions suffered more than ten percent layoffs in the first three weeks. The airline industry, already suffering the effects of the recession that began in 1981, was forced to postpone sharp rate hikes. Among the sicker segment, especially carriers engaged in international transport like Braniff and Pan American, the strike has produced a crisis. At the same time that passenger traffic was sharply curtailed, high interest rates on loan capital and inflation have cut deeply into the investment needed to modernize the equipment of the weaker corporations.

It is important to recognize the economic damage done by the PATCO strike in order to focus the fundamental question. Namely, why did the union's *economic* power fail to translate into a *political* and *ideological* victory? How did the Reagan administration forestall, despite the economic effects of the strike on the airline industry and the public, the political fallout that might have come from its repressive actions? The answer lies, I will argue, in the tendency within the labor movement itself to fail to link its economic struggles to politics and ideology. In the context of the general weakening of the labor movement's influence on American politics, the absence of this link becomes decisive. It is all the more important for unions that bargain with the state and are, therefore, directly dependent upon public discourse.

PATCO failed to seriously contest, let alone command, the public discourse from the moment it followed the tendency, widespread within the labor movement in recent years, to privilege, to the virtual exclusion of other tactics, reliance on the strike as an economic instrument of struggle. This very economism[3] made it relatively easy for the Reagan administration to set the discursive agenda for the conduct of the strike, especially its denouement—the firing of the controllers and the decertification of their union. Reagan posed the law—and the controllers' oath!—as a moral imperative that overshadowed all other issues. The media accepted the ideological framework of Reagan's agenda and put the PATCO leadership and rank and file on the defensive.

The union's inability to challenge the public discourse can be read in the posture of its president, Robert Poli, during the first days of the strike. Retaining a cool, self-confident demeanor, Poli refused to articulate the union's substantive position, claiming only that the rank and file was solidly aligned behind the leaders in pursuing the walkout. He predicted that the government would have to resume negotiations as soon as the cold and foggy weather set in, when the companies felt losses in income and the public experienced the inconvenience of hobbled air traffic. Even as the media became more sympathetic to the administration's hammering away at the legal and moral issue, the union persisted in its refusal to undertake a broad public education campaign to publicize its grievance and challenge the morality of the law prohibiting public employee strikes.

Like the rest of labor and progressive forces, PATCO greeted the idea that politics and ideology could take command in the American context as unthinkable. Relying on its economic power, the union failed to understand that Reagan was an ideologue speaking for a fraction of capital prepared to reverse the legacy of the New Deal along a broad front even if it meant temporary and deep economic losses. As heirs of that very legacy, the labor movement has become victim of the discourse of the "bottom line" with its claim that pragmatic considerations will always prevail within the business community whose last morality is profit. But this has never been true in American labor history. The great struggles have been conducted over the *principle* of the right of management to have free rein within the labor process. In the period of large-scale industry which dominated American production after the Civil War, employers were prepared to suffer economic losses to preserve their power at the workplace and in the market. Only when they saw their long-term interests threatened by a politically active labor movement did they back down from this stance and learn to use the labor contract as a rationalizing tool. The labor movement has rarely understood that U.S. corporations, despite their inability to command the world and national economy as a whole, are remarkably united regarding the issue of management's right to command production and distribution.

Reagan in effect trapped PATCO in labor's own ideology of contract unionism. The magisterial rhetoric of the law and the solemn oath resonates with conventional American trade union wisdom, which dictates that it is always in workers' interest to enforce the contract against employer infractions and that the rule of law in collective bargaining is part of "labor's magna carta." To break this ritual, the unions would be obliged to take the stance of the civil rights movement of the 1960's: "It is immoral to obey an immoral law," or labor's struggle for justice supersedes unjust and represssive legislation. Incapable of taking up these slogans and concepts, PATCO could not respond to the law and order theme.

The union, after Reagan's executive order to discharge the workers, did try to shift the discourse to the theme of public safety and the issue of whether the air transport system could be safely operated with reduced work forces. Only in this form did the union finally appeal to the public and for a time succeeded in keeping many prospective passengers from boarding aircraft. The administration moved quickly, appointing investigative bodies to certify the safety of the system and orchestrating testimonials from air traffic officials and pilots stating that safety was the first priority of the FAA and the airliners. By now the administration's command of the public discourse through the media was complete. The media concluded that the skies were safe—marginalizing any number of facts that indicated the opposite, from the poor training and overwork of the replacement controllers to an actual crash of small planes and several near-misses involving airliners. More significantly, the controversy over safety became the cardinal discursive practice surrounding the strike. As a result, all substantive strike issues disappeared from press and TV reporting within a month. PATCO had so dramatically lost the ideological struggle over public discussion that the press came to blame the union itself for the economic damage suffered by the airlines, the inconvenience to air passengers, and the reduction of schedules which the airlines sought and got from the government.

A summary of the decisive elements of PATCO's actions will illustrate the extent to which the union followed labor's general tendency to separate economic struggle from political and ideological struggle, a legacy that has become all the more disastrous with the emergence of ideological right-wing politics as the cutting-edge of the new fractions of capital who has come to national power: (1) In its negotiations for a contract. PATCO sought an "unwork" solution in the absence of an ideological grasp of the connection between the experience of stress and the denial of self-management. (2) Viewing the strike as a purely economic weapon, the union had no entry into the ideological and political context of public discussion except through its claim that it could bring the airline industry to its knees. (3) PATCO remained isolated from the labor movement as a whole due to the erosion of labor's political power in the United States today, and from the effective support of other airline unions, themselves constrained by contracts and laws forbidding secondary boycotts. (4) The Reagan administration, willing to privilege ideology and politics over immediate economic interest, took charge of the public discourse of the strike and pinned PATCO to the very law and order doctrine that the American labor movement itself, in its devotion to the negotiated contract, continually supports.

The PATCO strike is a case study of new tendencies within the composition of work and of the working class fractions. Only by relating these tendencies and the constraints imposed by American labor's own traditions can we begin to understand the convergence in American politics today between the devolution of the labor movement and the rise of the New Right.

The success of the PATCO strike was to have mobilized a new fraction of the working class to oppose both capital and the state. Its failure is a measure of both the ideological weakness of the labor movement and its traditional social and economic base. The labor movement represents the past era of industrial capitalism. Its grand achievement, the organization of workers in the basic, intermediate technology industries that once dominated the United States and the world economies, has been surpassed by social, scientific, and political transformations. The center of these transformations is the capacity of capital to mobilize science to replace manual labor as the chief productive force. Here the term "science" is employed not merely to refer to the scientific application to machine processes but to the organization of labor as well. What Max Weber termed *rational calculation,* whose central feature is the separation of design from execution or, to put it another way, the establishment of a sharper antinomy between intellectual and manual labor through the construction of the labor process, becomes as important as such innovations as numerical controls, memory chips, or robots designed to eliminate living labor.

In recent decades new developments in class structure and the recomposition of social classes have resulted from new forms of capital. Social theory has been obligated to account for these historical tendencies. European theory since the mid-60's has centered on the emergence of the technical intellegentsia as a new historical actor of first importance. In the

United States there has been only an action critique of the technostructure of late capitalism. The most important labor struggles of the past decade have occurred in the public sector among professionals as well as better paid clerical and professional employees. Teachers strikes outstrip virtually all others in length and frequency during this period; they have been conducted over a variety of issues bearing on working conditions, the principal category of which is either autonomy or a shorter working day. While wage issues are always important in an inflationary economy, these have not been enough to provoke major strikes except among the postal workers, who were notoriously underpaid until 1970.

At the same time struggles in this sector occur within more sharply delimited legal restrictions than for similar groups in Western Europe and Canada. The distinction between the private and the public has remained a critical element in the American ideology of economics and political relations. The concept of public service has been a major barrier to the new technical intelligentsia's emergence as a political force in the United States. There has been virtually no recognition in the United States that a strike in the public sector is, as such, a strike against the state and has broad political ramifications. The Reagan administration has, of course, recognized this fact, and its severe reprisals against the controllers were widely understood as an offensive against organized labor, not only in the public sector but against union power as such.

As I have been suggesting, the initiative and insight that the right enjoys today in the confrontation between labor and the state can be directly attributed to labor's own commitment to the ideology of contract unionism. Union officials accept the labor agreement as a solemn pledge. Only when management flagrantly ignores its provisions do union officials contemplate violating the boundaries of the contract. Not only is economic struggle separated from political action by the discourses and institutions that frame social struggle in the United States, but labor is also burdened by the doctrine of public and contractual responsibility. This raises the historic question of the potentialities of unions as a social movement when their character as voluntary associations has been so significantly altered by the juridical framework within which collective bargaining occurs, including contract provisions that require union membership as a condition of employment.

Many progressives hope that class struggle unionism can arise from the introduction of democratic processes into union governance and labor relations, a hope premised by the belief that the rank and file does not share its leaders' dutiful obedience to the law. There is, however, no evidence that union democracy or contract militance leads to left-wing working class politics. Labor radicalism remains limited by economistic assumptions so long as the ideological framework is imprisoned by the specifically American doctrine that class conflict is bounded by the parameters of the assumptions of economic growth and juridical responsibility. While American workers during the industrialization period of American capitalism did not always take this view as self-evidently in their interests, the basic discourse of American power has, since World War II, provided the limits of political and economic action. It is the dominance of this discourse, rather than coercive force, which has most constrained the labor movement.

A significant crack has been opened in the dominant discourse in the past twenty years. The ideology of public service, which had been able to contain the wage demands of public employees for decades, bolstered by the promise of secure employment and work that contained some technically based satisfactions, has broken down. Sections of the technical intelligentsia—call it the Professional Managerial Class, the new petty bourgeoisie, etc.—no longer accept their subordination, even in the wake of economic crisis. They understand their centrality to the economy and, less distinctly, their growing social weight. This awareness produced a wave of powerful public employees union organizing in the 1960's and 70's. The air controllers strike signals, from this perspective, a new reflexivity among members of this stratum. The resistance to job and pay cuts in the public sector has been markedly greater than in traditional industrial sectors. Industrial workers and their unions all over the nation are dolefully giving back wages and other benefits in the hope of hanging onto their jobs. Similar trends are somewhat present among clerical, blue collar, and some subprofessional workers in the public sector, as well as some teachers unions in the older centers of the northeast. The PATCO strike did not mark the beginning of a general countertendency, but the mood of resistance among sections of public employees in general and particularly among the most skilled certainly indicates that such a countertendency could develop.

The obstacles are indeed numerous. As the PATCO strike indicates, the process of self-organization on the part of technical workers is at a rudimentary level. Moreover, there is almost no evidence of private sector unionization among engineers and administrators. While the labor movement's most important organizing success in the last fifteen years was the enrollment of 3½ million public employees, these gains have not offset the loss of social weight that the working class as a whole has suffered because of the economic, social, and ideological devolution of the traditional industrial sector. Nor have these gains among public employees kept pace with the growth of the technical and administrative sectors which correspond to the realignment of the global economic order, in which the United States has yielded its preeminence as the industrial workshop of the twentieth century to Germany and Japan and become the coordinator of technology and capital. In terms of the new world economic order, the PATCO strike's importance lies in the fact that it was the first major internationally noted strike among the new "class" which has emerged as potentially the most powerful among the working classes. Its exceptional character is tied to the inability of these technical strata to organize themselves as a significant social force in American society.

LABOR AND THE NEW DEAL

I will now trace, in greater detail, crucial elements of the devolution of the labor movement. I will start with the role of the industrial union upsurge of the 1930's in transforming the Democratic Party from the second party of capital into a ruling coalition of class fractions, dominated to be sure by a fraction of industrial and finance capital, but given ideological and organizational form by the most dynamic section of the labor movement and the intellectuals allied with it. Essential to the formation of this coalition was labor's historic compromise with capital, its entry into a new social contract. After assessing the limitations that this new social contract, this new deal, imposed on the ideological and political potentiality of American labor, I will try to identify the elements of the decline and recomposition of the working class and its organizations—principally in terms of the labor movement's antagonistic relations with the American left, its increasingly detrimental adherence to the ideology of growth, and its failure to respond to the rapid social, economic, and geographical transformations of capital itself.

The New Social Contract. During the period of the New Deal's dominance in American politics, the trade unions, which had achieved a level of organization among the working class of some thirty percent by 1946, were not only crucial actors in raising real wages for industrial workers but also led the struggle for the maintenance and extension of the welfare state. Since 1936, when organized labor awoke from its twelve-year political nadir, unions had formed the key sector of the Democratic Party in many states. Its heavy organizational and financial contributions to Democratic Presidential candidates were indispensable aspects of the national campaign. From 1944 through the reelection campaign for Lyndon Johnson in 1964, labor formed the organizational backbone of the New Deal. As the most militant legislative champions of social reform, the trade unions became the center of the grand coalition that Roosevelt formed for reelection in 1936. Civil rights, youth, urban, and other movements relied on the support of organized labor to defend and extend their interests. Even though the alliance was largely informal, and other movements criticized the unions for failing to play an aggressive political role in their behalf, there was no more powerful or, in the final accounting, more reliable force than American unions for broadening the contours of social justice in America.

The critical issue for American progressives has, since the 1930's, been whether the American trade union movement and its working class constituency would remain ideologically committed to social reform, faithful to its decision to enter the New Deal coalition as a vital, socially powerful force. The unions' social power requires a high level of organization among workers, the retention of the legal preconditions for union organization and collective bargaining such as those provided by the Wagner Act in 1935, and the legitimacy of trade unions as representative of ideological, political, and economic interests among the rank and file. As I have argued, unlike European counterparts which have been linked to independent class political and ideological formations, such as labor, socialist, and communist parties, American unions have retained their nominal independence from party affiliation since the founding of the AFL in 1886. Unions have always represented themselves to workers as economic instruments; participation in electoral politics is always presented as an extension of the collective bargaining function, rather than in social or ideological terms. Socialism—or even a broadly anti-capitalist ideological politics—is strictly excluded from the daily discourse of the trade unions.

The long periods of U.S. economic expansion combined with the deep-seated anti-intellectual culture of even the majority of American intellectuals, much less the rest of the population, convinced the founders of the modern labor movement a century ago that the private sympathies of the leading trade unionists ought not to be confused with trade union practice. American trade unionism has, with the notable exception of the IWW, been fashioned from the combination of (a) commonsense economism in which political action may be undertaken, but only defensively; (b) an unusual labor militancy (compared at least to European counterparts) conditioned to a great extent upon the relatively favorable circumstances for protracted economic struggle (particularly among skilled workers, who were in chronically short supply throughout the industrialization phase); and (c) a strong orientation to the issues surrounding the legal protections of the right to organize and bargain without jeopardizing jobs of union activists. Opponents of this formula never challenged it *in toto* but focused on particular aspects: the IWW opposed the labor contract as a tool of class struggle but shared the AFL's antipathy to aligning the labor movement to electoral action except to protect its right to organize. For a brief moment, the social unionists grouped around the early CIO favored an offensive political strategy, especially the idea of constituting a left wing within the Democratic Party or forming a labor party, but accepted the legal framework of collective bargaining. The post-Gompers generation of AFL leaders tried to maintain union autonomy from the state and the political parties but remained quintessentially committed to contract unionism. The communists, bereft of a *theoretical* critique of trade union practice, made the principle of organizing the unskilled and semi-skilled their leading ideological precept but adopted the program of social unionism after 1935, a move which left them firmly ensconced in the contract union definitions of the labor movement after their political interventions of the 1940's failed.[4]

CHAPTER
5

THE POSTWAR PERIOD

IN Part I of this book I have shown how unions were obliged to become "state-like" apparatuses in order to serve their members' interests in the wake of the failure of Harry Truman's postwar Democratic administration to win the Congressional fight to extend the social welfare state. For the Clothing Workers, who had pioneered in creating a state within the state in the first decades of the twentieth century, such measures as jobless benefits, union-sponsored low cost housing, and health programs were grim necessities born of the labor movement's political weakness at the time. Progressive unions supported the New Deal as labor's best hope to create a genuine social safety net for workers displaced by capitalist crises, temporary unemployment, sickness, and old age. In industries such as the needle trades where the unions were obliged to take responsibility for these services, trade union leaders were well aware small employers were simply incapable of providing these gains individually. Nor could a union-run program match the resources of a liberal state committed to welfare.

Liberated from the Roosevelt myth by the distance provided by time and by the radicalism of the 1960's, revisionist historians rewrote the story of the New Deal, showing the administration's reluctance to press for welfare even in the depths of the Depression. Roosevelt believed that providing temporary "relief" from the massive effects of the crisis was the limit of the government's obligation to the poor. It was only the mass upsurge of the industrial unions in the early 1930's that made possible the "second" New Deal—Roosevelt's campaign to provide a legal framework for workers' trade union activity, minimum wages, unemployment compensation, social security, and housing construction. Mass unionism transformed the Democratic Party from an organization of professional politicians whose major commitment was to power into a party of modern liberalism which, for the most part, now became the functional equivalent of an American version of social democracy.

The New Deal did not create the CIO and other unions in mass production industries, nor did the unions create the second New Deal. They were formed by the growing militancy of workers who had suffered more than any other working class in advanced capitalist countries in the early years of the crisis, by the growth of the Left within the trade unions and other mass organizations, and by the radicalization of large fractions of the middle class, especially small farmers and professionals, which had in small and medium sized cities remained the bedrock of conservatism after the Civil War. Although there were substantial differences between the Left and the new populist right wing, which shared with the progressives the loyalty of the middle class, the movements together constituted sufficient political pressure to produce a new emphasis within the Roosevelt administration on social programs and regulation that promised to redistribute wealth and power.[1]

After 1935, the most successful struggles for union recognition were those in mass production industries. One of the reasons for these victories was that even during the Depression the citadels of "big" capital were relatively prosperous compared to the devastation visited by the crisis upon the small, competitive, and capital-poor sectors in light manufacturing and local retail establishments. Arrogance had replaced paternalism among the large employers in mass production industries in the wake of the Depression as they realized that their industries had expanded their international trade even as overall industrial production was down compared to the 1920's, they were profiting from the misery of the smaller scale employers, and that their labor costs were lowered by labor's fierce competition with itself. State planners regarded unions as part of the partnership that could lift American capitalism out of the Depression and a minority of capitalists agreed, but the message had not yet reached the overwhelming majority of large employers. For a large fraction of capitalists only the advent of the Second World War led to union recognition because the Roosevelt administration, by now allied strongly with organized labor, insisted that the price of government war contracts was their agreement to bargain collectively with unions.[2] Hillman, Philip Murray, the Steel Union and CIO President, R. J. Thomas of the Auto Workers, and the significant number of "left-wing" CIO leaders (most notably the United Electrical Workers, the Mine-Mill and Smelter Workers, and the West Coast Longshoremen) agreed to a wartime no-strike pledge, de facto wage freezes for the duration, and a substantial relaxation of informal work rules. These explicit compromises were considered principled agreements by the labor leaders because they wholeheartedly supported the struggle against the Axis powers; unlike the First World War in which a significant portion of labor and socialist movements opposed U.S. entry on the ground that it was imperialist, the overwhelming majority viewed the Second World War as a progressive struggle. Barely a handful of socialists opposed the war while the relatively powerful Communist Party, its trade union periphery, and the liberal center of the labor movement supported U.S. intervention, especially after the Nazi invasion of the Soviet Union in June 1941.

Despite general trade union approval of the new wartime terms of the social compact, the number of strikes, after falling precipitously in 1942 owing to labor's unbridled wartime enthusiasm, kept rising thereafter. 1944 witnessed the largest number of strikes in the twentieth century, reaching almost 5000, even though the number of working days lost declined in comparison to the 1943 figure. Highlighted by strikes among miners and auto workers, these "illegal" walkouts may be taken as an accurate measure of rising labor militancy in the wartime period. Patriotism aside (there is little doubt that workers supported the war) the no-strike pledge and wage control policies of the labor-backed Roosevelt administration were perceived by a rising number of workers as pro-management. By the middle of the war John L. Lewis, renegade in the labor movement, declared under pressure from working miners that the pledge was no longer binding. Although Walter Reuther, now a vice president of the Auto Workers, utilized the no-strike issue to defeat his opponents, he had stood behind it for most of the war.[3]

The major corporations in basic industries seized upon the no-strike pledge as an occasion for reasserting their power at the workplace, accelerating capital accumulation and weakening the power of the shop floor union organization. The unauthorized walkouts were not only actions of resistance but attempts by workers to preserve their carefully constructed steward system and informal work rules that restricted management's power on the shop floor. In addition, the strikes were elementary struggles for wage justice. Although the leadership held onto control over the unions despite considerable internal opposition, most unions were forced to lead the massive 1946 wage movements during which nearly all industrial workers conducted a general strike in the mass production industries and major sections of transportation.[4]

By the end of the war, it was becoming increasingly evident that Truman and a substantial fraction of the Democratic Party leadership were asking the labor movement to free its hands if the trade unions persisted in militant strikes. Truman invoked a rhetoric of national emergency even though armed hostilities had ended. On the one hand many economists and business leaders feared that problems of reconversion from wartime to peacetime production would result in a massive decline in investment, employment, and profits. On the other hand even before the last bombs had been dropped on Japan, Truman and Churchill were already making dark references to the new Soviet threat, implying that unless labor continued to moderate its economic demands, America might be plunged into a new crisis of both economic and political dimensions. Many labor leaders, pressed by the rank and file, began to search for alternatives to the Truman presidency although not to the Democratic Party. Their leading political spokesperson for the early postwar years became Henry Wallace, Truman's Secretary of Commerce and former Vice President.[5]

During this immediate postwar period, the dominant political group within the CIO was still the so-called left-center coalition whose leading figures were Murray, R.J. Thomas of the UAW, the UE leaders Albert Fitzgerald and James Matles, and Harry Bridges of the West Coast Longshoremen. On the other side, Reuther, who had given critical support to the Thomas leadership during the early years of the war, was beginning to split off in an anti-communist direction. He quickly became the leader of a new coalition within the CIO that included Catholic trade unionists, socialists, some Trotskyists, and an assortment of liberals both within the UAW and in other unions, most notably an insurgent group in the UE led by its former president, James Carey, now CIO Secretary-Treasurer. The conjunction of the increasingly heated up cold war and internal power struggles within the UAW and the UE combined to produce an open split within the CIO by 1947.[6]

At first, the center-left coalition stayed intact. Murray condemned red-baiting as detrimental to the unity of the labor movement. He announced his support for Wallace's policies of a new détente with the Soviet Union to preserve world peace, and an aggressive push for the completion of the social welfare state at home. By late 1947, however, Murray had retreated before the anti-communist impulse both within the labor movement and in the country at large. Unwilling to go into political opposition, the mainstream of the labor movement returned to Truman who, in turn, cemented his relations with the top leaders by vetoing the Taft–Hartley Bill, which in 1947 had been rammed through Congress by a shrill counterrevolutionary coalition of Republicans and Southern Democrats.[7]

Historians generally agree that Henry Wallace's third party candidacy in 1948 was an unmitigated disaster. The former Vice President entered the race only to find his early support evaporated among labor leaders and among blacks and liberals. Truman not only robbed Wallace's thunder by promising aggressive civil rights and full employment policies, he also captured the hearts and minds of Wallace's putative constituency by initiating the Marshall Plan to rebuild Europe and contain Russia.

Wallace had been close to labor's leadership, having been their favored candidate in the 1944 Democratic Convention when Roosevelt, already nearing death, bowed to cold war pressure and selected Truman to suceed him. With thirty percent of the labor force in unions and a much higher degree of organization in the leading production sectors, unions were plainly in a position to heavily influence, if not dictate, the Democratic candidate in the 1948 elections. They stayed with Truman not only because he bowed to their program on domestic issues, but also because they were won to his international positions against the "Left" which had argued for a détente with the Soviet Union. Even more profound, the labor movement was not prepared to break its collaboration with capital and the Democratic Party. The prospect of forming a new, labor-based party seemed to promise nothing but isolation and vulnerability in an increasingly anti-labor environment. Although no Democratic candidate could win without the support of organized labor, neither could organized labor "go it alone."

Left-wing critics have ascribed labor's reluctance to form a new party in the postwar period to the prevalence of the anti-communist hysteria that accompanied the cold war. Although this argument retains considerable validity given the structural position of the labor movement (economic, political, and ideological) in American society, I dispute the cold-war-as-causal explanation. Rather, I would argue that the persistence of the social contract negotiated during the 1930's is due to the continuity of the ideological and economic conditions that produced it. (1) The position of the United States as a world power, already strengthened by the Depression, experienced a quantum leap after the war. (2) The AFL, which initially resisted industrial organization, finally adopted its tenets with vengeance, while retaining the voluntarist ideology inherited from its origins. By 1950 the AFL had organized as many industrial workers as the more aggressive CIO, had expanded its membership in the building trades, and among retail and wholesale workers, and was on the verge of regaining the initiative among public sector employees. The Federation was almost twice the size of the CIO and with the rise of new leaders, George Meany and Walter Reuther, to leadership of the respective organizations, merger was only a matter of time. Lacking a distinctive ideological difference with the AFL that extended to a new conception of economic and political strategy, the CIO was considerably weakened in the postwar period. Reuther, the former socialist, was by far the most visionary leader, left or right, in the labor movement. His proposals to force companies to "open the books" during contract negotiations, his opposition to automatic price increases after wage settlements, his democratic style of trade union leadership were bolder and more imaginative than his opponents within the UAW and certainly made his voice the most articulate within organized labor. (By the 1950's Lewis had reverted to his bunker tactics of the 1920's, conceding control over the labor process to the mineowners in return for pensions, health plans and high wages.) (3) Labor's postwar legislative offensive failed to move an increasingly conservative Congress to enact national health insurance, a massive housing program, and other elements of the welfare state.[8]

As a result of the new social political contract the fight to extend the social welfare state was not only weakened by the cold war, but by labor's own traditions as well. As trade unions' legislative demands met with increasing opposition, the labor movement did not draw the conclusions arrived at by British workers a half century earlier—to form a new political party. Instead, those unions now firmly ensconced in the mass production industries struck a new bargain with the large corporations: labor would reduce its militancy in return for the corporativist version of the welfare state. Reuther, elected President of the UAW in 1946, signed the first five-year contract in mass production in 1950; after leading a militant strike in 1947, Lewis joined the coal industry in trying to preserve itself in the face of sharpened competition from oil and natural gas which had replaced coal as the leading home heating fuel and threatened its preeminent position in commercial energy production. Lewis exacted a price for submitting to the employer's demand that the union not interfere with the industry's further mechanization. Workers would share in the gains by raising welfare funds from the increased tonnage. Employers would contribute a certain amount per ton to such benefits as a modern hospital system administered by the union to treat the tens of thousands of miners suffering from black lung or victimized by accidents, and a substantial pension program that would give miners a decent standard of living after retirement. Lewis added a new principle to the old Amalgamated Clothing Workers' policy of making the union responsible for the survival of a sick industry: even though, under adverse economic conditions, technological change would result in mass unemployment among miners, those who remained would gain from the new collaboration. Lewis's philosophy became the foundation for later agreements between longshore unions and stevedoring companies in the 1960's and the pathbreaking Steelworkers' experimental national agreement (1971) in which the union exchanged control over the pace of technological change for high wages, sabbaticals, and job security for senior employees. This pattern was carried into the UAW–Chrysler agreement in the late 1970's and 1980's.[9]

The common roots of the Steel union and the Mine Workers are evident in this agreement. In 1938 Harold Ruttenberg, then Research Director of the Steelworkers Organizing Committee, had issued a handbook *(Production Problems)* for shop leaders that advised them on methods of gaining higher wages, especially within small and medium sized companies. Among the major provisions of a "model" contract were the following paragraphs:

1. The union agrees to co-operate with management in order to reduce costs, enlarge sales, improve quality and in general to advance the interests of the industry.
2. The management agrees to share equitably with the union any benefits so obtained, in the form of increased employment, better working conditions, increased wages or decreased hours.
3. Nobody is to lose his job as a result of any improvement that is installed.

Ruttenberg's argument was that smaller companies are often genuinely unable to grant substantial concessions to the workers without their active cooperation in increasing productivity through technological improvements, eliminating waste, improving "team play" among executives, and "better coordination of the various divisions of the enterprise—sales, purchasing, financing, and the working staff." The handbook contains a veritable plan for co-management of the enterprise in which workers, in exchange for cooperation with employers, would gain a real voice in the determination of major decisions, not only those affecting such issues as piece rates, but on all decisions affecting their jobs including company management.

The most important early experiment in joint management in steel was conducted between the union and the Empire Steel Company in Mansfield, Ohio between 1938 and 1940. *Production Problems* cites several other examples of how unions help "friendly employers to run their business better and compete successfully," especially the Amalgamated Clothing Workers and some shop crafts in the railroad industry, such as the Baltimore and Ohio plan. The major difference between the doctrine of what Ruttenburg and then Steelworkers Vice President Clinton Golden called "industrial democracy" and the postwar instances of labor management cooperation is that the earlier plan insisted that workers would be protected from unemployment and worsening working conditions when they agreed to increase productivity through labor saving machinery, improved quality, and other cost reducing measures. Moreover, the concept of industrial democracy was intended to bring workers into the management of the enterprise. *Production Problems* urges agreements in which employers are obliged to share information about the enterprise with the union, just as the union would establish a "research committee" to find ways to improve the quality *and* the quantity of goods produced.

There are two issues here: should unions "help friendly employers run their business better" and if so, under what terms? Since the 1920's the needle trades unions have recognized their obligation to prevent "their" industries from going under. Their main tactics were to control wages by employing specialists who work with management to set equitable piece rates that neither resulted in bankruptcy for the employer nor discrimination against the workers. The Clothing Workers and the Garment Workers restrained worker militancy in union shops because the leadership believed that the whole industry as well as individual employers faced competition from both non-union shops and other, more powerful sectors of the economy. In addition, the Clothing Workers' bank became a source of capital for hard pressed employers or those wishing to expand under union control. Of course, this arrangement could only remain effective so long as the industry controlled the national market for garments. In the wake of international competition, not only for clothing but also for labor, the entire edifice created by Sidney Hillman and David Dubinsky has crumbled.

We have come a long way since the publication of *Production Problems* and Walter Reuther's 1946 demand that companies "open the books" to prove their claims against substantial wage increases and fringe benefits. Today, unions have been willing to entertain contract reopeners that entail wage and benefits concessions but, except for a few cases have refrained from making demands for corporate concessions, particularly those bringing workers into management of enterprises. My concern is not to condemn unions for entering concessionary agreements, which in many instances may be necessary to save workers' jobs. The more pressing issue is whether unions are likely to evolve an alternative position to the concessions dictated by capital. Hillman's doctrine of collaboration and Ruttenberg's concept of industrial democracy were departures from traditional notions of both labor voluntarism and class struggle, but they were rooted in a conception of economic and ideological perspectives of labor as a broad social movement. The recent agreements are bereft of any concept of labor participation or control over the industry; they are neither democratic nor effective because they concede the continuation of management's absolute right to determine the policies of the company. Further, in the case of the UAW-General Motors deal where the company agreed to limited job security for most senior employees, the union consented to sacrificing the same employment rights of younger workers.

The pragmatic orientation of most of organized labor is firmly rooted in the postwar tradition that confines the task of the union to representing the interests of workers who remain on the job and those retired after long years of service. In this environment, hundreds of thousands of black workers, women, and younger workers have suffered permanent or long-term layoffs from industrial plants since 1979. In a period when the displacement of labor from industrial jobs is a function both of technological change and the economic crisis, this tacit union policy implies that these workers will be obliged to settle for substantially lower living standards because wages in the leading mass production industries have been much higher than in competitive sector manufacturing or services.

Within the working class, the postwar period was marked by sharper differentiation than during the Depression between those workers who retained levers on economic power and those stuck in industries that were unable to compete with the monopoly sector, much less survive within their own market. The decline of union organization in private sector, small-scale, low technology industries resulted in the formation of a distinctly separate underclass or sub-proletariat in American economic life. This group corresponds to the sectors of the economy that are locally or regionally based such as retail and wholesale trades; competitive manufacturing industries such as textiles, apparel, toys, and novelties; branches of the chemical industry such as plastics and paint; and small electronic assemblies. Most workers in these industries are unskilled or semiskilled and work in rural enterprises employing less than fifty workers. Under these conditions employers are extremely mobile because of relatively small quantities of investment capital in fixed assets and even the *threat* of union organization may result in overnight capital flight.

Lacking strong unions, workers in these industries were typically paid close to minimum wage depending on the threat of unionism and the relative shortage of labor in a particular region, while workers in heavy industries were able to make large strides in wages and benefits, even as their power over the labor process declined. Unionism for these workers was not only a means to bargain for wages, but became the vehicle through which the so-called *social wage* was procured, in contrast to other countries where such gains were made by political and legislative action. For example, in 1958 when textile workers earned $3000/year in an industry where only ten percent of the one million workers were organized into unions, steelworkers averaged $5000/year. Today, many auto workers have incomes of more than $25,000/year including overtime (or a base rate of $21,000 for a 40-hour week), while textile workers have reached only half that amount and apparel workers even slightly less.

I am not comparing skilled and unskilled labor. On the contrary, the skills required by a sewing machine operator may be somewhat greater than those of semiskilled assembly line workers, machine operators, and many categories of steel labor. The fundamental difference is the degree of union organization, the market position of the industry, and the sexual composition of the industry. The fact that unions failed to organize in the Southeast and the Mexican border areas of Texas and Louisiana, which had become centers of the textile and apparel industries, contributed to the growing disparity of living standards among workers in different production sectors. At the same time, private sector retail, wholesale, and clerical labor was falling behind in similar proportions because unions were unable to make significant inroads there as well.

In the context of the almost uninterrupted prosperity of the 1945–1970 period the character of the underclass remained poorly defined, except for the shrinking but substantial population of the permanently unemployed—single mothers, disabled workers, the elderly, and a large fraction of young (mostly black and Hispanic) workers. Young workers were part of the classic "reserve army" of labor, kept out of the labor force until capital needed them during periods of rapid capital expansion. In the quarter century following the war, millions of young and minority workers entered the mass production industries and shared in the wages and living standards of the basic working class. They enjoyed job security because of high levels of production and the seniority provisions of the contract and gained entrance into the consumer society—civic organizations and social movements such as trade unions, the church, and community political groups.

In the 1980's, as capital flight was no longer confined to a few regions and displaced workers could no longer migrate with high reemployment chances, the industrial reserve army was no longer an adequate description of the new underclass. As workers were displaced from steel, rubber, electrical, and auto plants they were obliged to take jobs in the non-union sectors. Miners laid off because of lack of work or technological displacement were unable to find a job at similar pay in South Chicago or Pittsburgh steel mills or in New Jersey chemical plants because these were also experiencing unemployment. Young male industrial workers found jobs in small plants or in the low wage, non-union residential construction industry and young women factory workers were forced to retrain themselves for lower paid office work, retailing, or hospital employment in patient care, housekeeping, or dietary services.

In contrast to the immediate postwar years when the formation of the "secondary" labor market was a marginal phenomenon, confined to the "blind, the halt, the lame" and the minorities, the *new* underclass may be defined as workers excluded from union organization and who lack professional or craft skills. These are largely full-time workers in the low technology, competitive manufacturing and service industries, agricultural workers and the underemployed. My contention is that with few exceptions (notably the apparel and textile industries where economic conditions prevent most semiskilled workers from rising from the underclass even if they are in unions), union membership marks the difference between the working class and the underclass unless the non-union industrial or service worker is employed by a paternalistic corporation such as Eastman Kodak or IBM.

One of the most stunning successes of mass unionism in the postwar era was the organization of the health industry and private sector services, such as food retailing, and among low wage public sector employees, where unionism facilitated the entrance of these workers into the mainstream of the working class. For example, hospital dietary employees earned less than $40/week in 1958, but twenty years later their wages had increased five times, exceeding the rate of increase for workers as a whole. Similarly, retail food employees, many of whom had been stuck at the bottom of the occupational and income ladders, had achieved a respectable working class wage by the 1970's. In 1982 a New York City government shipping clerk earned $15,000 annually compared to $3000 in 1960. Taken together, these three major categories of semiskilled labor brought about 3 million workers into the labor movement in the 1960's and early 1970's, but some 1 million textile and apparel workers remained outside unions and the public employees' unions had succeeded in organizing only a third of their jurisdiction. The extent of union organization among service workers is even more dismal; except in retail food services and some big city department stores, financial services and administrative workers, most of whom are women, are unorganized.

During the 1930's wage differentials within the working class were relatively small between various industries. Steelworkers, miners, and railroad workers earned about $25–30/week in 1929, all having suffered declines compared to the mid-1920's. Although textile wages were lower than those in basic mass production and transportation industries, New England textile workers earned about two-thirds the rate of miners, but in general regional differences in average wages were not substantial, except for the South. In the late 1920's and early 1930's the major differentials had been between skilled and unskilled but during the 1950's the gap widened within the ranks of the unskilled and semiskilled based on the degree of union organization, with many employed auto workers earning as much as skilled printers, garment cutters, or machinists in small shops. However, compared to these workers, millions of workers are earning the minimum wage or only slightly more. Today, differentials between union and non-union workers for the same level of skill is often two or three times. During the steep inflationary spiral of the 1970's these differences became tantamount to class differences. One could no longer equate the economic and social position of the working class and the underclass without subordinating the importance of living standards, political citizenship, and social organization. In the 1980's immigrants from Central and South America and Asia increasingly make up a large section of the underclass, joined by displaced workers from mass production industries who were forced to accept lower paying non-union jobs, and the army of women employed in retail and administrative services who earned some sixty percent of average male wages. Members of the underclass are more often not registered to vote, do not enjoy credit with financial institutions (since the Second World War the absolute precondition for home or appliance ownership) and are employed by companies constantly threatened with bankruptcy or subject to technological displacement. These workers are for the most part as distant from unions as they are from any other vehicle of economic or social power.

During the 1950's and 1960's the press, experts, and some politicians began to assert the evils of big government and big labor as replacing the traditional evil of big business. Liberals and radicals dismissed these characterizations as merely the latest example of anti-union propaganda and conservative hostility to the welfare state, and in part they were perfectly right. However, something more was going on in this widely held economic perception. Union members were becoming even more a minority of the working population, confined to fewer places within the economy so that trade unionism became isolated from some of the growing non-manufacturing private sectors. More Americans were defining themselves as "consumers" against the producers who were identified with manual labor, now a minority of the population. Perhaps even more important, unions were no longer representative of the working class as a whole. Their particularistic ideology corresponded to their sectoral isolation; they presented themselves as voluntary institutions whose sole obligation was to defend the specific interests of their members and the industries that employed them. Organized labor became an interest group that possessed inordinate power in some industries or crafts because it could control the supply of labor and drive up prices, thus holding the "public" hostage to its demands. At the same time, it had become painfully evident that unions were no longer representative of the now visible underclasses who appeared abandoned by organized labor.

My concern here is neither to validate nor to refute these perceptions since they are important only from a cultural and political standpoint. They were believed by large segments of all groups in the population including many workers themselves. The industrial worker was no longer identified with the oppressed; "he" was regarded as a new player in the game of economic power, having as little sympathy for the working poor and the unemployed as for the consumer. Whereas in the 1930's the trade union movement was a social and quasi-religious "cause" that enjoyed the sympathy of other social classes and strata, it was widely believed that labor had become part of the new power bloc, arrayed against other less well organized sectors of the population.

CHANGING PERCEPTIONS OF THE AMERICAN WORKER

The emergence of the manual worker as a new social type—no longer the victim as in Paul Muni's 1930's portrayal of an outcast miner—was signified in the 1950's by the figures of Jackie Gleason's Ralph Cramden and his friend Norton, and by William Bendix's *Life of Riley.* Comic characters rather than tragic figures, their economic problems were almost insignificant compared to their family conflicts, especially their marital woes. Cramden was almost an anachronism because the decor of his apartment corresponded to the 1930's, while the bare room with a few sticks of old (but not antique) furniture called attention to the newly won affluence of the American worker. While *Riley* concentrated on the family as such, Gleason's *Honeymooners* concerned the conflict between male friendship and an almost routinized marriage contract; Gleason's wife, played by Audrey Meadows, was prone to frequent outcries of prefeminist rage against the nearly misogynist attitudes of her husband. Proletarian in appearance, the themes of both *Riley* and the *Honeymooners* are eminently middle class family squabbles and friendships. We know the terms of the class struggle have unalterably changed from the absence of class discourses, the privatized existence of these working class characters, and the occlusion of social conflict. From these images militant leftists who were influenced by the experience of the civil rights movements, were to invent the doctrine of "white skin" privilege to encapsulate the social character of the postwar white working class. In turn, unionism was the new mask for privilege; union workers were now of society as well as in it, and the sigh of the oppressed was only heard off-stage from the excluded blacks and poor.

In the 1980's white skin was still a mark of hierarchy and status, but for an increasing number of workers it merely connoted degrees of degradation. In 1983, blacks were still unemployed at twice the rate of whites, but white unemployed had approached ten percent of the labor force so that the distinction, although still dramatic, no longer held the same sting as before. However, the labor movement remains immune to these changes. New simulacres of John L. Lewis have come to the fore to assert particularism. Bunkers are once more erected to protect labor's dwindling minions from the scourge of another depression.[10]

Contract unionism is not in itself an evil. The union contract is the measure of the workers' achievement of power at the workplace, and its provisions are the necessary compromise with employers to maintain the reproduction process. From a radical perspective, the elevation of the contract to the principle of the labor movement has occluded virtually all other elements.

The ideological contours of the American labor movement are over-determined by influences of American ideology in general, the specific historical features of American labor history, and the course of class relations during the rise of industrialism in the late nineteenth and early twentieth centuries. Virtually unlimited U.S. expansion at home and abroad has determined the specific features of U.S. capitalist development, which were unusually favorable to capital accumulation given this context. All ideological issues in American economic, political, and cultural life have been subsumed under the rubric of "problems" to be resolved through bargaining and compromise among social classes and groups. The epistemological position that informs social and political relations assumes that the larger framework of economic growth is sufficiently supple to make unnecessary the European concept of redistribution, which presupposes that a gain for the workers is a loss for capital and vice versa. Similarly strike struggles are considered exclusively in their economic context, rather than being perceived as issues of political and ideological contestation. The labor movement functions within a public ideology that prevents strikes from raising the larger social and political questions, except in the circumstances of national emergency. Since the war, these have been invoked in a relatively small number of instances: the coal strike in 1943, the rail and steel strikes in 1946, and more recently the national postal strike of 1970, and the air controllers' strike.

Since the 1970s the national emergency has appeared in the public sector, today the most dynamic section of the labor movement. Because laws prohibit strikes by public employees, the strikes at the federal level have taken on the character of political struggles, notwithstanding the modest claim of the union's merely seeking a decent contract. The unions themselves, however, have typically employed the discourse of private interest rather than proclaiming broad social objectives. They want private sector workers' rights to bargain and strike for wages and benefits. The government, under both Democratic and Republican administrations, has invoked the doctrine that public employee strikes are illegal disruptions of vital public functions. The government argues, in effect, that employees are civil servants, agents of the state. Thus their status as members of the bureaucratic "class" is inconsistent with the general rights of workers. Public employees' unions have no defense against this argument so long as they share the general union opposition to ideological appeals. Their public stance appears naive in the face of the ability of the state bureaucracy to invoke the twin appeals of right-wing nationalism and the doctrine of public service. In an age when the old expansionist assumptions that implicitly guided the labor doctrine of seeking "more" rather than marching under ideological flags are in serious disrepair, the ideological position of unions has deteriorated considerably, especially in the public sector.

The labor movement has, with important exceptions, become a more virulent opponent of communism than any other social organization, including the large corporations. Anti-communism results from the intransigent historical opposition of most trade unions to "mixing" (ideological) politics with economic struggle and from the adherence of most unions to the nationalist precepts of American ideology. Especially during the periodic anti-red struggle in the labor movement, conservative union officials have cited the Soviet ban on free trade unions as reasons for refusing democratic rights for leftists inside U.S. union ranks. Communists are not heretics, according to conservative union leaders, they are conspirators against freedom, including workers' rights.

At the root, American trade unionism has evolved under the assumption that labor's fate must be tied to U.S. global interests. Expansion is viewed as the condition for social betterment for union members and, by extension, the underclasses of society. The partial reversal of U.S. global fortunes has not altered this orientation despite the fact that the decline of U.S. power abroad has rendered the struggle for social reform a legislative dead letter, halted union organizing of new members to a trickle, and placed the "normal" course of collective bargaining, particularly the automatic wage increase, in jeopardy. Even as unions find themselves fighting for their survival much less making progress at the bargaining table or anywhere else, the force of nationalism and pragmatism maintains its hold on trade union policy. With each new attack against familiar trade union gains, the union leadership seeks new paths to accommodation and compromise, placing organizational survival above the defense of traditional benefits. Since the crisis deepened in 1975, some workers strike to extend their job rights, but many workers accept wage cuts to avoid layoffs, relax work rules won after militant job actions, and vote for conservative politicians as the last best hope to regain prosperity.

This withdrawal from political struggles in the face of state and corporate resistance is ingrained in the history of the American labor movement. With the exception of a brief period during the last half of the Depression, unions have never relied on political solutions to their problems. When the unions engaged in a determined effort to root out communists and other leftists within their ranks after World War II and gave full-throated support for U.S. foreign policy as the necessary context within which gains could be made, neither Congress nor the Democratic administration was inclined to reward this cold war loyalty with substantial legislative concessions to protect and extend labor's ability to organize workers, bargain under better terms, or enjoy an expanded welfare state. The cold war instead demanded a heavy shift to arms expenditures and a freeze on the social wage. After losing several important congressional battles for extended social wages, the unions sought these gains at the bargaining table. During the 1950's, labor concentrated its political energies on protecting its legal rights, which had been seriously eroded by the Taft-Hartley Act of 1947, and defending the welfare state. Whereas in postwar Europe the workers won pensions, health care, and many other amenities through parliamentary action, American unions chose to retreat to the bargaining table. The results were good for strong unions and disastrous for the rest.

Even at the bargaining table, the unions were constrained to forge a new social contract as the undergirding of the negotiated agreement. After 1950, signalled by the unprecedented five-year contract between the United Auto Workers and the car industry, unions exchanged shop floor power for pensions, health care, and rising real wages. In the 1950's workers and their unions moved decisively into consumerism and away from the incipient self-management ethos represented by a strong rank and file steward system, which protected informal work rules grounded in work groups able to control the pace of production as well as some of its technological means, and, in many cases, became weaker in defending the job security provisions of the agreement.

The new social contract exchanged workers' independent political and social power and their claims on central issues of the labor process for job security and a high level of consumption. In this context, anticommunism was more than an ideological proclivity among the bulk of American workers—it became a code of collaboration. Even if there were good reasons why workers might reject the Soviet system, the virulence of such views within American labor politics cannot be explained on the ideological merits. Most workers, with the important exception of many of East European origins, did not buy the claim that the Russians constituted an immediate threat to American security, nor were they militantly opposed to the communists within the unions on broad ideological principles. The ability of the longshore and substantial sections of the electrical, mine, mill, and smelter workers to survive the most determined efforts by the CIO leaders and its government collaborators to break them, is fairly substantial evidence that the red issue, although important in the postwar period, was not important in its own terms. Rather, it was the signal for the new social contract; it was invoked as part of a new kind of deal between capital and labor. Workers accepted simultaneously the cold war, curtailment of their shop floor power, the surrender of political autonomy, and a shift from struggle at the level of production to struggles around consumption. Here, I must enter a strong caveat. Surely, all trade union struggles are concerned with the terms of production relations, which, as Marx argued, strongly imply consumption. But the postwar working class surrendered its emerging goal of determining what is produced, how much, and by what means—in short, turned away from power over investment, particularly the questions of how technological change would be introduced and the equally important question of whether capital could employ surplus value extracted at the point of production at its own will. Workers in the basic manufacturing industries understood that giving up their hard won gains to limit production and their aspiration to challenge capital's investment prerogatives meant divesting themselves of those tendencies within the unions whose opposition to capital was global.

There were, of course, serious complaints against the communists, not the least of which was their penchant to subordinate workers' immediate interests to broad ideological concerns. But, as has been recently argued,[11] the CP's vigorous enforcement of the wartime no-strike pledge matched other progressive and conservative unionists who supported the war against fascism. The communists were also often accused of being bad trade unionists because of their political views. These accusations were far less valid than similar attacks against the racketeers in the unions, or soft liberal trade unionists for whom union democracy was always a pain in the neck. Only by understanding that, following the general strike of 1946 and the subsequent anti-labor offensive by a conservative Congress, workers entered into a new social agreement, can the postwar era in American labor be understood.

When workers did refuse the new social contract in practice, they never articulated its alternative discursively. The wildcat strike took on its ambivalent significance in this context: the wildcat strike was the protest of the rank and file against the tendency of the union leadership towards a strategy of political compromise in order to secure the means of consumption, but at the same time it was a measure of the hegemony that this strategy exercised at the level of discourse. The absence of an alternative discourse conjoined with the expulsions of left unionists in the late 1940's. It cannot be claimed that the Left, beyond its advocacy of a more militant brand of unionism, was able to articulate an alternative to the dominant discourse of contract unionism. As a result, workers occupied a place of truncated opposition to the leadership, challenging their policy of compromise only sporadically in the form of action critique.

The New Deal and Its Left Critics. The Kennedy and Johnson years revived the power of the liberal-labor coalition after a decade of political stalemate and defeat. But underneath the resurgence of liberalism, forces of disintegration were working to tear the coalition apart. Among them an important place must be assigned to the civil rights, student, and anti-war movements. By the mid-60's they found themselves opposed not only by traditional conservatives but also by significant sections of the liberal and labor movements. The new movements were breaking the rules of American politics through their intransigence, at least in political style, and more importantly, through their use of extraparliamentary means to project their demands and get them met. Sit-ins and disruptions of other types seemed to ignore the normal processes of parliamentary compromise by which liberal democracies get things done. This new loosely knit political coalition of blacks, youth, and a fraction of the middle strata made no attempt to form an oppositional political party, in part because much of the "movement" that emerged in the 1960's was persuaded that parliamentary politics was an impediment to democracy. The movement adopted a version of the doctrine of direct democracy. "Let the people decide" and "one man one vote" were infused with new significance. These slogans were made continuous with the old Jeffersonian ideal of the town meeting in which representative forms were cast aside for popular processes of governance. Although historians of the New Left have mistakenly called this a new form of populism and have proceeded to contrast it with traditional socialist politics (offering New Left doctrine as an alternative model for building American radicalism), it did have its European analogies in the anarchist and council communist movements that refused the path of parliamentary action except defensively and chose to build institutions of dual power.[12]

The student movement's leadership became a major force within the progressive coalition leading to its disintegration. Although SDS and other middle class movements maintained what they termed a "dialogue" with labor and Democratic Party leaders, their major strategy was confrontation with the prevailing forms of social action that had been invented during the New Deal. SDS organizers in slum communities fought for social reforms within state run social welfare bureaucracies, but refused to elevate this activity to the level of theory or strategy. Winning concessions for poor people was seen as a part of political mobilization but inferred nothing about the state that would change their antipathy to corporate liberalism, the term widely employed to characterize the alliance built during the New Deal.

When the student radicals formed the core of anti-war activists, the intransigence of the Johnson administration and the often active hostility of the trade unions only confirmed their earlier judgment. The state, the labor movement, and the liberals grouped around the Democratic Party were called reactionaries masked as progressives, and the old coalition was seen as little more than a force for the preservation of the privileges of the strata that constituted them. Neighborhood organizing, anti-war activity, and university reform struggles were interpreted in revolutionary terms by student radicals even if the content of their activity was consistent with the reformist goals of traditional progressives, the major exception being anti-imperialism which, in any case, could boast a rather wide following among progressives.

In the 1960's the cultural revolution that embraced youth and minorities and women briefly fashioned an alternative discourse that tore at the foundations of the progressive alliance from the left, just as the neo-conservatives challenged the alliance's implicit ideological foundation— guns and butter within an expansionist framework—from the right. The overriding importance of the New Left was its heroic effort to fashion a legitimate alternative discourse *within* American politics to the prevailing cold war social welfarism of the old progressives. The New Left's critique of the weaknesses of representative institutions led to efforts to create a political counterculture in the ghettoes and universities. This vision was best articulated in an SDS paper written by Tom Hayden and Carl Wittman, *Towards an Interracial Movement of the Poor,* a euphemistic goal that really signified a new coalition between intellectuals and the underclasses that defined stable working class strata, the middle class, and ruling classes as the enemy.[13]

I wish to emphasize the concept of political counterculture in contrast to the social counterculture or "youth" culture whose guiding slogan "sex, drugs, and rock and roll" was never really shared by most radicals whose principal identification was with the ideological Left. It is important to underscore the disruptive effects of this political counterculture on the old hegemony. For SDS and other organizations within the "movement," the working class, the liberal professions, and other elements of the New Deal coalition became "part of the problem" in eradicating racial and class oppression in America rather than part of the solution. While radical groups objectively derived much of their influence because they were obliged to engage frequently in mainstream institutional struggles in the course of their southern and urban organizing as well as in the anti-war and university reform movements, their politics was framed in a radically different discourse than conventional progressivism. The conflict between the progressives and the political counterculture became most abrasive at the discursive level, even when differences of strategy and program were intense. Progressives could reckon with a "nonreformist reform" such as community control of the police, black power over traditional resources and institutions, or the right of students to participate in hiring processes in universities. Even the war was a fairly clear cut issue, taken from the perspective of foreign policy. If the new radicals wanted a place at the councils of the various organizations of the coalition they would, like the civil rights groups in the 1940's, have to earn their seat. Since the coalition had always shown sufficient flexibility to recuperate any legitimate opposition, there was no reason to believe that the new radicalism was destined to remain in the cold. After all, it had proved sufficiently independent from both communist and socialist parties and was, to say the least, hostile to the Soviet Union and the Eastern bloc.

From the perspective of the progressives, the most unnerving aspect of student radicalism was that its revolutionary rhetoric suggested a profound corruption in the economistic goals of the coalition and blamed progressivism itself for the deformation of American values. It was the critique of culture that proved most devastating to the old progressives for whom the goal of increased consumption and redistribution was sufficient to define a politics. To have challenged ends as much as means was enough to engender the fissures that tore at the coalition's attempts to find a meeting ground with the radicals. Student radicals were opponents of bureaucracy as much as critics of the Great Society. Since the progressives regarded the consolidation of the various bureaucracies of the state and those institutions constituted around it as ideological apparatuses (the educational establishment, health care, the trade unions, the Democratic Party at the local level, the liberal political machines) as important victories in their quest for permanence in American life, the radical attack was perhaps more threatening than any conflict over particular issues. And even if Martin Luther King urged blacks to disregard immoral laws in their quest for freedom, the confrontation between student radicals and the authority of university administrators, big city mayors, and labor leaders was interpreted—not as an assault on the vestiges of a bygone era of which segregation was an anomalous, although powerful, representative—but as an assault on the liberal elite upon whom depended the hopes of the poor, the workers, and others who had been treated unjustly. The critique of law and order did not cause as much distress among liberals as the critique of the very achievements of the New Deal—their ability to inscribe the victories of the labor and progressive movements in institutions, to make anonymous the administration of social welfare so that even a conservative executive branch could not dismantle it.

It would be excessive to claim that the two countercultural movements of the 1960's were principally responsible for the weakness of the New Deal coalition after 1965. Nevertheless, to the extent that student activists and radicals in the women's movement no longer oriented themselves to the labor movement and, more broadly, to class politics, the labor movement was deprived of both the technical intelligentsia needed to develop programs, defend union rights in the courts, and perform the needed research to fight employers, and the coterie of organizers that had been recruited from intellectual ranks. In sum, if the cold war drove a significant fraction of the labor intellectuals out of the unions, the persistence of cold war discourse in the progressive coalition during the 1960's, at a time when anti-communism appeared more irrational than in the immediate post-war period, successfully estranged a new generation of radical intellectuals from the labor movement. Certainly, this intergenerational antagonism between the unions and the intellectuals could not have helped but weaken unions' capacity to meet the great historical transformations that were eroding their underlying strength within the recomposed working classes.

The black movement followed a historical path distinct from that of the New Left. While the most militant section of the black movement, the Congress on Racial Equality (CORE) and the Student Nonviolent Coordinating Committee (SNCC), shared basic New Left precepts and succeeded by the mid-1960's in imposing the doctrine of direct democracy on wider sections of the freedom struggle, this perspective was ultimately surrendered by black militants and radicals once the white left proved incapable of sustaining itself as a major force in American politics. After 1967, blacks moved toward legislative action as the best hope, within the framework of the apparently revived liberal coalition, for achieving legal rights and a measure of economic progress. The rupture between the black and white parts of the movement, taking the form of the enunciation of the new doctrine of black power, a euphemism for the strategy of separatism, was in fact the sign of a deeper fissure.

The organized black community, with the exception of a relatively small fraction of intellectuals, was moving back into the old coalition. Specifically, they chose to ally with the liberal fraction of big capital which promised blacks entrance into the low and middle levels of corporate management by creating a middle class able to assume social and political leadership in the black community and within the corporations. During the late 1960's and early 1970's, the historic coalition between the civil rights movement and the trade unions suffered considerable strain as the forces of economic decline afflicted the American economy, obliging the unions to defend their deteriorating position. In this environment, significant black organizations, particularly the churches, joined with business groups like the National Alliance of Business (NAB) and the banks to create job training programs, education programs, and employ-ment in the private sector, while retaining their foothold in such public institutions as the universities and social welfare agencies.

The early 70's were marked by a return to the basic outlook of the late nineteenth century black leadership whose undisputed spokesperson was Booker T. Washington. The struggle for equality through legislation and direct action yielded to joining with capital and, where possible, labor and government to produce credentials and skills for the black underclasses and middle strata. Black industrial workers, however, were not prone to these strategies since their fate was tied to the unions. In contrast, the middle strata and the unemployed were interested in the jobs being generated by the tertiary (service) sector and requiring skills training and academic credentials.

The white New Left remained deeply suspicious of electoral and legis-lative forms partially because of its philosophical rejection of the bureau-cratic character of representative democracy but equally because of its pejorative perception of the liberal coalition after the clear militarization of U.S. intervention in Southeast Asia in 1964. In the main, trade union-ists and liberal politicians not only backed Johnson's escalation, but formed much of the war's administrative and ideological apparatus. Under these circumstances it became difficult to separate personifications of representative forms from the forms themselves. On the other hand, true to American pragmatic tradition, most black militants refused, at first, to engage in the anti-war movement, arguing that the black freedom movement needed the liberal coalition's support for such demands as voting rights in the South, desegregation in schools and public facilities, and jobs. At the same time, the black freedom movement was obliged to engage in frequent collisions with the labor movement, especially over discrimination in the skilled construction trades. These tensions not only weakened the coalition, but revealed the deep seated racism of many sections of rank and file white workers, particularly those in construction trades, many of whom were descendants of southern and eastern Euro-pean immigrants.

The Discourse of Growth. I now wish to advance the thesis that at the ideological, that is, the discursive level, the chief category linking unions to the social and economic system of American capitalism was the dis-course of *growth*. In one respect, "growth" is a euphemism for capital accumulation. However, after World War II, it became a political pro-gram, a guide to action for social and business unionists alike. Union policy was constituted in and through the elements of growth ideology. Its political program was framed at the macroeconomic plane in terms consistent with those state policies that promoted growth. Unions became convinced that what was good for capital accumulation was good for workers, and this orientation led to an unbridled support for a foreign policy aimed at protecting markets for American goods and capital abroad, fiscal and monetary policies that promoted capital investment at home, and technological innovations that raised worker productivity, which unions understood as an insurance policy to protect foreign markets.

It might be argued that this open throated adoption of the discourse of expansion by American workers and their unions is conditioned by the depth of the Depression beginning in 1929, or their conviction that without such policies America would be reduced to an ordinary power in the world and their jobs lost. These causal relations are infinitely debatable, but the power of growth as discourse became itself a causal force after the war. It constituted a great historic compromise between labor and capital, and was the heart of the new social contract. The new social contract was, to be sure, not without opposition among militant unionists of the Left and among those for whom unionism was itself a democratic ideology. In order to surrender shop floor power, the recently won stewards system had to be modified by introducing full-time union administration of grievances and changing contracts to loosen union control over the scope and pace of technological innovation and guarantee that management "prerogatives" to control and rationalize the labor process would be protected from workers' challenge. At the political level, unions fought for an increased social wage within the rhetoric of growth rather than relying on the discourse of social justice exclusively. Although the argument that workers deserve a national health plan as part of their social security system was often invoked, union lobbyists employed the Keynesian arguments that growth could be achieved by increasing consumption; low interest rates for housing and other durable goods were supported as an economic measure stimulating investment.

To illustrate the way in which discursive hegemony becomes, under these conditions, the determining instance in political relations we might take the recent settlements in the Chrysler Corporation. In the late 1970's, the UAW, representing more than 125,000 Chrysler workers, faced the possibility that, owing to international incursions into the domestic car market, the weakest of the major auto companies might fail. The union had several choices in trying to protect the workers: as in Britain, where British Leyland was taken over by the government, it could have demanded nationalization as the best chance to save most of the jobs. At the same time, it could have demanded a voice for workers in the management of the company. Second, it could have insisted that the company pay union wage and benefit scales or go out of business. This would have been the militant "trade unionist" position for which the class struggle under capitalism is not to be betrayed by nationalization schemes. The union chose the third alternative—collaboration to save the company. The union entered a three-way partnership with the company and the federal government under which the state, in return for substantial loan guarantees to banks and other investors, demanded that the union accept wage cuts totaling some $400 million and agree to deep cutbacks in production and consequently employment. The union gained nominal representation on Chrysler's Board of Directors. Nationalization was not a real alternative because there has been no legitimating discourse of public ownership of production except in wartime, and then only in new industries where the private sector has no previous interest. The union chose to collaborate with the program of Chrysler's reindustrialization because accumulation/investment has been the dominant expansionist discourse in the industrial sector. Thousands of workers lost their jobs before the agreement and thousands have been rendered redundant since. In America, expansion has been linked to productivity, just another way of saying that what is good for accumulation is good for the country. The union succumbed, but without *feeling* that collaboration was somehow an act of betrayal. In its ideological lexicon, to have permitted the company to fail because of class considerations would have been infinitely worse.

The case of UAW-Chrysler negotiations of 1979–80 illustrates the universality of the *discursive rule* that all class interest must be subordinate to growth and industrial survival. By discursive rule I mean the informal imperative that political and other social relations be framed within the hegemonic discourse. This rule frames the boundaries of discourse, sets the agenda of debate, and has the force of a law insofar as other discourses are precluded from consideration. It is not, then, that other ideas have not been advanced in the Chrysler situation or in the recent struggle of workers and their unions to preserve jobs in the wake of capital flight. But the force of the discursive rule is to prevent these from being considered as practical alternatives because they do not meet the criteria of the growth ideology. Americans, including workers, have accepted the judgment that job creation is contingent upon growth and that expansion is a function of creating new markets and of increasing worker productivity in order to enlarge the volume of accumulated capital. As a result, programs that are predicated on the imperatives of social need, without offering new investment opportunities that promise a required rate of return, are simply ignored. In the labor movement, this rule has governed collective bargaining between companies and union leaders since World War II.

After the general strike of 1946, labor seemed headed for a sharp confrontation with the Democratic Party, which union activists accused of having effectively adopted the anti-labor, anti-New Deal program of the Republicans. This mood of militancy, however, quickly dissipated. The Steelworkers Union "pioneered" the concept that labor would approve corporate "pass alongs" of wage increases. The UAW initially led the fight against this practice and the notion that price increases were caused by wage increases, but capitulated in its 1948 negotiations. After unsuccessfully proposing that GM agree to "open the books" to the union and the public before it passed along price increases to consumers, the union bargained for a new provision in the contract. In return for agreeing to soft pedal its right to control the pace of production on the shop floor, the union won an "annual improvement factor" increase that recognized the right of workers to higher living standards. Secondly, the cost of living increase gave workers a hedge against inflation by tying increases to the Bureau of Labor Statistics Consumer Price Index.

This "breakthrough" in collective bargaining sealed the historic compromise that had been in the making throughout the New Deal. In terms of the discourse of class relations, it represented a profound class compromise in American labor history—the institutionalization not of class struggle, but of the integration of workers into the accumulation process. Workers hitched their star to production. Instead of demanding higher wages "at the expense of profits," unions agreed to "share the benefits of productivity" and so lodged themselves inextricably in the discourse of growth. The redistributive strategies of the old labor movement with its socialist and anarchist influences now became mere "rhetoric," and the radicalism of individual leaders or groups within the labor movement ceased to have political weight. Unions had become political organizations in the accepted meaning of the phrase; they had integrated themselves into the prevailing discourse of power.

This final phase of the historic compromise was itself the consequence of labor's legislative victories as well as its strike successes in the early and mid-30's. Political struggle had taken the form of transforming the state within capitalist society from an instrument of the bosses to one that protected workers' rights to a job at decent wages, better housing, and adequate health care, and the right to bargain collectively for job security and better wages. The concept of *economic citizenship* had always implied that workers needed civil rights at the workplace and the protection of law to enter unions. These were the ideological tenets of social democracy between the wars, and it is from them—and not the cold war house-cleaning of communists from the unions or the pressure of the old conservatives' offensive against labor—that American labor finally surrendered its class struggle traditions. Indeed, as early as 1933, the industrial union upsurge led by an amalgam of socialists, communists, and voluntarist trade unions had already abandoned class struggle or redistributive perspectives. As some old miners and craft leaders moved to the left, the socialists were on their way to the right. Together they helped forge the New Deal alliance. From its inception, this alliance enunciated the ideology of what C. Wright Mills called "syndicalism from the top."[14] The new nationalist discourse of the New Deal spoke of America first, a nation in which class struggle was imposed not by the working class but by the "economic royalists" who fought unionization, state intervention, and legislation enlarging the social wage, all in the name of the free market. Syndicalism from the top meant that the state, the corporations, and the organized working class would join in the common enterprise of economic recovery and growth—that is, of *capital accumulation* and *international expansion.*

Incapable of reversing its allegiance to the nationalist discourse of growth, the labor movement was ill-prepared to respond to the economic, social, or political crises of the past two decades. The present crisis—concentrated in Ronald Reagan's election to the presidency—is a measure of the New Right's capacity to take command of the discourse of growth itself. In the absence of an alternative to the very ideology that built the historic bloc, American labor can only preside over the demise of its own political power. The optimism that flourished in the 1960's is today without foundation. With John Kennedy's election in 1960 and Lyndon Johnson's thrashing of the first major representative of the new conservatism, Barry Goldwater, in 1964, the historic bloc could believe itself to be healthy. It was, of course, this environment in the mid-60's that engendered some of the key conditions for the emergence of the New Left and its conviction that the terms of political debate in America had finally shifted sufficiently leftward to permit another, more powerful dialogue, one in which liberalism would be challenged by a Left able to acquire a mass base. By 1980, it has become clear that beneath the surface of the war-induced prosperity of the 60's new forces of disintegration were playing havoc with the historic bloc and its social core, the working class and its organizations.

America in Transition. Just as the emergence of the new conservatism has depended upon the shift in the regional centers of the American economy, the break-up of the labor movement has been accelerated by this same geographical shift (capital flight) and by transformations in the technological composition of labor and in the international division of labor. The new conservatives based themselves on the burgeoning industries that grew out of the military—the advanced technologies of electronics, aircraft, and nuclear industries of the southwest; the oil and petrochemical industries situated in Texas, Oklahoma, California, coal regions of Colorado and Montana, and atomic metal mining in New Mexico and Arizona; gambling and real estate in the new towns of the southwest for which high property taxes and extensive transfer payments were significant retardants to their growth; the "old" new industrial South, with its traditional company towns employing nonunion textile, shoe, and lumber workers in furniture, paper, and sawmills. These have been the expanding sectors of American industrial production and have multiplied the powers of the construction trades, services, and transportation in the sunbelt. The old Democratic Party's grip on the South was broken, a splintering interrupted briefly by the Carter campaign because his roots in the old South were compatible with the cultural and economic shift of the country. However, the elections after 1968 were not merely frostbelt/ sunbelt contests. A much broader conservative drift developed among American working people and members of the middle strata. This transformation was rooted in three central elements:

(1) The long term decentralization of American industries has dispersed capital and labor from the large cities of the northeast and middlewest to suburban and rural areas. This development had already begun in the 1920's with the migration of the textile and shoe industries to the southeast and was only temporarily interrupted by the Depression. During World War II, California and the state of Washington were virtually industrialized by the decision of the military to disperse military plants from the traditional areas of concentration, ostensibly for security reasons. Overnight Los Angeles and Seattle became chief aircraft assembly producers, and the Bay Area in northern California was made into an important parts manufacturing center for the aircraft industry. The third stage of the decentralization occurred after the war: textiles and shoes resumed their flight away from the northeast, and were joined by the garment trades. But the dominant areas of the runaway shop shifted in the late 1960's to intermediate technology industries such as autos, steel, electrical and electronics, chemicals, and rubber and plastic products. During this period virtually all new plants with advanced technology in either the old sectors or the new petrochemical and electronics sectors were built in suburbs or rural areas, most of which were located in the sunbelt. Only the machinery sectors remained in the older centers because skilled workers were more reluctant to leave traditional communities within which their culture had been strong. In the 1960's even the historical locations of extractive industries such as coal and oil shifted as new processes for mining coal, such as strip mining, and for extracting oil from shale were discovered.

In the main, unions were not able to follow the capital flight in the low technology sectors such as textiles. Explanations for this failure of industrial union organizing in the South have been incomplete. The conventional wisdom points to the anti-union environment in the southeast, combined with weak federal enforcement of labor law protections for workers' right to join unions, as the principal causes of the relative weakness of labor organizations, despite some notable successes, most recently the Amalgamated Clothing and Textile Workers' victory at six plants of one of the giant corporations in the textile industry, J.P. Stevens. Certainly, it would be mistaken to ignore the failure of the unions and the progressive coalition to find a fraction of capital with which to ally in the pursuit of unionism and a liberal South. Dominated by ideologically recalcitrant textile employers, key states such as North and South Carolina, Georgia, and Tennessee remain to this day powerful bastions of the open shop. The repressive and ideological state apparatuses are solidly in line with this orientation, and workers know it. There is fear and trembling to join unions, even when the need is evident.

However, other issues are equally important to address. First, employers have become more sophisticated in their labor relations compared to the days of early CIO organizing drives. Wages and benefits in the vast nonunion sector of the textile and garment industries are equal to those of the unionized part. Further, the large conglomerates and multiplant corporations that now control American produced textiles have successfully defied government regulations prohibiting the use of the plant removal threat as a deterrent to union organization. Workers know that joining the union may mean losing their job to capital flight rather than discriminatory discharge.

Second, there can be no doubt that the American trade union movement as a whole failed to place organizing the unorganized high on its agenda after the CIO's Operation Dixie collapsed in the late 1940's. It was not only that labor's leadership despaired at their ability to organize in the deepening anti-union atmosphere after the war, but the increasing character of trade unions as business unions made organizing the job of paid staff instead of the rank and file. After the war, labor's education and political mobilization among its basic membership were sharply curtailed for various reasons, including the growing fear of the rank and file, virulent anti-communism, and the retrenched environment surrounding the union bureaucracy. In contrast to the 1933–45 period, when organizing was the principal activity of the unions and became the property of all union militants, the post-war era was marked by a division of labor between the staff—now assigned the task of handling union business, organizing only in their spare time—and the rank and file activists who had their hands full enforcing the contract's working condition protections and fighting a leadership that increasingly opposed shop floor militancy.

Third, in the absence of ideological and political education and with the erosion of union democracy, large sections of the membership became disaffiliated from the unions, even when they recognized the benefits of the contract. In the United States today there are many more contracts than trade unions, if by the term we mean a voluntary association of workers joined together to advance their economic, social, and political interests. Anti-unionism, deeply imbedded in American political culture, has found fertile soil for its appeals because the labor movement has lost its missionary zeal and has failed to ask its members to support union programs including organizing. Unions have not followed capital into non-union regions because they have lost their character as a social movement. Only the unions in the basic industries of auto and steel succeeded in maintaining the extent of their organization even though the new plants employed fewer workers because of labor saving technologies. The record of unions in the newer industries of electronics and chemicals was mixed; in those industries, wages tended to be higher because of advanced technologies requiring less labor, the character of labor was different from the old industrial labor process, and historically the unions were weaker. Militant unions with strong organizing traditions such as the United Electrical Workers and the Auto Workers were somewhat more successful in following runaway shops than the chemical workers' unions or the needle trades unions, whose organizing history was far less luminous.

(2) The effects of the scientific and technological revolution on the labor force have been to accelerate the historical tendency towards the "liberation" of manual labor from the labor process and its subsumption under intellectual labor. Unions were concentrated, until 1960, in those sectors producing means of production and means of consumption; this constituted the heart of the industrial working classes in the era of mechanization. Today these sectors have diminished in size. Among the reasons are the changes in the organic composition of capital and its technical composition, the latter being but the expression of the progressive displacement of labor by scientifically based technologies. Today, the worker in large scale industry is no longer defined exclusively as a manual worker. He or she is as likely to be a scientist, engineer, or technical employee; typically not part of the union that bargains for manual workers, these workers nonetheless do not exercise decisive management functions. In the continuous flow industries such as oil, chemicals, food processing, and paper, and those where the microprocessors such as the chip and numerical controls are becoming predominant, the weight of the old industrial worker in the labor process has given way to a new stratum: the *technical intelligentsia*, which is no longer composed of professionals such as doctors and lawyers, but by occupational layers in the private corporate sector that are concerned with the management or operation of the new technology and administration, distribution, and consumption, and by those in the state sector who manage and operate the forms of state intervention into the economy.[15]

The development of the public sector of the U.S. economy is as dramatic as it is complex. As in other advanced industrial societies, the public sector's economic and social interventions are by no means confined to the social welfare state. On the contrary, it is in the military and economic spheres, the sphere where goods and knowledge are produced, that the government as investor and coordinator has grown most. Reagan will cut back social welfare but not the other aspects of state intervention: that is, he will cut social consumption but not social production.

It is in technical administrative sectors that the labor movement has suffered its sharpest reversals. The trade unions have failed to make any significant dent in these growing sectors which, grouped under the rubric of knowledge production, administration, and management, now account for a majority of the labor force in the economy. The singular and important exception is the public sector, but even here only fifty percent of its employees have been organized into unions. The public sector amounts to one of seven jobs in the economy, and administration and intellectual labor (clerical, management, and knowledge employees such as computer programmers, etc.) half of all industrial sector jobs. In addition, the retail, wholesale, and financial sectors are largely non-union, save workers in some branches such as food, hotels, and warehousing. Here the concentration of union strength remains confined to the largest cities, most of which in the northeast and midwest are declining in population. The failure of the unions to extend their membership has profoundly affected their ability to maintain political influence among the working classes.

(3) These regional and technological shifts, responses to growing international competition as well as the strength of the workers to limit the power of capital on the shop floor, have come on the heels of a new international division of labor. I refer particularly to the changes that have made the United States a leading producer of technology and administration for the world production of goods but a declining producer of material goods. Having been the world's leader in minerals and industrial production, a role that shaped American political and economic hegemony, the United States is now primarily a producer of military hardware, computer software, information processes, and agriculture (which itself has become among the most mechanized of industries). This is not to claim that the United States has not remained an important producer of manufactured commodities, but, in addition to massive urban disinvestment and technological displacement of manual labor, there is a national industrial disinvestment and economic recomposition signalled by large losses in steel and auto production, a concomitant shrinking of the labor force in these and other related industries, as well as an international migration of those light consumer goods industries that were once the source of much union power, particularly the needle trades. Thus traditional concentrations of unions' political and social strength, such as New York, Detroit, Chicago, and Pittsburgh, are in serious disrepair. Industrial unions are replaced by state sector unions, but because labor has failed to organize in the new sectors of finance, knowledge production, and retailing, the overall political power of unions has declined dramatically. Union support is no longer the *sine qua non* of Democratic municipal and state politics.

THE TRANSFORMATION OF WORKERS CULTURE

The formation of social classes is a long historical process. In the *18th Brumaire,* Marx was fairly specific in delineating the conditions for class formation. A class is a class only insofar as it represents itself, rather than being represented by other classes as a "gift from on high." In turn, the class's capacity for self-representation is marked by common conditions of life, including, but not limited to, a common relation to the ownership and control of the means of production. Among other things, classes are, for Marx, formed by culture, understood here as modes of discourse, a shared symbolic universe, rituals and customs that connote solidarity and distinguish a group from others. Thus, the process of class formation is far more complex than the relation of a given group to the ownership of the means of production. The economic identification of social classes was the necessary, but not sufficient condition for their formation as historical actors. The working class could *become* capitalism's gravedigger only when its life situation produced a culture that enabled it to overcome its self-definition by craft, industry, race, or sex—a consciousness determined by the social and technical divison of labor. In the history of Marxism, various writers have tended to portray class formation as a function of the economic identification of social classes combined with the contradictions of the accumulation process. The central mediation of culture—that is, the actual process by which the working class may achieve a reflexive relationship to its own existence—is usually ignored as a social and political problematic.

The overarching virtue of E.P. Thompson's *Making of the English Working Class* was to revive considerations of cultural formation as a vital link in the general process of class formation. For Thompson, the workers' movement is constituted as a dialectic between the political and economic class struggle for elementary democratic rights and the social relations among the workers themselves that forged the bonds of solidarity at the level of everyday life. Implied by Thompson's history is the fundamental judgment that classes are effects of a system of mutual determinations (overdetermination), of which the question of relationship to the means of production is the passive element, while class struggle and cultural life are the active element.[16] For it is from cultural life that a working class public sphere is formed. This public sphere is the space where shared experience at the workplace and in the neighborhood becomes the common property of all; the issues arising from the economic relations between workers and bosses are displaced to tenants and landlords, consumers and merchants, and personal interactions among the group are named, given conceptual significance, and transformed into written or oral culture on the one hand and class organizations on the other. Factory and neighborhood are shared spaces within which and about which interactions are constituted, but these spaces do not constitute the relations themselves. There must be a common discourse that is, in part, separate from the national discourse. Workers produce discursive practices which, as a whole, form a cultural sphere that inscribes their historical solidarity as well as their structural difference from other social groups in society—

employers, landlords, and merchants on the one hand, and farmers and professionals on the other.

Thompson's critical achievement was to show how the formation of a distinct public or cultural sphere of working class life became a crucial constituent of the making, the self-making, of the English working class. Thompson's narrative leaves unanswered, however, the precise relation between the formation of working class culture and revolutionary class consciousness. How is it possible for the working class to constitute itself as a revolutionary subject pointing to a new future, rather than an oppositional class within capitalist society? Surely the English working class succeeded in the task of constituting a proletarian public sphere even before it organized its own political party in 1900. As early as 1832, the last year of Thompson's study, the organized labor movement was a growing influence in English politics and economic life, the Chartist movement having raised the demand for suffrage and other rights within the prevailing order. For our purposes, it is enough to note that the history of European working class movements demonstrated Marx's formula that the independent class formation of workers in the political sense was an outcome of the exhaustion of capital, its tendency to ever more frequent crises manifested not only by unemployment but by wars. The trade union movements which inscribe the elementary workers public sphere made the step to parliamentary socialism supported by the overwhelming majority of proletarians, who possessed the social weight to become leading forces in what Gramsci calls a *historic bloc* together with fractions of other classes. The greater the working class's solidarity, that is, the ability of the movement to unite its subfractions behind a program of self-representation—the more the perspective of social transformation becomes palpable at the level of discourse as much as political action.

In England, the working class succeeded in winning over a fraction of bourgeois intellectuals who became contestants for ideological hegemony within educational institutions, parliament, and the press. To be sure, these strata adapted working class culture, aspirations, and demands to a definite conception of appropriate political and cultural forms, such as were proposed by Fabians, Christian Socialists, and Marxists. For the purposes of this analysis, the appropriation of the working class movement by the intellectuals explains some of the diverse directions of the socialist and labor movement, but not the fact of the movement itself nor its capacity to intervene in the discourses of politics, education, and culture.

In the United States by contrast, the working class—though it did win over a significant number of intellectuals during its two great periods of upsurge, the turn of the century and the 1930's—never achieved sufficient power to evoke the articulation of a discourse of laborism. Instead, it was obliged to formulate its demands in a rhetoric and discursive framework that were the ideological property of other social strata.

"Late," "advanced," "monopoly" capitalism rather than socialism became capital's solution to its nearly mortal contradictions, except in its weak links. In the advanced countries, the capacity of workers for self-organization, political self-representation, and the formation of a (limited) proletarian public sphere were not sufficient to overcome the tendency of the working class to remain an opposition force within and not against the system. Whether the propensity of the workers movements and their political parties to conduct the struggle within the system is a testament to capital's ideological and economic innovations that successfully contain the scope of the workers movement or to weaknesses within the workers movement, including the political ambivalence of class culture—or both—it is plain that there is something missing in the formula *self-organization "plus" capitalist crisis "plus" autonomous public sphere "equals" revolutionary class consciousness.*

The history of the U.S. working class shows that the transformation from struggles about the economic conditions of workers to political self-representation is by no means automatic or linear. The American working class, for various reasons, only succeeded in forming powerful trade unions in the industrial sectors at the end of the upsurge of U.S. capitalism. I have argued elsewhere that the long delay in producing elementary class organizations is attributable to the diverse sources of working class formation—particularly the divisions based upon race and ethnicity.[17] Even when workers were brought together by capital into relatively concentrated geographical spaces, the racial and ethnic division of labor overlaid divisions based upon craft, sex, and industry to render more difficult the process of social class formation. The remarkable speed of trade union organization in the 30's and the rapid transformation of the labor movement into a core component of the New Deal—the American version of the historic bloc—are signs that the long struggle to overcome, at least partially, racial and ethnic divisions had finally borne fruit. The cities of Pittsburgh, New York, Chicago, and especially Detroit became sites for an incipient working class public sphere in the 1930's and early 1940's. On the national level, the AFL and CIO leadership was integrated into the power bloc, even if as junior partners. And contrary to the wishes of most radicals during and after this period, the mass base of the power bloc was more or less solidly in support of its leadership on questions of political representation.

Class formation required as one of its essential conditions the constitution of an everyday life that linked workplace and neighborhood so that distinct discursive practices could emerge. Upon this foundation American working people began to understand themselves in class rather than industrial, craft, or other terms. I would characterize the situation in the early 1940's as *incipient* class formation because the economic and political struggles of workers began to open the vista of a separate, reflexive political culture. There was no question of revolutionary class formation because of the specific features of late capitalism which began to dominate the landscape after 1936: specifically, the success of forms of state intervention designed to regulate the relations of labor and capital grouped under the rubric of the "social welfare" state; the development of consumer society which, while it signified a measure of the victory of the working classes in raising their level of material culture, also constituted a form of ideological domination as well as a terrain of cultural conflict; and the emergence of the United States as the undisputed world capitalist power.

On the one hand, working class political culture was assisted by the "one industry" basis of U.S. urban development (Detroit for autos, Pittsburgh for steel, Akron for rubber, New York for the needle trades and metalworking). In many neighborhoods of these cities there was a conjunction between common living conditions and common working conditions. When the UAW formed political action committees in the 1940's to elect its municipal, state, and national candidates, the task of mobilization was made easier by the working class bars, social clubs, and church organizations which auto workers frequented. The union had organized itself geographically as well as by shops. (UAW leader Walter Reuther was based in the huge West Side local that organized a large number of shops in the district.) As the ethnic divisions among blacks, Poles and other Eastern Europeans, Italians, and southern Anglo-Saxons, were overcome, under the slogan of "solidarity," elements of a working class political culture appeared even if ethnic culture presented itself as the displacement of class culture.

On the other hand, the relatively favorable conditions for class formation were short-lived. After World War II, capital began to decentralize to the South, the suburbs, and former rural areas, and by the mid 1950's began a massive movement overseas. Industrial concentration became unnecessary with the centralization of ownership and the profound advances in new means of transportation and communication, exemplified by the huge federal programs of the 1950's that linked east and west in a network of superhighways and airports. The "communications" revolution of miniaturization of electronic equipment, computers, and later the widespread use of numerical controls and robotization reduced the skills and the number of workers required for industrial production and administration. State investment in the military and the economic infrastructure accelerated capital decentralization. Auto, steel, rubber, and metalworking plants gradually disappeared from the older industrial centers. New

York, once a center of light industry and a powerful labor movement based upon key working class neighborhoods linked to the garment, metal, and transportation industries, was denatured. Now it is a financial and information processing city, an international city whose labor force is largely unorganized. Typical of several major cities, its primary labor force no longer lives and works together. Workers are dispersed in many neighborhoods within the city and many more commute daily from other cities and states.

Capital's diffusion played the role of breaking the link between living and working spaces. Social life is no longer organized around the common relation to the production of both culture and commodities. The old working class public sphere is dead, except in those rural industrial contexts, such as mining, which maintain the dominant characteristics of work/neighborhood linkages of the earlier period. In the mining areas of West Virginia, the southeastern region of Kentucky, and southern Illinois, the name "union" concentrates the economic, political, and cultural levels in a discourse of working class reflexivity. But this instance is becoming rare, confined to similar ecological environments that are today atypical of the new conditions of life and labor for the working class fractions.

In the new post-industrial environment, workers culture has neither the power nor the unity required for class formation in the sense that was relevant for Europe in the nineteenth century or the United States in the 1940's. Concurrent with the breakup of the historic bloc has been the displacement of workers culture to separate spheres. I want to comment, somewhat unevenly, on four such spheres—the culture of work-resistance, black culture, the culture of the middle strata, and women's culture—in order to emphasize the extent to which the conditions for forming a historic bloc in America have changed and to situate the power of the right in American politics today. The old progressive coalition has no possibility of integrating these separate sites of cultural formation; moreover, each has a distinct logic of its own, and includes elements openly antagonistic to the other spheres. The real segregation that preconditions both black culture and women's culture has not only given these sites of cultural creativity their oppositional capacity, but has at the same time made racism and anti-feminism powerful elements of the New Right's ideological agenda. The culture of work resistance has, in the United States, lacked any effective political articulation, and the absence of an alternative political discourse has made the middle strata's cultural life a terrain to be captured by the Right.

American workers culture has increasingly become a culture of work resistance. It has no political expression such as exists among the British, French, and Italian working classes or the Polish working class. For that reason, its moment of cohesion in the twentieth century as a universal culture rather than a sectoral phenomenon was confined to periods of upsurge. Even in these instances, union organizers were obliged to recognize the differences within the working classes that were not only those of divisions based upon occupation and skill, but also those based upon ethnicity, race, and sex. These differences were never obliterated by integrationist ideologies and remain the "actual" site of working class cultures today. Beyond the craft traditions of the last century, our time is marked by a diversity which is evident both at the level of work relations and social relations.

Today only blacks and Latinos share the same or similar neighborhoods, despite the dispersal of their workplaces. They experience a common oppression exacerbated by segregation and the racial division of labor that assigns the great majority to the secondary labor market, the underground economy, or the welfare rolls. Rather than restricting the problem of racism to the problematic of slavery or to the obviously privileged position of white workers in the social and technical division of labor or to the psychological displacements in social relations, I want to insist that a central category for explaining the conditions under which these "givens" of U.S. capitalism may be overcome is the *real praxis* of the social movements of opposition. The problem of culture thereby takes on its special significance, and in turn it becomes necessary to recognize the political obstructions or ambivalences or vulnerability that can affect the cultural sphere of a specific social movement. Despite occasions when black workers participate in mainstream occupations, they rarely share suburbs with whites. Even as black professional, technical, and administrative employees move out of the cities, they form middle class ghettos. More generally, the suburbanization of industry has produced increasing segregation because blacks and other socially constituted minorities lose their access to the labor and housing markets in proportion to the erosion of their political power. Like the miners, blacks maintain a close relationship to their churches, which often amount to centers for their political culture. Most churches are indeed centers of working class culture, including art, because they form a symbolic world distinct from that of other groups and classes, and have been a place of political mobilization as well as personal survival in a hostile social environment. While religion cannot be defined solely as a cultural form for workers, the dominant class location of black Americans is the working class and underclasses. It thus becomes clear that in the United States where class culture has been displaced to ethnic culture, the question of the role of culture in class formation assumes dimensions altogether different from those that governed class formation in England or Europe in the nineteenth century.

With the proletarianization of the middle strata, concomitant with the emergence of knowledge as a productive force, we are beginning to see the development of a new culture, or cultural sphere, among these salaried employees. Not only is this culture markedly different from manual labor's culture of work resistance and from the ethnic cultures of American minorities, but it is also marked with specific ambivalences that the Right has successfully exploited. The new technical intelligentsia still forms a work culture on presuppositions that are commensurate with, though not identical to, the old craft traditions. Computer people, air traffic controllers, portions of the medical professions, and engineers in advanced technological sectors often find their work intrinsically interesting and/or recognize its importance in the system of social material reproduction. This positive relation to labor derives from the wider scope of much intellectual labor and the wider autonomy enjoyed by the individual or small groups in the knowledge production processes. The technical intelligentsia does confront capital's tendencies towards rationalization, particularly the reduction of job assignments to reproducible operations, restrictions on the power of research or operations groups to make decisions based upon self-determined criteria and judgments, and the new health dangers produced by the mental fatigue that often results from a high degree of responsibility coupled with a shrinking measure of work autonomy. Nevertheless, these workers face different forms of alienation than manual labor and have not adapted easily to the technologies of managerial control over the labor process by inventing forms of unwork and ways to disrupt the smooth flow of the product. As we have seen, the response of the air controllers to untenable stress on the job has begun to resemble the demands of steelworkers and assembly line workers in auto plants: shorter hours and earlier retirement, both means of avoiding the pressures of the job. The dominant work culture of the technical intelligentsia is still expressed as camaraderie derived from the pride of skill, and the importance of the job in the new productive processes.

Even though the technical intelligentsia remains ideologically tied to professionalism (their particular mediation of class), and their few trade union affiliations are frequently professional associations that little resemble the older craft or industrial organizations of manual workers, the new context within which they labor has begun to disrupt many of their political and occupational perceptions. They have learned something about the issue that haunts the intelligentsia throughout history: the degree of their individual indispensability. The question raised by Reagan's actions against PATCO is whether intellectual labor differs sufficiently from manual labor to make ordinary degradation impossible or unlikely. Are they indispensable? Is a professional credential the ticket to economic security? The proletarianization of the intelligentsia began with the "subprofessions" of teaching, social work, and health, and is now extended to engineers and managers who face not only joblessness in a shrinking economy but sharply curtailed autonomy as well. Yet, in contrast to France and Great Britain where large sections of the emerging technical intelligentsia have supported various left and radical parties and movements in consequence of their growing proletarianization, their American counterparts have moved instead to the right, because there is no viable left discourse within which to explain their situation. The Right explains the effects of inflation on the real incomes of these strata by blaming "big labor and big government" when it does not rest its ideological appeals on bald racism. The middle strata, rendered more or less defenseless on the job by the deterioration of the international position of U.S. capital, have become an integral component of the so-called "tax revolt" whose tentacles have enveloped the suburbs. It may be argued that the growing social weight of these strata has produced a situation where they have succeeded in imposing their vision upon fractions of the working class, which shares some of their conditions, notwithstanding substantial differences, especially the fact that most skilled manual workers are union members. As the New Deal alliance continues to fragment and lose its political force, erstwhile liberal politicians anxious to retain their offices are constrained to move to the right since there is no progressive movement to keep them and their middle strata constituents in line.

The cultures of the middle strata are focused on the workplace through the ideology of professionalism, whose elements—credentials, rank and office—are understood as part of the baggage of economic security, but also of community. Home and family are entwined with cultures of consumption rather than "neighborhood." The bifurcation of work and home militates against class ideology. And the employed middle strata remain "represented" by fractions of the capitalist class since their own organizations are ensconced in issues of economic well-being. In recent years, what might be termed the rentier classes have successfully mobilized important segments of the middle strata to support tax reduction initiatives, budget cutting at the local and state levels, and have built a broad base among these strata for conservative economic doctrines.

Let us turn finally to the question of women's culture, for it is here that the gap between the political potentiality of a social movement, grounded in a distinct cultural sphere, and the contemporary Left's organizational capacities has become acute. The rise of the modern women's liberation movement poses a serious challenge to those who would resurrect the old progressive coalition or construct a new one on the basis of economic justice alone. For the central innovation of the new women's movement has been its insistence that sexual liberation and the struggle for social equality are inseparable from the struggle for job opportunities for women and wage parity with men. The New Right and the neo-conservatives have made the social and sexual gains of women a primary target in their quest for ideological and political domination. This ideological attack has been drawn on the deep ambivalence that most of us raised with patriarchal culture harbor regarding the many questions of sexuality. The progressives, lacking an ideological perspective that would legitimate sexual freedom on other than civil libertarian grounds, have been drawn into the conservative orbit. The defense of the family has become a mainstay of many progressive intellectuals who, like Christopher Lasch, have carried out the critique of consumerism in a way that leaves them with no sense of possible community except one grounded in traditional forms of family experience. We have arrived at a point, visible in the divisions that now afflict the women's movement itself, where the Right understands far more clearly than the liberals and the progressives the truth of Marx's remark that the measure of social progress is the degree to which society has liberated women.

The real segregation of women begins in the home, a condition not fundamentally altered by the tendency over the past forty years for a majority of women to enter the labor force as part-time and full-time workers. This segregation carries with it the reproduction of the domination of men over women and at the same time produces a separate women's culture. The old working class neighborhoods, no less than the suburbs, are the terrain of women's social relations marked by the absence of men, except in the taverns and pool halls among workers or the clubs inhabited by members of the ruling and managerial classes for which the distinction between social life and business is moot. "The family" is the relation of women to each other realized in shopping centers, parks and the streets, and in their collective interaction with children. Women are the clients and the immediate political constituency of the public schools, health institutions, and other social amenities. Their sphere is quite separate from that of men for whom the home is a resting place since male labor is defined in terms of wage earning.

This social and cultural separation carries over to the workplace, where women inhabit not only the lower paying jobs together with blacks and other minorities, but also perform different tasks from men. They not only comprise the preponderant labor force among clerical and administrative sectors, but are in the majority in finance, retail and wholesale, and the public sector. Yet their unions are characteristically male-dominated since men occupy the skilled manual or technical jobs. Like the rest of the labor movement it is these employees who run the unions. As a result, women are usually not only estranged from their work because of its degraded and sexist structure, but from the labor movement as well. The fact that this pattern has been broken in a scatter of instances shows up the degree to which women have been separated from the core of the old progressive coalition.

Thus, the women's movement was obliged to establish itself autonomously in the late 1960's, repeating the experience of the suffrage movements earlier in this century and nineteenth century progenitors as well. The recent accommodations of the organized liberal feminist movement cannot obliterate the force of a separate women's culture, particularly among those for whom liberation remains, if not a conscious goal, a practical activity as well as a utopian vision. Women have expressed this will for liberation in many ways over the centuries ranging from the widespread practice of illegal abortion prior to the 1976 Supreme Court decision, to the advent of an open lesbian culture after centuries in the closet, to the growing mass of single women who prefer being alone to male supremacy. Women have created institutional forms for their culture in the middle classes while preserving informal networks built around the neighborhood and the workplace that are not subsumed by unions or other male-dominated organizations among the working class women. Even as mass-mediated culture and consumerism have made profound inroads into women's autonomy even in their "private sphere," women's culture tries to preserve the home against this intervention because this is not only the space of their oppression, but the site of their autonomy—at least for a time each day.

Like any culture, women's culture lives the contradiction between the fact that it owes its formation to conditions of domination—a condition imposed upon oppressed groups by hierarchy and segregation—and, on the other hand, the fact that the modes of interaction, ritual, and discourse are the only free space. Conservatives and right progressive intellectuals have seized on this contradiction to exacerbate the ambivalence among women and to organize an ideological offensive against the genuine liberation movement. In the black movement the contradiction takes the form of the conflict between integration and nationalism. Among women there are tendencies to integrate by surrendering their newly won legitimate social power and to return to the underground of the rusty coathanger on the one hand, and to advocate cultural separatism on the other.

The present crisis cannot be explained adequately by economic categories for it has resulted as well from specific ideological and political tendencies. It remains important to examine the enormous appeal of right politics and culture in the United States, but the fundamental reason for the Right's ascendancy lies in the decline of the labor movement and particularly its inability to hold together the strands of the old historic bloc. It has been my argument that labor's decline stemmed from the very tendencies that forged the New Deal coalition itself principally, the devotion to contract unionism and to the dominant discourse of power and growth. As the economic and cultural conditions of class formation have changed, the labor movement has steadily found itself incapable of integrating workers from the new regions of capitalist growth, workers engaged in intellectual and technical labor, minorities, the underclasses, or women. The absence of an ideological alternative to the national discourse of power and growth has left labor bereft of organizational capacities within these new sites of class formation and of antagonism to the prevailing society. This loss of organizational capacity was accentuated by the business union precepts of organized labor in the postwar posterity, which have eroded workers education and rank and file participation in organizing efforts, and by the unions' confrontation with the New Left.

Culture, I have argued, is fundamental to class formation and to the organization of political consciousness within the working class. The tendencies that I have traced, including the problems of race and sex, defy older nineteenth century concepts of workers culture. It is not surprising that historians and sociologists have refused to explore our century; one cannot revel in the evidence of self-organization as in previous periods. Nonetheless, there is much work to be done. The separation of workers from their own traditions, recovered today only by the scholars, has also meant that a new worker was born from the ashes of the old culture. We need to define workers culture within the workplace under the new conditions of degradation not merely as resistances to the logic of capital but as a different cultural logic. Historically capitalism had to inculcate a work ethic, whether on religious or secular grounds, but it has found only consumption and mass culture as the substitutes in the age of mechanical production and reproduction. Old socially minded trade unionists or academics do not find encouragement in the new ethic of unwork that capital itself has unwittingly generated by weakening the social and political consciousness of workers. Nor has the technical intelligentsia been integrated into the old coalition. In contrast to their European counterparts, these new workers have in America drifted to the right, giving the contemporary political situation one of its most striking features. The ideological and programmatic assumptions of the New Deal coalition cannot serve to organize those workers who have abandoned the work ethic or those now forming the technical intelligentsia or those belonging to a generation that has become disaffected from politics as such. Nor will the old coalition's precepts answer the fundamental task of giving ideological and political direction to the cultural spheres, particularly those of minorities and women, that have the potentiality, however obstructed and threatened, to oppose the entire social and moral order of contemporary capitalism.

There is no turning away from the dissonance or the discontinuities that define the cultural and ideological tendencies of social classes and movements in America today. It is from these alone that can develop the conditions, which I will discuss in the last section, leading *toward a new historic bloc.*

THE DECLINE OF LABOR'S POLITICAL CLOUT

By the end of the first year of the Reagan administration, political experts, labor leaders, and Ronald Reagan himself had concluded that the old progressive coalition that had set the agenda for American politics for two generations had finally collapsed. In retrospect, Jimmy Carter's defeat in the 1980 presidential election was merely a symptom of the crisis. More than forty percent of traditional Democratic voters, especially "blue collar" workers, had defected to the Republicans despite the fact that Reagan was the most ideologically conservative presidential candidate of any major party since Goldwater in 1964. Labor's political clout, which had sustained the coalition built by Franklin Roosevelt and Sidney Hillman appeared to be dissipated. Several large unions, principally the Teamsters and others in transportation such as the Maritime union, had deserted to Reagan; they did not even feel pressured to remain neutral as AFL-CIO President George Meany and the building trades had during McGovern's defeat by Richard Nixon in 1972. The turnout among black voters, an important factor in any possible Democratic victory, was relatively small though overwhelmingly pro-Carter. A symptom of the malaise was the unsurprising pro-Reagan and pro-Anderson support of nearly half of the traditionally Democratic Jewish vote which responded to Carter's apparent drift to pro-Arab sentiment, and the economic conservatism of a growing proportion of middle class voters for whom nearly runaway inflation had become the leading political issue of that year.

Of course, the doctrine that became known as *Reaganomics* was already guiding his three immediate predecessors, each of whom lacked the Gipper's audacity. But it was Nixon, Ford, and Carter, not Reagan, who had presided over fundamental changes in economic philosophy compared to both the Roosevelt-Truman eras and the Kennedy-Johnson decade. (Even Eisenhower had not altered the basic outline of the New Deal although he froze its forward march into a full blown welfare state.)

Reagan's unique achievement was to have given ideological shape to the new policy, reversing the pragmatic approaches of his predecessors. He not only declared the end of the Keynesian doctrines that had guided U.S. economic and social policy since the thirties, he also made concrete proposals to speed their demise. Whereas the deeply conservative Richard Nixon had railed against "big" government even as he increased federal spending in health, education, and income maintenance programs, Reagan jammed through Congress sweeping welfare cuts, declaring that not only was the welfare state inflationary and big government contrary to American traditions, but the poor were undeserving. More salient to his offensive, he proposed radical new policies—tax cuts amounting (over three years) to the abolition of corporate profits taxes, unprecedented high peacetime levels of military spending (spelling the end to Presidents Ford and Carter's efforts to achieve arms control and an eventual reduction in nuclear weapons), and massive transfer of government-owned lands to private investors on the grounds that only by resource exploration could America become energy independent and the private enterprise system be preserved.

The progressive coalition was too busy licking its wounds to offer more than token resistance to this sharply ideological offensive. Moreover, its political legitimacy had been seriously undermined by the defections among traditional working class and middle class voters who in an inflationary economy regarded the emblems of the welfare state—the commitment to end poverty, provide a safety net under those expelled from the labor force by economic vicissitudes, and make the government the employer of last resort when the private sector failed—as an oppressive burden. The widespread belief among voters that inflation was the leading issue of the 1980 elections was a sign that the progressives had run out of more than solutions. The social and economic changes of the 1970's had combined to erode the traditional base of the progressive coalition, the organized industrial working class, and its middle class periphery in the northeast and midwest where such basic industries as steel, auto and rubber as well as electrical manufacturing and chemical industries were centered. As capital fled these regions, leaving in its wake half-filled or closed factories, their white population base was similarly shifting to the southeast, the southwest, and Pacific coast (all except California traditionally non-union, deeply conservative areas). Thus the labor movement, which had in the previous thirty years provided the major funds and political cadre for the Democratic Party, was caught in a "scissors" crisis. It was both weakened by ideological defection among those workers in the monopoly sectors who were convinced that a program for economic revival required cuts in welfare spending and by the loss of membership due to technological change and the developing economic crisis.

These fundamental shifts in labor's economic strength and ideological coherence were partially offset by the rise of public sector unionism in the 1960's and 1970's which, by the 1980 election, comprised a quarter of union membership. The million member American Federation of State, County and Municipal Employees (AFSME) had together with the Machinists and the Auto Workers become the most articulate representative of the old progressive commitments of the labor movement. However, these unions were only effective at the local level where budget cuts were affecting both members' jobs and community services. In the 1970's, the public sector unions forged coalitions to limit the size of welfare cuts (with community groups, the black community, and liberal professionals), but were often frustrated by the reluctance or inability of other private sector unions to join the fight. In the end, many of them felt obliged to make substantial concessions in wages and benefits in order to save members' jobs. The cutting edge for this partial retreat was, of course, the New York City fiscal crisis of 1975. Afflicted with capital flight in manufacturing, shrinking tax revenues, declining state and federal assistance, and a growing, dependent population of aged and poor, New York City government teetered on the brink of bankruptcy. In order to prevent default, the government was forced into receivership by its creditors who demanded control over the budget as the price for saving the city's credit status. One of the major elements of Reaganomics was first implemented in New York—the balanced budget. The banks and real estate corporations did not, of course, offer to surrender their substantial tax deferments in order to make up the shortfall; nor did large corporations whose major offices were located in New York assess themselves additional taxes to prevent substantial cuts in services. Instead, unions were asked to fold a portion of their pension funds to pay the debt service, defer scheduled wage increases, and accept considerable layoffs and subsequent service cuts.

By the end of the decade, business takeovers of many urban governments through mechanisms emulating New York's Financial Control Board became the rule in the wake of the fiscal crisis of American cities. The crisis was the result of the shift of capital investment in manufacturing to rural southern areas and overseas as much as the Ford and Carter administration policies to "bail out" such corporations as Lockheed, a major defense contractor. Carter actually came through for New York City, but not the dozens of other cities facing similar problems. In some places teachers and other municipal and state workers resisted political and corporate demands for concessions, but the pattern set by New York prevailed. New York unions accepted a virtual partnership with big business and the political directorate to salvage the remnants of gains obtained in the militant years of the 1960's and early 1970's. When the floor was mopped after the fiscal bloodbath of 1975–6, the unions had wrested an agreement from the administration to reduce the labor force by attrition rather than furloughs, in return for submitting to the control over bargaining by the newly established Financial Control Board.

With the election in 1977 of former liberal Congressman Ed Koch, the unions were confronted by a popular mayor who had already adopted the rhetoric as well as the policies of fiscal conservatism. Koch began to squeeze union members in their workplaces by reorganizing the labor process to expand responsibilities for many job classifications with small pay increases (a "reform" called broadbanding) that strengthened the power of management to direct the work forces arbitrarily, and to undertake "workfare" programs that required welfare recipients to perform jobs formerly held by union members on the threat of being cut off the rolls if they refused. The partnership among unions, business, and government was severed when Koch, a Democrat, revealed that Reaganomics was a doctrine that respected no party. The city unions finally joined a coalition that unsuccessfully tried to unseat Koch in his bid for reelection. However, the seeds planted by the trade union/black/liberal primary campaign in 1981 led to Koch's defeat in his bid for the Democratic gubernatorial nomination the following year at the hands of Lieutenant Governor Mario Cuomo who rode to victory on a coalition effort that was widely hailed as evidence of the revival of the old New Deal alliance. As the economic crisis deepened, it was evident that the sweeping political changes of the early Reagan years failed to fulfill their promise of economic revival. Nationally, the Democrats' midterm victories in the 1982 election, especially their capture of seven new governorships formerly held by Republicans and their 26-seat gain in the House of Representatives, temporarily confirmed the progressives' optimism about their chances for regaining power.

While it is entirely possible that the 1980's will prove a victorious decade for the Democrats, it may not spell the death of neo-conservatism in economic policy or social issues. The Democrats may survive, but the labor movement remains in a precarious situation and its traditional allies are not faring any better. The first years of the new decade have been disastrous for small business which has suffered more failures than at any time since the 1930's. Black unemployment, traditionally double that of whites, is now more than twenty percent. One out of every two black youths is jobless. The trend begun in the late 1970's for older industrial cities of the midwest to become ghost towns has not abated.

Clearly, the conjuncture of the economic crisis, technological change, and political events made urgent the tasks of finding solutions that could become the basis of a new political agenda. In the aftermath of the steady defeats suffered by labor and its partners, progressive intellectuals and liberal political leaders in the 1980's are focusing on developing alternatives to Reaganomics, and I shall discuss some of these proposals in the final section of this book. But until now most of the new work in economic policy from the left side of the debate has assumed that the major problems in the demise of liberalism are programmatic. I wish to offer an alternative definition of the problem before making a contribution to finding solutions that represent a genuine alternative to neo-conservatism. While it is important to stir an intellectual debate around programmatic issues, progressives are prone to focus exclusively on the "fetish" of program as if the constituency to fight for these measures already exists and simply needs to replace its old solutions with new ones.

I wish to argue that the rise of the new conservatism is as much the result of labor's loss of its powerful position both among its own membership and within the coalition as it is of the historic failure of Keynesian economics of growth. Therefore the question concerning the prospects for labor's revival and, concomitantly, specifying the conditions for creating a new alliance capable of setting the agenda for American politics, should precede any debate concerning program.

PART III

TOWARD A NEW BEGINNING FOR AMERICAN LABOR

CHAPTER 6

ORGANIZING THE NEW WORKERS

JUST as the rise of the industrial unions in the 1930's constituted the fundamental condition for the emergence of a progressive agenda in American national politics, the revival of the labor movement in the 1980's is the prerequisite for a new alliance. By "labor movement" I refer chiefly, but not exclusively, to the trade unions. I include such organizations as Working Women, a Cleveland-based feminist organization devoted to organizing among women clerical workers; a new but not yet formed movement of the unemployed in which some trade unions must play an important but not perhaps a dominant part; professional organizations such as the National Education Association, engineers' and scientists' groups, and nurses and other predominantly women's groups all of which may assume traditional trade union functions to the extent that they become collective bargaining agents; and black workers' organizations that have in the past taken the forms of civil rights movements as well as trade union caucuses.

In the past thirty years, as the intermediate technology industries were displaced to other regions of the world and those which remained became automated, the trade unions were unable to take root in the growing sectors of the economy. Unions have not organized extensively in private sector financial services, administration, communications, or in the new knowledge industries because of the steady decline of unionism as a political culture in American society. Trade unionism does not yet present itself as a logical alternative for new groups in the labor force that seek organizational means for the redress of their grievances against employers or their working conditions. We need only cast a cursory glance at Great Britain and France to find contrasting instances. Among the most powerful of French unions is the bank employees union and the major growth unions in Great Britain are those that organize among scientific, technical, and managerial staffs in private industry. These new unions are not merely replicas of the craft or industrial organizations but combine professional with trade union functions; in addition to collective bargaining, they are concerned with informing members about new developments in their industries, new certification requirements, issues of technological transformations that may affect their employment and, equally important, the political environment in which the professions are obliged to function.

There are, to be sure, a number of American unions that have taken the professional interests of their members seriously—notably those that became collective bargaining agents after a prolonged period of traditional professional activities. However, except for public employees unions and a minority of the older industrial unions, union leaders often consider professionals, managers, and clerical workers in the private sector as unorganizable. The hard fact is that the American labor movement has been too preoccupied with the survival of its traditional jurisdictions to pay much attention to the growing sectors of the economy.[1]

The idea of the professional as a member of the controlling apparatus of the labor process is deeply ensconced in industrial and labor relations. Indeed, the Labor Relations Law excludes managers from the jurisdiction of the Labor Boards (a provision which makes it necessary for managers to gain union recognition by strikes or be effectively deprived of representation), and requires that intellectual, clerical, and manual workers be organized in separate locals, and that they negotiate separately with the same employer. The Labor Relations Law has become more than a vehicle through which workers may gain legal protection for self-organization. It has constituted an *ideology* about who may be considered an "appropriate" subject of union organization.

As for the professional occupations, they were more or less safely subsumed under two distinct but closely related ideologies: the profoundly American notion of individualism which ironically became the basis of a collectivist practice in the twentieth century—meritocracy—and professionalism which reified the distinction between intellectual and manual labor by asserting the superiority of the former because it usually implied higher education credentials. Professionalism buttresses an individualist mentality on the basis of a highly social and bureaucratic process—the successful completion of a prescribed curriculum that legitimates professional status. However, in recent years there is some evidence that the effectiveness of large corporate paternalism and professional ideology has suffered due to the developing economic crisis and technologies that have reduced their autonomy. As a result, some professionals have organized unions and others have indicated in opinion polls their belief that unions are needed to ameliorate their grievances. Despite such signs of change unions have been slow to organize among these groups.

Clerical workers in the financial and administrative private sectors are also largely unorganized. More than ninety percent of these workers are women and their absolute numbers have increased dramatically in the past two decades as the role of the United States in the world economy has changed from industrial production to administration. Clerical labor, more than any of the so-called "white" collar occupations, has been subject to elimination by means of labor saving technologies. Despite relatively low pay, sexual harassment, and onerous working conditions, union successes among these workers have been sporadic. Until recently, few unions mounted large-scale campaigns among private sector clerical groups; like professionals they were considered beyond organizing except in companies where traditional industrial unions had established their economic power and social legitimacy, and in the public sector. Unions have been deterred by three major factors: legal restraints which often required that organizing include more than one workplace in companies that are chains, such as banks; corporate domination through paternalism; and the sexism of unions who themselves refuse to hire and promote women to responsible leadership and organizing positions. (Some unions are making serious efforts to change their way of operating among working women, especially changing the old "common sense" that regarded women as secondary wage earners beyond the pale of union organization.)

Finally, union organizing among the working poor has simply disappeared since the end of the Second World War, with the outstanding exceptions of the farmworkers' campaign of the late 1960's and early 1970's and the equally impressive hospital workers' drives of the previous decade. To be sure, the Textile Workers Union, some of the needle trades unions, and the tiny but militant Furniture Workers Union have maintained some commitment to organizing among low paid southern workers and the Clothing and Textile Workers' campaign to unionize the notorious anti-union bastion, J. P. Stevens, met with some success in the late 1970's. But with over a million textile and garment workers still outside unions in the South, and thousands more in furniture, lumber, and other secondary industries, the few victories recorded in that region can hardly be counted as evidence of intensive organizing. In addition, millions of workers in retail and wholesale companies in major cities remain unorganized and in recent years the sweatshop has returned, bringing hundreds of thousands of new immigrants into conditions of semi-peonage. I will argue that the dedication of labor's leadership to legalism as well as its loss of militancy is as responsible for the proliferation of non-union shops as the recalcitrance of employers.

I contend that unless a new wave of militant organizing is moved to the top of labor's agenda, not only are unions threatened with a return to the situation that prevailed in the 1920's when trade unionism in many industries virtually disappeared and the rest were obliged to knuckle under to employers' demands as the price for survival, but the condition of working people as a whole is likely to deteriorate rapidly, while the chances of reversing the situation will continue to decline.

THE DISMAL 1970's

Labor's earlier integration into the structure of economic and political power was unstable because it was conditioned on historical circumstances which have been surpassed; moreover, the trade unions' malaise, particularly with the deep membership losses in this era of deindustrialization and realignment in capital investment, has weakened the power of all but a minority of unions to protect workers' gains effectively. From 1970 to the end of 1982, the combined effects of the economic crisis, technological change, and capital flight resulted in reductions of between twenty and thirty percent in the membership of major industrial unions. The UAW reported a loss of 300,000 members or twenty percent in this period, down from 1.5 million. The Oil and Chemical and Atomic Workers, which claimed 180,000 members in 1970, had about 120,000 members ten years later, a loss of one third. The Machinists were losing about 10,000 members a month in 1981 and 1982, largely caused by business conditions and the introduction of computer-based technologies in machine shops; the Hat, Cap and Millinery Workers prepared to merge with the Amalgamated Clothing and Textile Workers. Its 1979 estimated membership of 7,000 contrasted to 32,000 members in the late 1960's; the United Rubber Workers, once 200,000 strong, was reduced to about 90,000 members by 1982 because, among other things, the tire business declined with auto sales.[2]

Membership losses in the public employees' unions were not as deep, in part because budget cuts, although substantial, have not yet been accompanied by massive technological change at the public workplace. Still, Reagan has successfully stemmed the growth of the public sector while at the same time federal, state, and local bureaucracies began the process of mechanizing administrative tasks, introducing word processors, computers, and centralized services in health, public welfare, and such institutions as libraries which resulted in workforce reductions. Similarly, the fast growing private service employees' unions, especially in the retail food industry, were confronted by corporate consolidations that resulted in store closings, the most dramatic of which was the massive paring of unprofitable A & P stores. The warehouse industry, heavily organized by Teamsters, Retail-Wholesale, and Longshore unions, computerized inventory records, order picking, and eliminated labor. And, of course, the earliest example of large-scale automation occurred on the docks which had been subjected to containerization in the 1960's. By the late 1970's, only income guarantees to senior employees provided a floor under longshoremen's living standards on both coasts. In San Francisco, where the legendary and once powerful Local 10 of the West Coast Longshoremen's Union once had 6000 working members, only 1500 workers were actually employed in any week in 1982 and many of these did not work full weeks. Those not covered by income guarantees were fortunate to work two or three days.

This incomplete but characteristic inventory of trends in some key production and transportation unions' memberships gives a fairly accurate picture of the situation. In the face of the membership slump, unions have tended to consolidate to relieve financial pressure and to increase bargaining strength. The Steelworkers—only a third of whose 700,000 members are in basic steel production compared to more than 600,000 in 1965—have led the movement towards union mergers. In the past twenty years, the Steelworkers have merged with several smaller international unions, notably the 40,000 member Mine, Mill and Smelter Workers which had been expelled from the CIO in 1950 on charges of being Communist dominated, and District 50, a potpourri of construction, chemical, and metal workers which once was a part of the Mine Workers. More recently, the Auto Workers took in the Distributive Workers' Union, the largest of whose organizations was New York's District 65, a "general workers' union" with about 35,000 metropolitan area members in cosmetics, corrugated, and other smaller production industries and the wholesale trades including warehousing. District 65 also had pioneered in organizing publishing houses, legal workers, and university workers in New York and Boston, and attorneys working for Legal Aid. The merger movement has united unions in similar industries. For example, the Meatcutters and Retail Clerks formed the Food and Commercial Workers. The unification of Clothing, Textile, and Shoe unions inspired the large union to rejuvenate organizing among some Southern textile corporate giants such as the fiercely anti-union J.P. Stevens chain. In the J.P. Stevens campaign, the traditionally innovative union enlisted the aid of the Corporate Campaign headed by Ray Rogers, whose tactic was to put pressure on members of the company's board and its financiers to force the company to bargain with the union, which had already won a Labor Board supervised election for six plants. Without the financial and organizational resources of the Clothing and Textile Workers, efforts to form unions in Stevens, Deering-Milliken, Burlington, and the other recalcitrant textile employers in the South would have surely remained frustrated. The Stevens victory was a breakthrough for which the labor movement fought since the 1930's and which confirmed the value of united efforts to achieve justice. Similar mergers have been proposed between the Oil and Chemical Workers and the Paper Workers. Another long time proposed merger would unite the two major electrical unions who deal with General Electric, Westinghouse, and other multinational corporations. Mergers of this kind make more sense than those which merely strengthen the power of union leaders to overcome membership losses in their traditional jurisdiction, but for some unions mergers have become a substitute for organizing. The Steelworkers' incorporation of

District 50 makes them one of the largest chemical workers' unions in the United States, but it does not affect the overall negotiating power of workers in the industry; the proposed OCAW/Paper Workers merger is less responsible than a unity measure that would bring together chemical unions with the Rubber Workers whose members increasingly overlap with many branches of the chemical industry.

ORGANIZING: THE SOUTH

The AFL-CIO and its Industrial Union Department (IUD) have, over the past twenty years, sponsored coordinated campaigns which sensibly try to concentrate energies in regional organizing. Organizing drives have been mounted in Greenville/Spartanburg, Los Angeles, and more recently Houston. The Federation brings together organizers from a number of participant international unions which agree to surrender their operational autonomy to a staff director. A committee of participating unions decides which successfully organized plants will be assigned to particular unions, and the director assigns organizers, regardless of affiliation, to campaigns. Coordinated organizing is a tremendous step forward for trade unions and it has yielded some positive results. But most of the efforts have suffered from a series of weaknesses which the leadership is not willing to face.

Among the most serious problems are the lack of sufficient funds which restricts the number of organizers and the talent of the organizing leadership. Although the IUD has tried to emulate the "blitz" organizing tactics of the CIO drives of yesteryear, resources are often inadequate to do the job properly. For example, despite earlier AFL-CIO sponsorship of radio shows, the unions usually do not sponsor radio and television shows not directly related to the campaigns in order to improve the labor movement's public image. Second, individual campaigns are thwarted by legal obstacles and company coercion designed to discourage workers from joining. The law is simply too lenient in granting companies delays in holding representation elections or delay bargaining after a union election victory. Among the barriers to organizing are the relatively innocuous punishments for those companies that flaunt the law. Union officials are right to argue that, until the law makes its violation a serious matter of contempt and penalties would affect profit margins or result in jail for perpetrators of anti-union coercion, the prospect is dim for organizing the South and other regions where corporate power extends to the courthouse and the statehouse as well as churches, the media, and other local institutions.

However, while labor's complaints of the external barriers to union organizing are valid, they are not adequate to account for the almost dead stop in Southern union organizing in recent years. The flight of capital to

Southern states has successfully reduced the extent of union organization among workers in a number of "soft goods" industries because the political and economic environment in this region has been unfavorable for years. In fifty years the agricultural South transformed into a major industrial region, bringing a new labor force into cities and company-dominated, one industry towns. The companies that migrated to the Carolinas, Tennessee, Alabama, Georgia, and Florida not only created an atmosphere of terror against workers who sought union organization, they carefully cultivated a paternalism in which workers were persuaded that their welfare was linked to the interests of the company. In company towns of the Deep South, most local institutions are dominated by the company; its managers and line supervisors are leaders in municipal governments, the churches, and civic organizations. The second major feature of the South was its overtly racist social oppression. Historically, blacks were effectively excluded from textile and other plants that had constituted the New South. These institutions were bastions of white supremacy long after federal civil rights laws were enacted. Many of them provided the space for segregated public schools after the Supreme Court decision ordering integration of public schools was issued. The ideological environment of the Southern industrial town retained visible signs of the racial division of labor. White workers were hired by the company as skilled workers and machine operators; blacks were hired, if at all, as laborers in the dirtiest and lowest paying occupations. As concentration of ownership and mechanization swept Southern agriculture after the war, many black workers were forced to migrate north or to larger Southern cities in order to make a living. Their exclusion from the mills made combatting unions much easier because employers had little difficulty showing the remaining white workers that organized labor supported civil rights, a position that invited fantasies of blacks taking white workers' jobs if the union came in.[3]

Union organizing strategy in the South was to try to circumvent racist propaganda by declaring the race issue irrelevant to union organizing. Consistent with its traditions, the labor movement attempted to limit trade union appeals to their economic dimension. But as long as the labor market remained organized hierarchically by race as well as skill in Southern textile, clothing, wood, and paper mills—the largest industries until the 1960's boom—the attempt to ignore or minimize race issues was bound to be a losing tactic. I am not claiming that the task was easy. Major union successes in the South have been confined to highly skilled crafts such as construction, long haul trucking, and machinists on the one hand, or industries such as steel, mining, aircraft, and clothing where union power was able to force local branches of national corporations to conform to agreements negotiated elsewhere. But the failure of the frequent union organizing drives aimed at Southern industrial plants since the war is as attributable to the labor movement's fear of the race issue as it is to the effectiveness of the carrot and stick approach of paternalistic corporations.

In contrast, the Clothing and Textile Workers confronted J. P. Stevens at a time when the industrial boom of the 1960's and 1970's had forced the corporation to hire black workers at all levels of skilled and unskilled production labor. The war had stimulated sharp increases in the textile labor force despite the simultaneously increased mechanization. Young whites were migrating to larger cities and more lucrative industries such as auto, steel, and electronics, or moving up the class ladder to expanding technical and professional occupations as a result of opportunities provided by the development of new colleges and technical schools. The weakness of textile workers' unions corresponded to the weakened place occupied by consumer goods industries in the national and international economy that made textiles, apparel, and shoes relatively low paying jobs. When black workers moved into these openings, Southern union organizing received a shot in the arm. Now it was in the unions' interest to advertise their strong civil rights positions; further, the wage gap between the predominantly non-union industries and the strongly organized sectors was widening in a relatively inflationary economy. Although unions still had trouble negotiating union contracts with companies which freely used legal loopholes to delay serious bargaining, threatened plant removal, and granted wage increases to keep the union out, textile workers, furniture workers, paper and lumber mill workers were joining in record numbers and the unions began to win Labor Board elections. The buoyant economic environment, combined with the large numbers of newly employed black workers for whom unionism had become part of the civil rights struggle, offered a new ray of hope for organizing the South.

Some unions recognized the opportunity and poured significantly larger resources into Southern campaigns, but the labor movement as a whole failed to invent a new organizing strategy. Despite some aid from the AFL-CIO, the affiliates were still mainly responsible for their own organizing and many, such as the Furniture and Wood workers, were too poor to do the job. Despite full employment in the mills, evidence of worker support for unions in the 1960's didn't lead to a massive effort similar to that which had brought millions into the labor movement in the 1930's. Labor still complained about the objective obstacles to organizing which, of course, were considerable, but with some exceptions union officials were blind to the new opportunities.

Given the fragmentation of the efforts, only farsighted leadership with a strong position in the AFL-CIO hierarchy could have made the Southern drive the occasion for a new burst of organizing. All of the ingredients were present: a favorable economic environment without which labor organizing is traditionally difficult, a labor force that was distinctly oppressed in comparison to other workers, and, most important of all, a powerful social movement among blacks which would have provided the ideological glue without which an upsurge is impossible.

In addition, dedicated, ideologically committed activists coming out of the civil rights and anti-war movements were prepared to enter the struggle for economic and social justice. The sixties were not only a time of student activism in new social movements, they were marked by the recovery by some young people of older labor traditions. Many of them had "graduated" from campus-based protest to community organizing, specifically in older cities with large minority populations such as New York, Chicago, Oakland, and Washington, D.C. Others had found jobs working for unions, particularly such new organizations as the United Farmworkers that did become a new social movement in the late 1960's and managed to attract thousands of young activists to the cause of migrant Chicano and Mexican farmworkers. Other unions that extended their hands to these activists were the National Hospital Union, which consciously linked itself with the wing of the civil rights movement led by Martin Luther King and others who believed in direct action to achieve justice; AFSCME and other public employees unions that desperately needed skilled organizers and negotiators to keep up with their expansion; and rank and file movements in the mining, steel, trucking, and other industries where workers fought to democratically control their own unions and their policies. In these instances where unions made organizing a *calling* linked to the conception of trade union as a social movement rather than a business organization, some of the most energetic and dramatically successful union growth occurred.

ORGANIZING: PUBLIC EMPLOYEES

Unfortunately, the most dedicated, experienced young organizers were not flocking to the crusade to organize the South, the traditional bastion of the open shop, although there were a few who saw the need—Bruce Raynor of the Textile Workers, Peter Brandon who worked for several unions and, most important of all, a substantial number of rank and file textile and furniture workers who in the last analysis take credit for most of the victories. Instead, the historic organizing of public employees unions succeeded in attracting a substantial number of "veterans" of movement struggles particularly in the midwest and on the West Coast. A major reason was that in post-student days many activists and others who had been politicized in the 1960's needed jobs and the public sector offered careers in teaching, social work, and health services. These jobs paid decent salaries and often involved socially useful work. Some joined the organizing staffs of these unions and were later to obtain elected posts. For example, student leader Paul Booth became associate director

of an AFSCME district council in Illinois; a number of veterans of the
early women's movement and anti-war activists on the West Coast are
full-time officials in several SEIU locals; Bob Mullencamp is organizing
director for the National Hospital Workers Union after having been the
first president of the progressive Teaching Assistants Association (TAA) at
the University of Wisconsin, which in 1969 staged the first TA strike and
led to the first contract in any major university for this group. Karen
Nusbaum and Ann Hill are feminist activists who helped form SEIU's
Local 925, dedicated to organizing women clerical workers.

The great upsurge of public employees organizing in the 1960's and
1970's was the outcome of a conjuncture of economic, political, and social
changes. Economic progress among public employees was painfully slow,
and well into the 1960's, in most states public employees were not only
barred from strikes, but were unable to bargain collectively on issues such
as wages, benefits, and working conditions. In the few cases where some
negotiations had been permitted by law, these were confined to so-called
"meet and confer" procedures. Union representatives or attorneys for
aggrieved employees could present their case to supervisors and other
officials, but there was no legal mechanism such as arbitration that
obliged management to resolve these disputes. The right to sue was the
only recourse available to workers and their unions. This option was in
most instances impractical because of high costs and the reluctance of the
courts to handle such cases or because labor faced hostile judges in many
of the more conservative states. As a result, employee organizations were
obliged to confine their fight for better wages and conditions to the legislatures which, faced with much stronger state, municipal, and corporate
lobbies, were generally unresponsive to labor's demands. Such unions as
did exist prior to 1955 were little more than professional associations
employing full-time legislative and lobbying staffs at best, or organizing
committees that had labored throughout the century with little success.

Among the most important gains secured by the AFL-CIO during John
Kennedy's term as President was his executive order granting the right of
federal employees to collective bargaining which obliged government
agencies to recognize unions showing majority support among its employees. Although some states and local communities had already enacted
laws enabling unions to secure bargaining rights before Kennedy's order
in 1962, the flood of union organizing that brought nearly a third of the
more than 16 million public employees into unions at all levels of government followed this clear signal from the White House. The Executive
Order was analogous to Section 7A of the Labor Relations Act because it
gave public employee organizing the imprimatur of the national political
directorate. Although unions did not go into the field claiming that Kennedy and Johnson "want you to join the union," the implication was clear
that unions had reentered full partnership in the exercise of national

political power. The first conjuncture of the vast expansion of public sector employment with the reassertion of the hegemony of the old progressive alliance at the national level gave a fundamental boost to union organizing.

Perhaps the most important organizing impetus was provided by the fact that the overwhelming majority of employees hired in the 1960's were women and national and racial minorities, particularly blacks. These workers occupied clerical and manual labor jobs in government, the most important of which were the Post Office at the federal level, and state, county, and municipal administration which was growing faster than any sector of public employment except education. From the point of view of mass unionism, the rapid expansion of AFSCME tells the main story of this period. In 1959, after about five years of active organizing, the union had 173,000 members, many of them concentrated in recently organized New York City, Philadelphia, and a scattering of Midwestern cities. Two decades later the union reported nearly 900,000 members. By the early 1980's, despite layoffs and job freezes, AFSCME had become one of the largest unions in the Federation with over one million members.

The surge of organization among public employees is attributable to the fact that major new social movements energized labor organizing among women and blacks. This was underlined by the fact that almost all major public employees unions are part of the "progressive" wing of the AFL-CIO, a designation that has been marked by the receptivity of these unions to the new social movements of the 1960's and 1970's. These unions, with the notable exception of the Teachers, were among the opponents of the Vietnam War as well. In short, they identified union organizing with the struggle for equality at the workplace, social justice, and opposition to the major drift of U.S. foreign policy. Although the degree of politicization among public employees unions is uneven, depending on the ideological complexion of its leadership, the particular history of the union, and the racial and sexual composition of its members, public employees have on the whole been among the most politicized of all trade unions.

Of course, much of the interest in political action stems from the fact that every strike by a public employees group has profound political consequences, unlike conflicts in the production sector which appear to be bi-lateral private agreements except under wartime conditions. The fact that, in the main, public employees are barred by law from striking, that their livelihood may vary with electoral outcomes, that the climate for bargaining depends more saliently on the ideological climate, has made these unions more militant and more conscious of the links between political power and economic struggle. Perhaps the most innovative demand made by any union in recent years was that of San Jose AFSCME members who in 1981 struck for equal pay for comparable worth. The overwhelmingly female membership of the union confronted a woman mayor with the injustice of the job classification system in the city's government. The union showed that "women's work" was widely classified below that of men and wanted to reclassify these jobs by comparing the degree of skill, responsibility, and other elements in order to establish more equality of pay and status. (The workers contended that, for example, a secretary's job was worth no less by these criteria than a male technician's job.) The union imposed traditional job evaluation standards in which tasks were weighted regardless of the traditions that degraded women's jobs on non-rational sexist grounds; by separating the ideological traditions from the job components they were able to show institutional sexism and win wide public support for their case. The union struggle challenged a major barrier to women's equality—the concept of "women's" work—and became a model for women facing the same discriminatory practices. In this instance, as well as many others, the feminist program of the women's movement provided the inspiration for union gains.

The most celebrated example showing the merger of the civil rights and labor movements was the strike of Memphis, Tennessee, sanitation workers in 1968, which tragically became the site of Martin Luther King's murder. The workers struck for union recognition and the traditional demands of better wages, dignity on the job, and job security. William Lucy, now Secretary-Treasurer of AFSCME, was then an international representative of the union assigned to assist in the strike. Employer opposition to the strike, combined with racist violence against the workers, their families, and the black community, provoked a national response by civil rights and labor movements around the country that made the struggle a symbol of the link between the two movements. King came to Memphis on March 18, 1968, at the urging of the local civil rights coalition formed to support the strike, Community on the Move for Equality (COME). When King arrived he was greeted by some 10,000 people at the Masonic Temple and, "extremely impressed by the large and lively crowd . . . [King] told them that what the Memphis movement needed was a general work stoppage on some chosen day."[4] On March 20, he led a mass march through the city of movement supporters and workers, which was marked by some missiles thrown by younger marchers in local windows. On April 1, 1968 King was murdered.

The Memphis collaboration of Lucy and King signalled a new departure for both the labor and civil rights struggle in the South. David Garrow describes the influence of the Memphis strike on King as the change from "reformer to revolutionary."[5] In the last five years of his life, King had become more convinced of the link between the struggle for legal rights and economic and social freedom. His support for the labor movement's campaigns to organize among the black workers and his pro-

posal for the formation of a national "poor people's movement" were signs
that the freedom movement was entering a new stage in which race and
class were explicitly linked.

After King's death militancy among black workers gained momentum,
reflecting the degree to which the freedom movement and the labor
movement had joined. The 1970–71 national wildcat strike among postal
workers, an industry with a large concentration of black workers in major
urban areas, and the rank and file movements among black workers in the
auto and steel industries began to translate black power into trade union
terms. At the same time, the struggle of Chicano workers in the lettuce
and grape fields in California and Texas was gaining ground against agribusiness which threw millions of dollars into the fight against unionization.

In the early 1970's the formation of the Congress of Labor Union
Women (CLUW) and the several regional organizations of women office
workers, most notably Working Women in Cleveland, were signs that
feminists were beginning to take the labor movement seriously. In turn,
women trade union officials, inspired by the new feminism, began to
assert women's demands in the labor movement. In 1980 one of the most
dynamic of the private sector unions, the Service Employees (SEIU),
"merged" with Working Women and chartered Local 925 as a national
women's office workers organizing campaign.

The third major intersection between the trade unions and a social
movement was with the rising new professionals. Until recently the most
characteristic examples were in the education and health sectors, particularly the expansion of the American Federation of Teachers (AFT) and the
National Education Association (NEA), a classical professional interest
group that was pressed by the surge of teacher union organizing to become, in part, a labor organization despite the large number of educational administrators in its ranks. Today the majority of America's more
than 3 million school teachers are union members. Although the AFT did
not become the majority union in the field (notwithstanding its membership increase from 50,000 in 1959 to its current 500,000), there is no
doubt, even among its detractors, that it is the spark of teacher union
organizing. As Irwin Pollishook, President of the Professional Staff Congress, New York City University's AFT affiliate, has stated,[6] the union has
prepared the ground for the growth of the other major organizations in
the field, especially the NEA and the American Association of University
Professors, AFT's major competitor for jurisdiction in colleges and universities. The pattern is this: AFT begins an organizing campaign, forms
committees, petitions for an election. Under state labor relations laws,
most of which parallel the national law, competing unions may intervene
in the election if they show minimum support among the proposed bargaining unit. In many cases, several competing associations have formed

coalitions to oppose the AFT because the union least resembles the conservative structure of a professional association and for this reason is perceived to be too militant for people of professional status (or aspiration). Unionism still represents an "outside" force in American education which traditionally has been jealous of its curricular and ideological autonomy. AFT has countered these arguments by showing that teachers and other school professionals need a trade union which is independent of the educational bureaucracies that dominate the NEA and AAUP. Against the usual expectations that intra-union rivalry destroys the chance for successful organizing, the reverse has been the case in teachers organizing. The overwhelming majority of teachers in elementary and secondary school systems in major metropolitan areas have selected union representation in the past twenty years and the trend among university teachers in public systems is towards joining unions rather than relying on professional groups to represent their interests. However, a recent Supreme Court decision declaring professors in private universities part of management has effectively disrupted the trend towards unionism that by the late 1970's had begun to make significant strides on some major private campuses such as Boston University, and in Catholic colleges and universities and a scattering of liberal arts schools. In most representation elections, the presence of two unions on the ballot has altered the terms of debate; in most instances, the issue is not *whether* teachers shall join a union, but *which* union can better represent them.

The capacity of public employees unions to broaden their scope to include workers' aspirations on a variety of levels is the key to their success which has continued after the initial upsurge. Unlike most industrial and craft unions which have gradually abandoned not only their character as a social movement but the conception of the union as a worker's public sphere and as a cultural center, many public employees unions have engaged in educational, cultural, and political activities, making the union hall a place where workers congregate even after they retire from active employment. To be sure, these activities have become more important in the 1970's and 1980's when gains at the bargaining table became more problematic. And as I have pointed out earlier, the service orientation adopted by many unions is, to some degree, a sign of the passing of the militant phase. Despite these reservations, it is also true that the typical public employees union means more to its members because they have recognized that workers' needs are not confined to better income, as important as this demand remains in the repertoire of labor's aspirations.

ORGANIZING: THE HEALTH SECTOR

The health workers' organizing differs from teachers' unionism in that the organization of health institutions and service delivery is similar to those in production sectors because the labor process has been rationalized. As Susan Reverby[7] and others have shown, the hospital is organized like a factory: the technical division of labor is hierarchically arranged with nonprofessionals in patient care, housekeeping, and dietary departments on the bottom; jobs defined as technical and professional are on the next rung; and administration is on the top. Within each of these broad categories small hierarchies serve to divide labor from service and from itself. For example, the tasks of various nursing occupations possessing different credentials may not be qualitatively different, but pay, status, and degree of authority are differentiated by professional credentials whether there is a union or not. Even the general classification "professional" is hierarchy-ridden: in recent years many critics have shown that the technical preparation of a registered nurse and a physician are similar but that the authority, pay, and status of the doctor is much greater. The struggle of professional nurses to achieve better salaries and more prestige has often been misdirected against practical nurses, nurse's aides, and orderlies (a male nurse's aide, whose title differs because of machismo). Their real battle is against the administration, most of whose officials are physicians. The rationality of the credential for determining places in the job hierarchy is constantly strained by the actual performance of tasks. Although various categories of nurses are barred formally from administering certain medications and performing surgery, these prohibitions are increasingly viewed as arbitrary by students of the health labor process and by health workers themselves. The recognition that credentials do not the physician make is shown by the evidence of a whole new class of doctors that has come into health institutions in the past fifteen years. The *physician's assistant* (PA) is permitted to administer medication and perform surgical procedures under a physician's supervision.

The entire PA occupation was produced by a severe shortage of battlefield doctors during the Vietnam War. The military was obliged to use "nonprofessional" medical orderlies to perform most superficial medical procedures. When these experienced "barefoot doctors" left military service, many hospitals, hard pressed by funding cuts and the chronic shortage of doctors produced by restrictive admissions policies of medical schools, urged local medical associations to relax the rules. Equally important, the federal government applied considerable pressure in the 1970's on the medical establishment to establish physician's assistant programs and accept them as part of the patient care team. The government was concerned both to cut health care expenses and accommodate the returning veterans whose morale had been seriously damaged by a losing war. Equally important, the physician's assistant provided a way to meet the growing demand for health care services produced by prepaid insurance programs such as Medicare, Medicaid, and trade union sponsored benefits, without undermining the top of the professional hierarchy. Registered nurses were the major group threatened by the innovation. Their professional status had already been shaken by the massive infusion of paraprofessionals in the 1960's boom years. Now they feared they were being superseded by a group of men whose credentials were considerably inferior to their own.[8]

The American Nurses Association (ANA), the leading professional association of registered nurses, had resisted unionization among its constituency on the basis that unions were only for manual or nonprofessional workers. The ANA held that professional status demanded more subtle methods to preserve the integrity of nursing. The ANA tried to emulate the medical associations by focusing on professional educations to establish standards for credentials, and thereby raise wages by controlling the labor supply. During the 1960's registered nurses in many states were required, for the first time, to obtain advanced academic degrees in addition to professional training; specialties were established in such fields as psychiatric nursing, obstetrics, and surgery; and the association worked without much success to persuade state legislatures to restrict the physician's assistant programs in state universities and to make them subject to supervision by RN's. However, despite these efforts, the politics of guilt about veterans, the galloping fiscal crisis, and the powerful medical associations that wished to avoid confrontation with their own restrictive practices, conspired to defeat the ANA's campaign. At the same time budget cuts, feminism, and the growing strength of nonprofessional and blue collar unions were forcing nurses to consider union organization and collective bargaining as weapons to replace or supplement professional tactics. In many places, when the ANA refused to lead the organizing movement, nurses turned to more militant AFL-CIO affiliates, particularly the Hospital Workers Union on the East Coast which had spent the 1960's in a series of visible, militant struggles to organize the nonprofessionals, and the Service Employees which played a similar role in the Midwest and on the West Coast. Finally, the ANA, following the example of once reluctant professional associations, turned much of its attention to competing for bargaining rights with these AFL–CIO affiliates.

Doctors employed by New York and San Francisco hospitals also recognized that they were increasingly caught in the squeeze between the mass of nonprofessionals who had flocked into unions and the administration seeking to limit rising health care costs by reducing the relative salaries of its unorganized professional employees. Underlying their immediate reasons for organizing into trade unions was another longer range development—the tendency towards the *proletarianization* of physicians. In the 1970's doctors saw their aspirations for lucrative private practices threatened by the high cost of going into business, the growth of group practices (such as Health Maintenance Organizations, prepaid health insurance plans sponsored by corporate and union benefits packages), and, emerging out of the irresistible pressure to increase the labor supply, expanded enrollments in medical schools that threatened to overproduce physicians relative to the market for the first time since the Depression.

Doctors' unions are by no means as widespread as unions among teachers and nurses, but where they organize interns' and residents' unions and form staff physicians' associations they are equally militant. Today doctors' strikes are not uncommon and when called produce serious political problems for public and private health agencies. The quandary is this: when doctors strike, who has the authority to supervise patient care since other professionals and nonprofessionals are not authorized to perform certain functions? The political environment has prevented other unions from withholding their labor (secondary boycotts are against the law in all states and at the national level), and the moral environment in health care services prevents most doctors from withholding their labor in serious cases; like striking truck drivers who deliver milk and bread to children and the infirm, doctors are constrained to mediate their protest by "humanistic" considerations. But the *fact* of doctors' unions is a sign of a new self-perception by a growing number of members of this priest-like profession that their privileged place in the economic and social hierarchy is fast becoming a thing of the past. Even with the gradual disappearance of the general practitioner from most large and medium-sized cities, only the minority of physicians with specialized training beyond general medical knowledge are able to establish flourishing practices because of skyrocketing purchase costs. And even here this elite position is not secure everywhere. The flood of specialists in Southern California, for example, has resulted in sharp competition among some categories—ophthalmologists in San Diego and internists and dentists throughout the area. Half of all doctors leaving medical school after 1970 can expect to become a member of the professional salariat and there are indications that an actual market surplus of doctors will appear by 1990. There is no prospect of a surplus based on need, but since the market determines "scarcity" and "plenty," this is the only economic criterion of surplus. Under these conditions of relatively full employment but also status degradation, doctors' unions will almost certainly grow in the next decade.

LABOR AND WOMEN WORKERS

The rise of public sector unionism has preserved the base of organized workers from which a new labor movement could arise. The sharp increase of membership in this sector, combined with the more modest growth of unionism in such services as communications, retail and wholesale trades, and substantial organizing achievements in the "voluntary" non-profit health and social service agencies, most of which have become dependent on public funds, means that the membership losses in the production and building trades sectors have not reduced organized labor to complete enfeeblement. A second consequence of the new unionism has been a major change in the sexual and racial composition of organized labor. The most important change of the postwar era work force has been the avalanche of women in the full- and part-time wage labor. Not only has this movement changed the sexual complexion of the workplace, it has also produced a social crisis in the home. Despite the desperate efforts of neo-conservatives and the New Right to spur a movement back to the kitchen and the nursery, women have been obliged to enter the wage labor market in accelerating numbers. The transformation of the role of the United States in the new world economic order, which has resulted in deindustrialization in traditional intermediate and low technology industries in which men predominated, has also produced jobs for which women have traditionally been recruited—in financial services, administration, and public sector jobs. The irony of the current job market is that women are privileged by sex role definitions of appropriate wage labor. To make matters more complex, efforts to find a common ground between male pride and traditionally "female" jobs have been unsuccessful, except in a few instances, especially in traditionally higher paid professions such as nursing and teaching. Unlike the immediate years after the Second World War, when women were pushed out of heavy factory labor, substantial male unemployment in the 1980's has not yet spurred a similar movement today. Part of the reason for this difference is the fact of unionization among large numbers of women office workers in the public sector, in utilities, and in the services. In addition, the job security and seniority provisions of the union contract prevents laying off women to make room for men.

Nonetheless, union organization has failed to substantially close the gap between men's and women's wages. At the close of the war, buoyed by high factory pay, women had achieved 65 percent of male wages. As industrial jobs declined and women entering the labor force found service jobs, their relative position deteriorated, primarily because the overwhelming preponderance of private sector administrative and retail labor is non-union. Women now earn only 59 percent of the wages earned by men, despite the fact that they are no longer classified officially as secondary wage earners. Many women in the labor force are heads of households, a result of divorce, single motherhood, or being unmarried. Others are in households where they are not considered "heads" even though, in most cases, their income is necessary to meet expenses.

In sum, the experience of public employees' organizing successes in the past two decades, in contrast to the snail's pace of most other trade union recruitment, suggests that unions can only grow by allying themselves with social movements whose critique of the prevailing order includes but is not limited to the struggle for economic justice. The degree to which women, blacks, and proletarianized professionals comprehended unions as vehicles through which their social as well as economic needs could be met determined their willingness to affiliate with the labor movement. In contrast, unions that maintained the narrow, economistic orientation of the conventional trade union practices of the postwar period, were overwhelmed by the profound changes that afflicted the American economy.

Another way of putting the case is that when trade unionism loses its character as a social movement and reduces its activities to sectoral economic action, workers outside the labor movement get the signal that unions are not for them. Until the 1960's public employees were convinced that trade unionism and civil service were conflicting forms of status, just as most professionals identify union organization with the images associated with manual labor. In instances where public service professionals have joined unions, their decision was often prompted by a new perception that collective bargaining was their last chance to preserve status continuity. Similarly, racial and national minorities who have joined public employee unions in large numbers in recent years were able to link the struggle against sexism and racism with affiliation with the labor movement. In the 1960's and 1970's large numbers of women entered the labor force as primary wage earners. In a growing number of instances, women are the only working adult because their partner is unemployed and less likely to find work in the future.

This situation has been exploited by the ideologues of social conservatism, and they have found fertile soil among men for whom the sexual division of labor has suddenly worked against them. The proliferation of households in which the male could perform the role of houseworker but forces his working spouse to perform two jobs, has produced the kind of male resentment of which right-wing movements are made. At the same time it has made women more trade union and politically conscious, a fact noted by recent survey research. In 1982 several public opinion polls found that women tended to be more "liberal" than men, were less inclined to support the foreign policy of the United States, especially the arms buildup and were more radical on social issues such as abortion, the death penalty, and other traditional social conservative policies.

ORGANIZING: THE WORKING POOR

While black women in service and public jobs have benefited from union protection as well as the fact that the immediate results of the economic crisis have not been as deeply felt in service sectors as in production, black men have been hit hard.

One of the most important developments arising from the wartime expansion of leading mass production industries in the 1940's was the entrance of large numbers of black workers into these heavy, dirty, but highly paid jobs. By 1965 blacks comprised 40 percent of steelworkers and a similar proportion of auto workers. In both industries black men occupied all levels of skill in the manual labor force and accumulated considerable seniority protecting them against layoffs. Blacks were employed in light production industries as well where unions had succeeded in making substantial inroads. Until the 1970's the composition of the black working class in production jobs revealed a sharply different profile from the 1930's. For millions of black men *economic opportunity* did not mean the chance to get white collar or professional jobs but fairly good paying jobs in the mines and mills and the post office. Of course, black men still held many low paying service jobs, comprised a larger proportion of unskilled labor in non-union factories than whites, and suffered twice the rate of unemployment as their white counterparts, but the proud achievement of industrial labor was also a testament to the strength of the civil rights movement and militant black union caucuses which pressed for upgrading and for an end to hiring discrimination in the 1950's and 1960's.

By the 1970's mines and factories closed down in New Jersey, Pennsylvania, Ohio, and Michigan, and the flight of production capital decimated New York State's industrial base. Compared to the diversified manufacturing sector that marked these regions, black workers were affected disproportionately to all others. For example, in the Mahwah, New Jersey, Ford plant, which shut down in the early 1980's, black workers comprised nearly half the work force, were an important militant force in the local union, and had become a significant factor in North Jersey politics. The loss of the plant to the region's economy was deep, but the impact on the black community of northern New Jersey was equally powerful. Similar consequences on a larger scale have accompanied massive plant closings in Detroit and Youngstown where black workers played a crucial and often dominant role in the union, the economy, and the politics of the respective cities. Apart from the mass economic deprivation suffered by the workers, the effects were felt by the entire strata of small businesspersons and by the black churches. After several years of chronic unemployment, many communities have revisited the Great Depression after a brief period of jobless benefits. There simply was no safety net under steel and auto workers who often were forced to leave their homes, sell their cars, and bid a permanent farewell to the dignity earned as industrial workers. Many of these workers have been obliged to accept low paying, non-union jobs in local retail establishments or construction, and do other forms of casual labor that pay the minimum wage or below since many of these jobs are part of the mushrooming underground economy of business and labor activities that are worked "off the books."

The fate of black workers in the contemporary crisis is symptomatic of a pervasive tendency in the U.S. economy to create an underclass not only through immigration but by the impoverishment of stable industrial workers. Poverty has revived as an emerging public issue in American economic and political life. The coherent and largely successful efforts of Reaganomics to reduce the size of the welfare state in a period of high unemployment and massive social, geographic, and economic transition has exacerbated the fundamental tendencies towards the formation of an underclass in American society. The underclass may be understood in a number of dimensions: its traditional activities were drugs, petty crime, and prostitution; sometimes it is described as those unemployed or marginally employed in legal and illegal service and production industries. Many of the members of this class receive public assistance payments even when they work because their jobs pay less than minimum standards provided by law. But the underclass is a much broader category of Americans. Many older Americans fall in the underclass. It also includes workers employed full time in the low technology, low wage sectors, such as the non-union needle trades, local retail and wholesale businesses, agricultural labor, as well as that part of production which takes place outside the law. In thousands of basements, lofts, and homes in urban and rural areas men, women, and children may be found working in the new sweatshops. They may work ten, twelve, or even fourteen hours a day and are often paid wages well below the minimum. They work for employers who are able to keep them in virtual bondage because many of them are in this country illegally. As undocumented workers they are subject to blackmail: protesting an unfair piece rate or the lack of ventilation in the shop may result in deportation. Since the shop falls outside the law, children labor without working papers. In many shops, the employer has revived the family wage: the parent(s) bring the kids to work in the shop or press them into homework in order to earn enough to keep the family's body and soul together.

In other shops single mothers on welfare put in a few hours at a machine or behind the counter of a retail store, trying to earn some extra money to supplement the welfare check which provides rent and food stamps but little else. In the fields in California and the Southwest, New Jersey and the Pacific Northwest, entire families struggle to eke out a living. The Farmworkers Union has been obliged in recent years to consolidate its gains and prevent both employers and other unions from reducing its strength. As a result there is little organizing going on today in the major agricultural states. In "tramp towns" in the sunbelt thousands of families have built houses made of cardboard and pitched tents at the edge of towns and in public parks waiting for a job to turn up. Most of them are migrants from Michigan, Ohio, and other states of the industrial Midwest. They were told by newspapers, recruiters, and rumor that the area bounded by Florida and Arizona was where a tremendous expansion was taking place. After their unemployment insurance and supplementary union benefits ran out they packed up and went South rather than accept the "humiliation" of social welfare. They are mostly white and some of them are former professionals and shopkeepers whose businesses failed. They are the newest entrants into the underclasses.

Fifty years ago the communists and socialists organized the unemployed movements that became the hope of the hopeless. While AFL President William Green in 1930 denounced unemployment benefits as a sign of worker dependency on the state, and refused to lead the fight for a genuine federal relief program or for public workers, the ideological left filled the vacuum created by a demoralized labor movement. The Veteran's Bonus March in 1930, the nationwide unemployed demonstrations a year later, and the small leagues and councils of the jobless organized in neighborhoods throughout the country were not powerful enough to change national policy immediately, but they were effective on the local level where they prevented evictions, set up soup kitchens, and filled the vestibules of city halls and state capitals with the unemployed demanding relief.

There are some efforts underway in our own time: New York's Union Theological Seminary and other church-related organizations have set up soup kitchens; some Steel and Auto union locals have formed committees of the unemployed in Western Pennsylvania, Michigan, Ohio, and Indiana; and New York's public employees unions have recently joined hands with welfare rights organizations to oppose workfare programs that take union members' jobs and subject recipients of public assistance to peonage. But the labor movement on the whole has not seriously considered either a new campaign to lead a movement of the unemployed or to organize among the working poor.

The underground economy has flourished at the expense of the legal manufacturing industry because America is in the midst of a major new wave of immigration. Although immigration quotas restrict legal immigration to 425,000 persons per year who can obtain "green" employment cards—chiefly in skills and professions that are in short supply within this country—more than one million illegal immigrants each year have entered the United States since 1970. Unlike the earlier European migration, the new immigrants emanate mainly from economically depressed agricultural regions of Asia and parts of Latin America, chiefly Mexico, Central America, and the Caribbean. Some are political refugees from Korea, Cambodia, and Vietnam, but these are often admitted under quotas on political asylum regulations. On the other hand, the Haitians and Salvadorians are called "economic" migrants who have often been denied refugee status because the Reagan administration has made clear its intention to seek reconciliation with the authoritarian regimes in the region which, ironically, are considered bastions of the free world's struggle against "totalitarian" communism.

In the main, the new immigrants are part of the underclasses but are often employed in full-time work. From the point of view of a large section of the labor movement, they are beyond the pale for unionizing precisely because of their illegal status. Further, some union officials claim that organizing these shops will merely put them out of business and force the workers out on the streets, while many progressive unionists regard the task as worthy but beyond their resources. It is refreshing therefore that the International Ladies' Garment Workers Union (ILGWU) has taken an active role in tackling both the problem of illegal immigration and organizing among the working poor in New York's Chinatown, a leading center of the sportswear branch of the industry. The union has suffered deep membership losses in the past twenty years because of imports, plant closings in its major markets, and the near-permanent depression in the industry. Although these conditions have undoubtedly influenced its decision to press for a broad program of amnesty for undocumented workers and a vigorous program of organizing Chinese workers, this explanation is insufficient to account for its singular activity in this area.

Like many other examples of imaginative and aggressive labor organizing, both leadership and social tradition play an important role. A vice president of the union, Jay Mazur (who also serves as manager of its Sportswear Local 23-25), is a man with a strong political and moral sense combined with a clear vision of the future of his union. While many locals in the Garment Workers and other needle trades have retrenched as membership and income continue to fall, Mazur has tackled this difficult task. As chair of the ILGWU's committee on immigration, he has played an active role in the major coalition fighting to win amnesty for all undocumented immigrants. Although the battle is not yet won, the organizing with a political program to advance the interests of many of the workers who are affected by the repression that dominates U.S. immigration policy, has built an honorable reputation for the union among many Chinese and Latin American workers. In addition, since these workers comprise a large proportion of the industry's labor force, the central task is to deprive the employers of their principal anti-union weapon—the threat of deportation.

Second, in the spring of 1982 when some of the contractors in the Chinatown market attempted counter union requests to renew existing union contracts by making unacceptable demands such as eliminating the arbitration clause in the agreement, refusing to grant increases and rejecting other proposals, the union boldly counterattacked by calling for work stoppages and threatening a general strike to bring the employers back in line. The tactic not only brought victory for the union in the shops where agreements had existed, it also resulted in bringing a large number of previously non-union shops under contract. Further, the direct, militant stance of the union warned other employers who might have followed the lead of the Chinatown contractors.

Third, Local 23-25 relies on a staff of young, socially conscious organizers who were able to defeat the employers together with rank and file committees. The union has an extensive literacy program for its Spanish-speaking, Chinese, and Haitian members, indicating that the leadership understands that making the union a cultural and educational center is a vital part of its survival and growth.

Fourth, the union's victory would have been impossible without the support of the Chinatown community. The close relationship between the shop and the neighborhood made possible the mobilization of small businesspersons and "civil" leaders as well as workers. The Ladies' Garment Workers grasped the fact that work arrangements and living arrangements are part of the same social fabric among the working poor. The high cost of transportation prevents many workers from finding employment outside their immediate neighborhood—childcare arrangements are easier to make, hours can be more flexible, and lunch can be eaten at home. Further, the community provides a measure of job protection for workers that the centralized industrial plant located far from their residence destroys. The informal network of neighbors, friends, and relatives constitutes a kind of extended family that helps with locating jobs, providing for emergencies that might otherwise prevent them from going to work, and other support. The communal environment is, of course, made far stronger by the homogeneous ethnic environment of many ghetto and slum neighborhoods. Union organizing among the working poor that does not integrate itself into the rhythms of the community is bound to fail because the key leaders are located within the neighborhood networks as much as in the shops. To build relations of trust, unions must become part of these networks; their leaders must be the community leaders.

The working poor will not be organized by reliance on Labor Board elections for recruiting new members. When Teamsters Local 810, another New York City local of production workers in diverse industries, finds a group of workers, many of them foreign born, who want union organization, its major organizing tactic is to strike for union recognition. Unions unwilling to spend the money and risk the long strikes for recognition will not enter this arena. In the long postwar period when many unions abandoned the "old time" religion of class combat for the strategy of partnership with employers and the state, they were unable to organize among the working poor because the kind of struggle that could achieve results entailed a different social and political mentality than the concept of the union as a broker between the workers and employers.

Part of the problem was that the new workers in the organized shops, many of whom resembled those in non-union plants, were culturally different from the union leaders. Many Spanish-speaking and black workers may not have been illegal aliens but they were certainly the "other" to the older Jewish and Italian leadership that had come up from the shops when the majority of workers were of similar ethnic backgrounds. The gulf separating leaders from members meant that few unions could form rank and file organizing committees to assist the full-time officials. Education programs, once the pride of the old socialist led unions, either disappeared entirely or were confined to a) providing services to retirees; b) providing such skills as basic education and technical training to prepare members for better jobs; or c) steward's training to handle shop floor grievances. Yet the key to organizing is not the full-time official but an active rank and file willing to spend the time needed to reach out to fellow workers in the community and the shop and able to explain the union's economic and social program. As unions have downplayed even their own official social and political philosophy in favor of limited versions of contract unionism, the fundamental task of preparing new union leaders has not been fulfilled. When unions bring active shop leaders into full-time staff positions, they are usually employed as business agents or representatives whose major job is contract administration and internal political fence mending. With few exceptions, organizing has been made a low status staff position reserved for either young or new union employees or political appointees not considered capable of negotiating and administering contracts. Only in unions like the Farmworkers, the Hospital Workers, and the Teamsters have organizers enjoyed recognition as the lifeblood of the union.

The best tradition of trade unionism has been to regard the unions as a means to bring millions of workers into the democratic economic and political process. Apart from the achievement of a higher living standard, unions once sought to advance the cultural and political power of the workers through union organization. Union education programs taught English to the foreign-born and prepared them for citizenship, transmitted the philosophy of progressive political action, and conducted voter registration campaigns to bring their force to bear on legislation and on elected officials. More important than any specific benefit, the union provided community at the workplace and in the union hall that had been only partially fulfilled by social clubs, nationality groups, and civil rights organizations. In the old socialist tradition, these organizations had to be linked to the labor movement if the influence of the Democratic political machine was to be vitiated. And the labor movement was a better advocate for workers' interests than the social reformers who fought for such measures as child labor legislation but were not interested in helping workers empower themselves as a class.

With the current flood of new immigrants into the United States, the labor movement is once more called upon to become one of the vital components of a working class community. The task is made more urgent by the near total collapse of the urban political machines and the decline of the settlement houses which at the turn of the century had been, in the absence of a strong labor movement, one of the institutions that protected immigrants from the ravages of unemployment, poverty, and repression.

Today, the slogans of assimilation which guided earlier social policy regarding immigration have lost their ring. America is not destined to reproduce the melting pot (either as fact or ideology) that marked previous waves of immigration. As American cities have become the meeting ground for global labor and the ideology of cultural autonomy has replaced assimilation among the immigrants themselves, the challenge to the labor movement, particularly its social visionaries, is greater than ever. The immediate task for labor is to commit itself to reaching out to organize the unorganized working poor, but this will remain an impossible dream unless unions dedicate themselves to finding new leaders among the immigrant workers and recovering their own activist orientation.

THE NEW WORKERS

The historical achievement of the socialist movement and the industrial union movement had been to show the way for the organization of skilled and semiskilled workers into their own unions. The CIO and progressive AFL leaders knew that the key to industrial organization were the immigrants or the recent migrants from the rural South and Appalachian regions who had entered auto and steel plants in the Midwest. The task was difficult but the terrain was familiar—after all, many of the leading CIO organizers were from the same immigrant and Southern backgrounds. Today, the most serious challenge to trade unions is not posed by its old problems but by the sweeping transformation in the international division of labor, which makes the United States the world center of administration and the producer of scientific and technological knowledge rather than its leader in the production of metals, autos, and soft consumer goods.[9]

Although the one million members of the United Food and Commercial Workers, the 600,000 member Service Employees union, and the smaller Retail, Wholesale and Department Store Workers have made substantial inroads into retail trades, American unions have made little or no progress organizing in the two most dynamic sectors of the economy, administration and financial services, and the growing research and development branch of high technology production. The French and German unions succeeded in recruiting bank and insurance employees and the British have been notable in building a strong 400,000 member union of scientists and engineers, the Association of Technical and Scientific Staffs (ATSS) and MANA. In contrast, the American Insurance Workers Union reported 17,000 members in 1979, its strength concentrated in a single large company (Metropolitan Life), and the combined membership of unions of scientists and engineers in the private sector (excluding auto, steel, and electrical manufacturing companies where the industrial unions have recruited considerable numbers of technical and engineering employees) is about 50,000. In 1979, the Office and Professional Employees, the largest union in the private administrative sector, reported only 83,000 members, many of them clerical workers in small companies, union offices, and non-profit organizations.

The image of American unions composed of production, building trades, and maintenance workers has been partially displaced by the substantial growth in public sector and retail unionism. However, the intentions of the Service Employees, the Professional and Clerical Department of the AFL-CIO and the smaller organizations to the contrary, trade unionism is not part of the discourse of administrative, scientific, and technical employees in the private sectors of the economy. Actually, there are several broad categories within what has popularly been called "white collar" employment. The first and by far the most numerous are those occupations grouped under what Louise Kapp Howe has called "pink collar" labor, so designated because women dominate it. Most administrative workers are in clerical occupations—file clerks, bookkeepers, and machine operators who "process information" to clients and vendors or within business organizations. In financial service institutions such as banks and insurance companies information processing is the primary activity. There are also a considerable number of employees engaged in the retail side of finance, exchanging money, obtaining credit information, and performing the clerical tasks associated with loans.

In a recent report on office automation, Working Women reports "over 50% of the 20 million new jobs projected between 1980 and 1990 will be in white collar work: managerial, professional, technical, sales, and clerical. The Department of Labor expects clerical work to grow more rapidly than any other occupation in the 1980's—with 4.8 million new positions in jobs dominated by women." Clerical workers numbered 18 million in 1979—"equal to eighteen percent of the total labor force."[10] In 1950, sixty percent of clerical workers were women. By 1980 women constituted eighty percent of the clerical labor force. Clerical labor is the lifeblood of the entire administrative and financial services sector.

These occupations are the most susceptible to mechanization and automation. As early as the 1950's, much of the hand labor in the office was replaced by machine work; the Burroughs bookkeeping machine and other calculating machines had already become the characteristic mode of producing financial records in small and medium-sized offices, while IBM and other computers were handling payrolls and billings in larger companies and government agencies. In the 1970's the tendency to replace secretaries, typists, and file clerks with word processors operated by women workers organized in large impersonal pools had reached maturity. The old relationship between the manager and the secretary that was built on paternalistic authority had yielded to a highly rationalized workplace. Typically, word processor operators are isolated in carrels where their most direct relationship is to the machine, but though their tasks became narrower and more repetitive than those that prevailed under the old technologies and forms of work organization, there was no degradation in skill levels, as Braverman and others have argued. Operating a word processor is no less complex than the individual tasks of filing and typing on conventional machinery; moreover, word processors are more fun than standard office work. To be sure, those who work in the "office of the future" have less personal contact with supervisors; the personal office is gradually giving way to a central information system for answering the telephone and assigning calls automatically and other measures designed to achieve greater office efficiency. The large corporate office resembles both a factory and (from the perspective of managers) a hotel.

The proletarianization of clerical workers has encountered resistance from both managers and secretaries for whom the old relationships were important means of making their work more enjoyable. For the managers the rationalization of the office in the image of the factory is often taken as status degradation because, in large organizations, not only salaries but space allocations and personal services have been conventional signs of power and prestige. But the assumption of those like the authors of "Race Against Time," Working Women's report on office automation, is that some of the old relationships and work processes are worth preserving for clerical workers as well. The argument is that rich social relations at the workplace are more desirable than "cockpitlike modular workstations," where the machine replaces the supervisor to limit the worker's autonomy. The report quotes a study that describes a typical large office where centralized management and extremely decentralized work stations prevail:

> Clerks rarely move around to observe workers in other parts of the building. Messengers deliver and pick up communications. At Big City Insurance, clerks must stay at their desks except during designated break periods. These arrangements are defended on the grounds of efficiency. However, they also limit workers' opportunities to form face-to-face relationships with other workers.

Corporate managers replaced the old typing pool or individual secretaries with word processing centers in the 1970's to reduce the proportion of labor in the production of administrative and financial services. Considerable resistance has occurred at the workplace among those who perform "computer-mediated work." Computer mediation results in the abstraction of work from concrete experience of the object. The contrast between the new "information" workplace environment and the old one may be understood by employing craft as the central metaphor from which the worker derives satisfaction: "The potter who turns a pot with his or her own hands has direct experience of the task object through continual series of sights and tactile sensations." Even machine operation did not remove the sensuousness of the work experience. "Those who work with paper and pencil usually feel 'in touch' with the objects of their tasks through the activity of writing. . . ."[11]

But computer mediated work, such as word processing and programming, provides only *symbolic* feedback, which results in feelings of frustration among those engaged in these tasks. From the perspective of designing a work environment that is more efficient, worker frustration and resistance is an obstacle even if hypothetically more effective for facilitating management's control over the labor process. Thus the technology of computer mediated work is no neutral innovation; it enlarges management control and surveillance of the entire labor process. The woman who works at a video screen is deprived of the grasp of the entire flow of information of which her tasks are merely a part, and of the rich social relations on the office floor that have historically sustained psychological satisfactions. Equally important, the direct sensuous relationship between the worker and her object provided clerks and line managers with a means to vitiate the arbitrary authority of top management.

Some proposals focus on the middle and line managers themselves, who have discovered that computer mediated work entails loss of their skills, primarily their ability to exercise independent judgment and maintain their autonomy from the system's inexorable flow. Since the new technology will gradually eliminate most of those jobs for which craftlike skills were once needed, Shoshana Zuboff advocates an educational program to prepare the employees likely to remain (the technical and professional staffs) for creative participation in the new work environment, to simulate elements of craft culture. She wants broader "theoretical comprehension of the task" because this is a necessary skill for the efficient "utilization of the information system."

Contrast this "progressive" management approach to the trade union demand of Working Women for a moratorium on further introduction of video display terminals (VDT's), not only because they displace labor but because the working environment of clerical workers in the new information environment produces occupational stress and serious back and vision problems. Most experts like Zuboff assume the transformation of the office is historically inexorable but fear that the new system will suffer an excess of authority—a degraded professional and managerial labor force.

Local 925's program is focused instead on the shop floor and the economic consequences of office automation for women clerical workers. Fearing that multinational corporations such as banks, insurance companies, and major industrial conglomerates will introduce the new technology and management systems too fast for effective organized resistance to be mounted, the union's program resorts to government as its only recourse. Of course, the demand for investigations, and moratoria on introduction of new technology by the Department of Labor and other federal agencies presupposed an administration responsive to the labor movement. This assumption could no longer be made with the Reagan administration, but the effects of computer mediated work on clerical workers, programmers, and other computer technicians remains a burning issue.

The once glamorous computer occupations have become subject to the same rationalization and management control technologies as have clerical and industrial labor. According to one computer programmer:

> I remember that in the fifties and early sixties I was a "jack of all trades." As a programmer I got to deal with the whole process. I would think through a problem, talk to clients, write my own code, and operate the machine. I loved it, particularly the chance to see something through from beginning to end.[12]

The same development that marked the transformation from craft to industrial labor, the separation of design from execution, has become the norm in computer work. A new occupational hierarchy has been created, resulting in the degradation of the proto-craft that programming had been in the early generations of the technology. At the bottom, the computer operator follows orders. With all judgment shifted to the programmer and systems analyst, the computer operator becomes "just like any other machine operator," especially because in many workplaces the operator is not permitted to assist with designing programs. In recent years, programming has been rationalized by the simplification of languages, task standardization which consists of specifying the boundaries of operator's and programmer's authority. But language simplification has had contradictory effects. On the one hand, the introduction of new languages upgraded their skills and, in the short run, increased their pay. But in the long run the reduction of language complexity has the effect of proletarianizing the entire occupation since some of the new computer languages can be learned rapidly by a larger number of people. Such older languages as COBOL and FORTRAN have been partially replaced by BASIC and PASCAL which, while not simple, require less training and prior education.

Organizing computer people in the public sector has proven easier than in the private sector. Many municipal and state governments have large computer centers where computer people work in a more or less collective work environment; their interactions are more frequent on the office floor, their work more task interdependent. For these reasons, the explosion of union organizing in other classifications of public employment since the 1960's has favorably affected professional and technical employees organization. Computer people in the private sector have suffered all of the same problems as those in public employment, with the rationalization of tasks proceeding as inexorably as that for manual and clerical workers. Concomitantly, thousands of computer technical programs have been offered by colleges and universities. As the economic crisis of the 1980's gained momentum, the rate of increase of computer jobs began to slow both for operators and for programmers. Although the median long-term employment outlook for data processing of all kinds remains far more favorable than that for traditional production, and computers are becoming the fulcrum around which nearly all advanced production techniques, large scale administrative and data processing in financial services revolves, the technology itself is labor saving. The demand for computer people will grow but not as fast as job displacement due to the introduction of computer mediated technologies. This implies that employees in the computer industry are beginning to feel the conventional problem of job insecurity. In addition, in contrast to the 1960's when most computer programmers and systems analysts believed the "sky is the limit" on wages, the 1970's brought them down to earth. With the exception of a small number of research workers and engineers for whom computer work is a "science," the great mass of computer people are not considered "true" professionals. Their pay is downgraded in proportion to the degradation of their status and the increased supply of labor. Despite these indications that the computer industry may be ripe for organizing, unions have been more impressed with the obstacles than with the opportunities.

Although many companies in both industrial production and administration are replacing the older machine technologies with computers, much of the computer work is performed by subcontractors. Consulting firms produce programs for everything from numerically controlled machine tools that have decimated large chunks of the machinist trade and inventory controls for warehousing, to payroll and accounting procedures and national and international investment evaluations. While the large corporations employ computer analysts, programmers and operators, they also "outsource" considerable portions of the work to small companies. Many of the subcontractors do not pay health and pensions to their employees even if their salaries are competitive with those of large firms. Their administrative overhead is much lower than that of large organizations. Like the apparel industry, the contracting system is cheaper for the larger business enterprise, not only because of savings in overall labor costs and overheads but also because the decentralized knowledge production discourages union organization.

The *experience* of autonomy in the relationship between the worker and object has been broken by symbol manipulation and the loss of the concrete object. Computer people suffer from the same occupational stress as air traffic controllers, middle managers, and women obliged to sit in front of VDT's all day. But like the controllers they still are able to experience the creative side of their work; for many programmers and analysts even the accelerating tendency towards boundary specification imposed by information systems has not removed the imperative to making judgments, pacing their own work, and retaining methodological choices in selecting routes to job closure. The technical division of labor in which the programmer discovers the limits of autonomy raises the whole question of the distance between managerial authority and the competence of the worker in a way that was not possible in the old technology except among those crafts incorporated into industrial production. If the programmer's labor is entirely degraded, the issue of power over the labor process will appear, like manual workers, as a *job security* issue: manual workers want to control the pace of work, methods of production, and investment decisions in order to prevent capital flight and management's superexploitation of their labor. But there is little chance of manual workers actually possessing the theoretical capacity to manage the entire process without the collaboration of technical and scientific labor. The labor of technical and professional workers still involves considerable knowledge and generates the requirement for autonomy in order for the worker to perform the job satisfactorily. As I have argued earlier, stress, lower morale, and other emotional barriers to work motivation are the major occupational hazards of the new strata who now have the central role in the labor process. Management can succeed in status degradation and lower salaries by encouraging educational institutions to overproduce the supply of technicians and professionals, but, as Mallet pointed out in his introduction to the 1969 edition of his now classic work on scientific and technical labor originally published twenty years ago, advanced technology has produced "new types of jobs . . . for which the traditional hierarchical classifications (worker/technician; blue collar/white collar; secondary/tertiary) [are] almost completely useless contrasted with the old . . . factories. . . ."[13]

Drawing on the French experience, Mallet's argument was that management's efforts to rationalize the intellectual labor process are bound to fail because the new worker must be multivalenced in order to develop prototypes—the main work of research departments of large corporations. This assumption requires modification when considering computer mediated and other technologically advanced work in operational departments. IBM information systems have been applied widely to occupations on both the lower and the higher rungs of the labor hierarchy. When computer people in both design and execution functions recognize that management has set boundaries to their autonomy and insisted that they be subsumed under managerial authority, the foundations for rebellion have been laid.

Joan Greenbaum and Phillip Kraft have demonstrated convincingly that "the transformation of programming is not the result of technological imperatives inherent in the logic of programming or computing. Programming has changed because managers concerned about profits have set about systematically and carefully to change it."[14] Here is the case for self-management in a nutshell: the training and professional culture of programmers contains, as one of its cardinal features, the pleasures of puzzle-solving, the ethos of creative labor. Kraft argues that management's objective was to have programmers "who work like machines." The only way this objective could be accomplished was to replicate Taylor's project for dequalifying and degrading labor.

The absence of a set of institutionally inscribed standards such as are provided by union contracts has meant that this process has been extremely compressed in comparison to the century-long struggle that resulted in the degradation and the partial elimination of craft labor. At the same time, as Zuboff notes, when managers, who are often recruited from among technical and professionally trained labor in the new information-based environments, are deprived of broad theoretical comprehension of the flow of work, the system is threatened with anomie because a tiny elite is the only repository of knowledge about the entire process. To this observation I would add that the managerial elite in the present economic climate is less able to use material incentives to integrate the disgruntled even if they are less likely to quit the job.

One of the main features of proletarianization is the closing of mobility options, not only vertically but horizontally as well. The new restrictions faced by computer people and others in technical and low and middle management suggest the environment is ripe for union organizing. However, better wages and working conditions, the traditional basis of labor's demands, are necessary but not sufficient to provide a program for these strata. The conflict between the expectation that intellectual labor implies work autonomy, a wider range of tasks, greater responsibility for the entire labor process, and the actuality of rationalization opens wide the door to struggles over democratizing the workplace beyond such important issues as investment decisions.

The question is whether management is capable, given its own ideology of hierarchy and control, of *democratizing from above.* Even if it is in their own interest to do so because low morale produces low productivity, it would be an error to assume that the profit imperative is always the winner. On the one hand capital needs to expand and its reward structure is to link hard work and productivity to personal gain; on the other hand the "personal gain" of the professional is not reducible to monetary rewards or status honor. Skilled labor of all types has been the most rebellious with respect to these definitions. The formation of the technical and professional intelligentsia is entwined with the promise of *work* satisfaction whose key element is the ability to control the labor process if not the product of the labor and at least comprehend the relation of the part for which they are responsible to the whole. The proliferation of computer crime, a form of rebellion in which the knowledgeable worker tries to reappropriate his labor by alienating it by theft from his employer, the common incidence of mental stress resulting from the conflict between enlarged responsibility and restricted autonomy, and high turnover in times of relative prosperity all attest to the difficulties in enforcing further rationalization among intellectual strata.

The hope that top management in its own interest can be persuaded to share knowledge and thereby some power with middle and line managers upon whom the new information work environment depends contains both logical and empirical flaws. When capital surrenders some of its power to the servant as a gift, such as assigning administrative control of the enterprise to a manager, the manager is still dependent. Despite administrative power his freedom is limited by external authority. On the other hand, when the workers collectively force employers to share power at the workplace through the exercise of their autonomous power to withhold their labor or other means of refusing authority, they make permanent gains. The contemporary scientific and technological revolution is marked by the centrality of intellectual labor which now dominates manual labor as the motive force of material production. The dream of the democratic workplace which arose during the industrial revolution among workers and intellectuals for whom the factory was the last vestige of traditional authority, was surely prefigurative of current possibilities. The socialist goal of workers' self-management, which appeared utopian in the wake of the dequalification of labor, has now been resurrected on the promise offered by the new technical intelligentsia.

The empirical objection is connected to the advent of the multinational corporation as the prototypical form of capitalist enterprise. Capital no longer requires the cooperation of a national labor force to reproduce itself, global reach having become the mode of its existence. If the first stage of the organizational revolution was the change from family-based businesses to large corporations, the second stage has been the advent, more than seventy years after Hilferding announced its arrival, of organized capitalism. The multinationals announce to their own cadre that their dependence on the decisions of the commanding heights of the corporation has become absolute, that they are no longer indispensable because their labor must now compete with others in advanced capitalist countries on the one hand, and professionals recently arrived from the Third World who are eager for their jobs, on the other.

The labor movement has not yet conceptualized these questions, much less made concerted efforts to organize among the workers in computer mediated occupations and professionals, many of whom are called managers in technologically sophisticated workplaces. But the designation "manager" in such corporations becomes ambiguous and raises some serious questions of class location and organizing strategy. Despite its aversion to class ideologies, the American trade unions locked themselves into definitions of legally appropriate bargaining units that excluded managers. Indeed, in the complex history of the administrative labor relations law, management sought to defeat union organizing drives by including their own cadre. NLRB decisions and the Labor Relations Act have excluded managers from its purview; even foremen on the assembly line are not accorded legal protections of the law such as bargaining rights. Instead, the self-organization of managers occurs in the form of professional associations and within informal groups. But their exclusion from the labor movement no longer corresponds to the new conditions of the workplace organization. A careful study of the history of recent Labor Board decisions, as well as the literature on professional, technical, and managerial labor, demonstrate that in many large corporations the distinctions between management and labor have been blurred by changes in authority relations, particularly the centralization in few hands of such decisions as hiring and firing, promotions and transfers, standardization and segmentation of tasks, computer mediated labor process choices, etc. At the same time, the boundaries between professional, technical, and middle managerial employees are no longer sharply defined. Corporations such as AT&T call many of their working clerical and technical people "managers" and the research scientists who supervise clerical and technical staff are similarly named. But the range of authority in supervising day to day labor is considerably narrowed by rules imposed from above. Decentralized production and research is ever more tightly controlled even when widely separated geographically because the preprogrammed computer mediates once autonomous problem-solving functions. The middle manager and the professional are increasingly subject to the concept of interchangeable parts by corporate controllers for whom each option is weighed against an international balance sheet. Under these circumstances the exclusive orientation of trade unions towards organizing among "non-supervisory" employees requires revision. The questions arising from the new modes of corporate power, the configuration of technological changes, and the new information based workplaces, suggest that both the factory and the office of the future will be occupied by knowledge workers for whom the major issues of both simple economic justice and work democracy will dominate their concerns.

Just as public employees and service workers evolved different models of unionism that corresponded to their needs, so unions among technical and professional employees are obliged to consider the specificity of the occupations and sectors within which they work as a guide to union structure and program. When the AFT and the unions of hospital workers began to recruit professionals, they did not oppose the professional associations for the work they *were* doing, such as providing assistance for members wanting more credentials, technical knowledge, debates within the field, and appropriate legislation. The unions criticized the associations for the absence of militant economic struggle, accusing them of substituting professionalism for trade unionism.

In nearly all instances where trade unions have become bargaining agents for professional and technical employees, they have continued programs for the professional interests of their members as well as traditional trade union bargaining services. The AFT has entered public controversies on questions of class size, school governance, budgets, and other issues of education policy. Of course, much of the justification for these political concerns has been made on trade union grounds: a reduction in public school funds often entails teacher furloughs, increased class size, and fewer support services such as decent textbooks and learning equipment. However, the union has also proclaimed the responsibility of teachers to remain concerned with issues associated with teaching and learning and professional development. For example, the union has criticized the use of visual and computer techniques in the classroom on grounds that go beyond the threat of layoffs for its members; it has argued that there is more to education than the 3R's, that learning is a cultural experience, and that the social relations of the classroom are relevant for cognitive development. The implied learning model of those advocating wide application of individual, computer mediated modules rather than the collective modalities of the old-fashioned pedagogy is the IBM information center approach for large corporations. Some who have advocated the return to "basic" education as the primary focus of elementary and secondary schools have, indeed, invoked machine methods as effective for socializing students to the office and the factory of the future where the interaction of the worker with the machine replaces human communications. The AFT's hostility to machine mediated teaching and learning is not based exclusively on narrow economic self-interest. The union was formed in the philosophical traditions of "progressive education" and the political traditions of democratic socialism. Although most of the half million members are probably unaware of these aspects of the union's origins, the traditions are still an important ideological component of its current policies. Of course, the AFT has been subject to the same economistic influences that have shaped the modern labor movement; here, too, contract unionism has defined its essential character. However, as decisions affecting schools are increasingly political and ideological questions, AFT leaders have moved back to the original ideas that motivated the organization: the idea that education is more than a job training regimen, that it is also a means to strengthen democracy through wider citizen participation.[15]

A major new issue has been raised by the Committee of Interns and Residents (CIR), New York's doctors union. In 1981 interns and residents employed in the New York area voluntary and public hospitals conducted an unsuccessful strike to improve the quality of patient care. They did not strike for pay issues (although this has remained a sore point for the union) but demanded more equipment and more personnel, not only among physicians but also in nonprofessional and technical categories. Despite the strike's loss and the considerable price paid by the union (a major hospital decertified it as bargaining agent during the dispute), it was a landmark in the history of professional unionism. Badly reported by the press, the strike failed to capture the imagination of other unions, health professionals, and health consumers. In fact, the doctors were isolated from the rest of the labor movement which refused to honor their picket lines and those of the few community groups that supported them. Nevertheless, the action showed the differences between struggles of what have been called "service providers" and industrial workers. When health or education professionals are guided by a set of ethics that specify the necessary conditions for excellence, these standards may constitute a basis for forming alliances with community groups interested in improving the institutions. Here we can see the two-sided character of professional ideology when placed in the context of political combat: on the one hand, as left critiques of professionalism have argued this ideology is inscribed in the apparatuses of job hierarchies that are often constructed at the expense of both the non-professionals at the bottom and the "clients" of the service. Professionalism as a discourse for controlling the supply of labor replaces the craft tradition; it has become an exclusionary rationale that often has racist and sexist overtones and, equally important, it has become a deleterious opponent of those who wish to democratize the workplace by organizing the division of labor along non-hierarchical lines.

On the other hand, in these times even most liberal administrators have been obliged to manage the progressive shrinkage of social services so that the major difference between liberalism and conservatism is that the former shed some tears while applying the shears to service budgets. The close link between the budget and the quality of services means that a fight for quality is also a political fight. When the doctors took on this issue, they challenged the entire practice of planned shrinkage on the basis of precepts that derived from their professional ethics. Since the pervasive social service cuts of the 1970's these ethics have become subversive barriers to neo-conservative policies and a strong appeal encouraging collective organization among professionals for whom unions were once anathema.

THE NEW ISSUES

As I have already indicated, the new issues among professional and technical employees in the private sector combine traditional concerns such as job security, wage stagnation, and occupational health hazards with issues arising from the problems associated with new forms of labor process organization in computer mediated work both in the factory and the office. Professionals are deeply affected by rapid technological transformation that makes their skills obsolete every four or five years. Each new generation of technology reduces the autonomy of the professional as well as threatening his or her job. To build a union among these employees requires a whole new approach to union issues and new styles of union leadership that approximate but are not identical to the public models.

First, contract unionism, although necessary for negotiating some of the traditional issues, is clearly inadequate to dealing with such problems as work organization, professional training, and the larger social consequences of the new scientific and technological revolution. The British Association of Scientific, Technical and Managerial Staffs (ASTMS) has distinguished itself by its interest in promoting democracy at the workplace. Although acting as a traditional trade union among private sector professionals including managers, the union has also argued that "workers have an absolute right to a voice [in management] in two crucial areas: the allocation of resources within the company, including manpower, plant and capital investment; and the appointment of senior personnel, the quality of whose decisions directly affects their jobs." Union leaders point out that co-management of enterprises is not a partnership—"The presence of union directors will produce decisions different from those that would have been made without them. In its turn that implies a conflict of interest between staff and shareholders' representatives." Workers' power to influence investment decisions implies considerable conflict—in the direction of technological changes, workers will be interested in whether the proposed investments reduce or enlarge the work force; allocation of the labor force assignments becomes a subject for workers' decisions; and the selection of "senior personnel" means that the union will assume a strong role in management.[16]

The fact that unions in Britain, France, and Sweden have been raising issues such as democratizing the workplace, especially among members of the "salariat" of professional, technical, and clerical employees in the private sector, reveals the originality of the new unionism. Thus far, these issues have been discussed only among writers of the labor process and some union officials in the United States, yet the issue of workplace democracy is one of the major new concerns that could lead to an awakening of union interest among the salariat and those industrial workers faced with the widespread introduction of computer mediated work.

As we have found in examining public employees unionism, the convergence of professionalism and trade unions is among the key elements leading to successful organization. For example, large multinational banks and insurance companies are making substantial profits but have reduced salary increases and closed mobility routes for their professional and technical employees. As one computer programmer reported, "the high unemployment makes the manager more cocky. Maybe I could find another job, but I'm not sure." His department is reorganizing and he's not sure where his next assignment will be.

Among the more than 80 percent who are women clerical workers, unions would raise issues concerning the work environment, but these are not confined to the occupational hazards such as vision problems and back ailments resulting from the prevailing VDT technologies. They also include such problems as sexual harassment, improvement of sanitary facilities that take women's physiological needs into account, and demands for upgrading. Since the new technologies are knowledge-based, women who want to develop their skills require, in most cases, educational credentials. Since women are poorly paid, company reimbursement for college programs is an essential demand. But many women are not able to take advantage of these opportunities even if companies are prepared to pay tuition. They need released time to attend school during working hours and many also need day care facilities for their children.

One of the recent innovations introduced by some companies to accommodate the scarcity of child care services is "flextime." Rather than requiring women to come to work at a fixed hour and leave on a definite schedule, many employees have been encouraged to synchronize their working hours with their children's school regimen so they are able to work both jobs without disruption. Under these circumstances, unless they have released time for school attendance, most women lose the chance to upgrade their jobs until their children are grown. Flextime is often important for the single mother or the woman or housemate whose husband cannot or will not share child care, but it does not replace the need for company supplied child care. At the same time nonstop work prevents her cultural and intellectual development.

As I have noted, some unions have converted their headquarters to education, cultural, and health centers where members can receive college degrees, technical training, prescription drugs at a discount, and enjoy a Friday night film. These services are made part of the contract, including employer reimbursement for tuition, preparation for civil service examinations, and health services. However, company paid day care services have not been included in the union contract. Of course, among the reasons unions have been unable to raise child care services as a contract demand is that in recent years workers have been forced to choose between modest salary increases and maintaining the social wage, of which child care is a part. In the inflationary economy of the last half of the 1970's wages did not keep up with prices and the choice was to preserve purchasing power. But union resistance to making day care a major legislative as well as bargaining proposal is a function of the still limited influence of women in the leadership of the labor movement. Although CLUW President Joyce Miller, a Clothing and Textile Workers vice president, is the first woman to sit on the AFL-CIO Executive Council, this gain has not yet reflected a qualitative change in the extent of women's leadership at the local level. While women have drawn closer to the labor movement because of the progressive orientation of many unions, they have not wielded power at the bargaining table, except in a limited number of cases.

Organizing among the salariat in the private sector requires more than a lot of money and staff; it also will take new ideas—new concepts such as the struggle for regaining autonomy for employees who have been subjected to increasingly centralized authority, despite their ostensible high status; closer working relations between unions and the new social movements, especially among women and racial minorities; and the invention of new forms of unionism in the private sector that meet the specific needs of workers in multinational corporations engaged in administration as well as production that is marked by computer mediated work. Paternalistic corporations have kept unions out through highly sophisticated techniques, including careful attention to the problem of communications.

Unlike the old industrial robber barons who were characteristically contemptuous of manual workers and helped organize the industrial unions by the arrogance of their exercise of arbitrary authority, few of the newer potential targets of union organization have made similar mistakes. They are acutely aware of the threat of unions even when the labor movement has averted its own eyes from the target. Corporations pay considerable attention to planning personnel actions, technological shifts, and work reorganization. They maintain large internal communications staffs responsible for transmitting news of changes in the corporate structure to its employees. They have devised intricate systems of job evaluation to guide salary determination. And they appear to "decentralize" work groups to give employees the semblance of autonomy even as they concentrate power at the top. Some employees are offered profit sharing plans in which they have some kind of vesting, and the corporation reaches out to make sure some employees are brought closer to its objectives.

Unions aspiring to organize in banks, insurance companies, and head offices of large corporations cannot ignore the challenge posed by the pseudo-public sphere these institutions have created, even as they have organized the workplace in a way that divides workers from each other. There is a popular belief among unionists that non-union workplaces are "unorganizable" and that those workers are subject to the arbitrary authority of management without effective redress, even if wages and other economic benefits are equal to those of union shops. This misconception arises because unions have come to regard the NLRB as labor's Magna Carta, a view that places a premium on the juridical framework of trade union struggle. Employers resist unions because they are unwilling to subject managerial prerogatives to the contract's constraints, even if unions have formally conceded the right to manage to the company. Despite the arguments made in this book about the frail partnership between unions and employers, every provision of the collective agreement concerning wages, benefits, and working conditions limits the power of management to direct the work forces, unilaterally determine the size and location of its investments, and make changes in work organization and machine design without considering union positions. The contract becomes an occasion for workers to limit the authority of management and this structural feature has meant that corporations have been obliged to seek union concessions in order to restore these elements of their authority. In this sense, from management's point of view a depression is a felicitous moment for conducting the power struggle because unions are likely to be softer.

However, in workplaces not subject to collective bargaining, workers still possess power, through informal work groups, to restrain the company. Lacking formal authority to participate in making a variety of decisions affecting the labor process and their income, they are forced to resort to underground resistance resulting in lagging productivity, white collar and specifically computer crime, high turnover rates, and (in industries that are highly organized) threats to join the union if the company does not heed their grievances. The presence of the labor movement has been an important factor restraining corporate authority even if it lacks formal power in specific workplaces and industries. Corporations in the new sectors that aspire to avoid the institutional constraints posed by collective bargaining are still obliged to act as if their employees were potential antagonists—trade unionism does not determine class conflict, it only provides a specific framework for its course. Conflict is inherent in the social relations of domination, even if the superordinate possesses the preponderance of power resources to maintain mastery.

Since the early 1970's trade union organizing has virtually come to a halt. In a period of economic crisis, massive technological change, and capital flight, the prospects are dim for union recruitment in those industries that are most adversely affected by the new world economic order. However, in the growing sectors organizing opportunities will probably get better because large financial service as well as international communications and information corporations are likely to remain strong. On the one hand, control of banks, insurance companies, and communications (publishing, recording, film, television, and the new computer games and cellular radio) are being concentrated in fewer hands. The publishing house, newspaper, film company is merely an item in the investment portfolio of the large corporations that become communications holding companies; consequently, the old relationships are breaking down, weakening the paternal ties between employer and employee. In this environment clerical and professional employees tend to experience their proletarianization in an immediate way: editors are subordinate to marketing executives, and the computer becomes an editorial arbiter. On the other hand, the acceleration of computer mediated financial service jobs both recomposes skills and, from the perspective of authority relations, reduces the autonomy of middle managers as well as professionals. The "professional/managerial" class which as late as twenty years ago was expanding its authority as well as its numbers, is now subject to both kinds of cuts. In the context of a rising sector, the turmoil now underway among these employees improves the environment for collective organization. The question is whether the old style trade unionism, forged by craft and industrial workers in the era of expanding industrial capitalism, will suffice for the new situation.

Another way of stating this problem is that the labor movement must address the questions associated with *form.* Just as the IWW, the CIO, and other proponents of industrial unionism challenged the old craft model, and the public employees unions evolved a new service-based form to supplement contract unionism, prospective organizers and intellectuals, as well as organizing committees among financial service and administrative employees in the private sector, will have to confront the specific problems of their situation. To conclude this chapter I will offer some reflections, most of them speculative but grounded on an analysis of the current prospects for clerical and professional organizing.

NEW FORMS OF UNIONISM
The problem with organizing among new clerical and professional employees in the private sector is that there is not yet a native labor or

industrial tradition in the new industries. The rate of technological and organizational change is so rapid that occupations, skills, and authority relations have not had the time to sediment such traditions. This presents a unique challenge to the unions. The organic intellectuals of these sectors have yet to emerge.

Thus the first task for a prospective union movement is to identify the organizers who, in the classical mode, are people steeped in their communities who are willing to become part of the labor movement as well. The recent history of clerical organizing reveals patterns and practices that have already departed from the recent model: Working Women, Union Wage, and other organizations addressing themselves to problems of clerical workers began as organizations that combined feminist and traditional labor concerns. They dealt with sexual harassment and the lack of child care facilities as much as with the occupational issues such as low salaries, limited job mobility, problems women faced staying on the job, and the acquisition of new skills. After a decade of advocacy for working women's issues, particularly among clerical workers, some of the feminist organizations made connections with progressive contract unions, chiefly the SEIU and District 65. Some of the working women's leadership subsequently became staff members of these unions who are working to bring feminist issues to the fore within the framework of trade unionism.

Organizations among professionals that are independent of, but oriented to, trade union concerns had been among the more important sources of organizing cadre in the doctors' and lawyers' organizing successes of the 1970's. For example, District 65 organized 600 Legal Aid lawyers, most of whom entered the profession in order to work with poor people, racial minorities, and political dissenters. Their trade union affiliation presupposed both economic grievances and ideological orientation. Similarly, the current leaders of independent doctors' unions on both coasts were long-time medical activists in the civil rights movement.

These instances suggest that organizing among the new workers may take the form of small professional, feminist, and civil rights groups before trade union organization becomes possible. The contract union orientation may be inappropriate to these groups who could instead find alternative modes of association more congenial to their conditions, at least at the beginning. In banks, insurance companies, and many information processing and communications corporations the culture of contract unionism still has an alien ring, and the idea of collective consultation and action has not taken root among these workers.

Of course, I am not opposing contracts as one of the means by which workers gain economic and social justice, but unions in these industries must create organizations that meet the special needs of the employees, especially those that the large companies have ignored or repressed. Since turnover in any individual company remains fairly high because of poor wages and working conditions, occupational communities may be more important for organizing than communities based in the single workplace. Programmers and word processing operators often change jobs, yet they stay within the same industry and continue to share skill formation, knowledge, salaries, and working conditions with others performing similar work. Similarly, middle managers caught in the organizational and technical squeeze are no longer able to remain dependent on a single corporation for their security or to protect their authority. They find conditions are the same throughout the industry because centralized organizational methods have become globally applicable regardless of the company.

Unions would recruit individual members among these groups. The union would become a place to share experiences, receive professional and employment information, fight for legislative remedies for such abuses as occupational health hazards in the office, job security violations, and needed changes in the labor law to facilitate union organizing. The union might apply some of the features of the service model developed in public employees' unions, offering pension and health care programs, educational opportunities, and other benefits not offered by the company. In addition, the union would become an educational center for clerical and professional workers to learn about the labor movement, social and economic issues, and acquire a broader cultural formation. They would invent their own organizational forms to prepare for larger campaigns in their industry.

The challenge to those aspiring to organize among the new employees in the private sector is whether they possess the patience and the resources needed to undertake the long, slow, and probably painful process of recruiting and building unions of a new type, which are as much concerned with professional and women's issues at home as at work; providing intelligence on questions affecting clerical and professional labor such as new technologies; changes in corporate organization for communications people; discussing problems of the organization and content of the production of culture itself.

These examples indicate the possibility that new unions would be voluntary associations that collect dues without necessarily having achieved collective bargaining. In contrast to industrial workers' and public employees' unions, which frequently lost their voluntary character when they chose to enforce union or agency shop provisions within the contract, the new unionism would insist that membership in the union be associated with the professional, educational, legislative and social welfare services even prior to bargaining. In this sense they would partially reproduce the actual history of many public employees' unions that were originally civil service associations, nursing associations, and more informal groups. Such an organizing strategy would employ some of the most successful existing modes of organization among these groups rather than impose a contract union orientation on people who are not prepared for it. When workers felt ready to organize for collective bargaining they would surely join such efforts just as they have in the past.

This perspective could easily be mistaken for the old "soft" anti-union model of the older professionalism. Nothing could be further from the truth, for the actual evolution of unions has been preceded by the slow formation of a specific occupational or industrial culture in public as well as private sectors. The problem with current contract union strategies is that this historical process has been forgotten even by many who participated in it. The elevation of the contract to the exclusive goal of working class organization has become reified into the sum and substance of unionism.

For unions accustomed to finding ways to organize in corporations employing hundreds or thousands in a single workplace, the new work relations present an entirely new situation. The strategic issue here is whether unionism can take root when the opportunity to organize the employer has been subverted by radically different work arrangements. Like musicians, the union is obliged to recruit at both levels. Except for a tiny minority, most musicians are employed on a freelance basis, with the restaurant, club, or bar hiring a new group or performer on a daily, weekly, or monthly basis. Even if the owner signs with the union, the strength of the arrangement depends on the ability of the union to recruit the most talented and sought after musicians without which owners cannot attract customers, although this does not imply that musicians' or writers' unions must focus on the so-called stars in their fields.

American labor needs a new ideology, a new common sense. Unfortunately, the common sense of contract unionism corresponds better to the older craft and industrial sectors than to the new workers, professionals, and managers. Thus, while the contract union traditions of the labor movement inherited from Gompers are already a century old and hard to displace, the tradition of unions as democratic and voluntary organizations is today all but lost.

The results have been devastating for many of the older unions that are losing their contracts to capital flight. The identification of the labor movement with the contract has meant that workers no longer, except in rare cases, turn to their unions in times of hardship. The outstanding exception remain the craft unions which maintain hiring halls and active social ties, and who possess the remnants of a skill culture that binds their memberships. In contrast to many industrial unions that have virtually disappeared with deindustrialization of their sectors, the crafts have an unusual capacity to bounce back despite frequent adversities.

To the extent that professionals form occupational rather than industrial communities, the best traditions of the older crafts can be revived—

naturally minus the sexism and racism that was rampant among them. At the same time the character of the contract would resemble the industrial union rather than the craft model because technological change makes the occupations increasingly unstable. Thus, the new unions would take the best of both traditions. They would be democratic and voluntary associations that provide important services while stressing the need for industrial and class organization in the wake of the increasing concentration of capital ownership and control.

CHAPTER
7

RADICALIZING AMERICAN LABOR

AMERICAN social reform, including successful union organization, has traditionally presupposed economic prosperity and expansion. The struggle for redistributive justice has always been linked to the economic perceptions of workers and the poor that the pie has expanded sufficiently to make room for their demands. However, while workers will risk their jobs when the chance to obtain another one is good, when the labor market is tight, they tend to hang onto their jobs even when wages and working conditions are poor.

Another important issue for union organization and social reform generally is whether the political climate is favorable for union organization. During the Depression economic conditions had already improved as the mass industrial union upsurge got underway, but unemployment remained high, wages were still falling, and the employer arrogance that had soared in the 1920's and early 1930's was still powerful. The New Deal, despite skepticism among radical critics, offered a social and political climate that favored labor organization and other forms of collective action. The crisis had shaken confidence of the large corporations, and leaders of corporate and political power made significant new spaces for bold radical and labor leaders. Industrial unionism grew on the soil of hope for a better future that was nurtured by the Roosevelt administration and the radicals of both the socialist Left and of the populist Right.

In the early years of the Depression, the basic program of the Left called for redistribution of the still considerable wealth of the giant monopolies and for massive state intervention to relieve the hardships suffered by working people. Trade unionism was one of the central vehicles promising, if not immediately, economic and social justice. Like the decades around the turn of the century, all factions of the labor movement presented themselves as representing all those historically excluded from the process of capital's rapid expansion. As I have shown, in the important postwar spurt in organizing public employees, labor once again presented itself as a new social movement—this time incorporating the demands of the civil rights and feminist movements. Thus the program of the labor

171

movement coincided with the social reforms of the Kennedy and Johnson administrations, and for a few years labor was able to reconstitute the same New Deal alliance in which trade union growth had previously occurred.

I have insisted that the elementary trade union demands of workers have always been linked with struggles for social reform and have always implied a program for justice that extended far beyond the purview of the unions themselves. As unions entered progressive political alliances in the Depression and its aftermath, they became capable of organizing new constituencies. In turn, strong industrial and public employees unions formed the heart of the progressive alliances that set the terms for political debate until the mid 1960's. When workers perceived unions as representatives of their global interests as well as their sectoral and occupational needs, the unions were able to make deep inroads among groups normally regarded by union leaders and intellectuals as beyond the pale of labor organization. Thus, unions have historically been required to adopt an explicit political strategy that organized around *class* interests in order to organize *particular groups*. It was only when unions became established institutions within the social order that they reverted to the older business and contract union models.

Revitalizing today's labor movement is the key task for revising the agenda for American politics. However, if unions are to both defend the interests of their current membership and extend the promise of the labor movement to new groups, labor needs a new social philosophy, a new political and economic strategy, and a program that is radically different from that of the old social contract unionism. My contention is that the old contract no longer fits the new conditions. Some labor leaders know this to be true, and certainly many "enlightened" corporate leaders are similarly convinced that the smooth path to higher wages, the extension of the social wage within the framework of collective bargaining, and a powerful safety net under the income and living standards of the poor, is now in need of radical revision. The labor movement is being asked to cooperate with the so-called neo-liberal program for revising the social contract that offers a partnership of planned shrinkage. Thus far, the unions have developed no serious alternative to the various proposals for reductions in wages and other contract benefits, a trimmed social welfare state, and uninhibited investment in technological development that will reduce jobs.

The climate for revitalizing the labor movement will not be produced by improved economic conditions, for America is once more mired in a profound economic crisis. Instead, politics must take command of the process by which the nation as well as the unions are revived. This chapter discusses some of the leading options offered to workers, their unions, and social movements that have mobilized among excluded groups such as racial and national minorities, women, and discontented professionals. It proposes a radical break with the assumption that contract unionism or the old social unionism can survive the probability that economic growth will not save the day. I am not advancing a program that could have dominated the discussion as long as American capitalism was capable of accommodating reform through expansion. My position realistically grasps the fact that American workers and their unions are not prone to independent political or economic action as long as they identify their interests with those of capital. However, since even the most liberal fraction of capital is asking a price for cooperation that even the most compliant unions find difficult to stomach, much less sell to the membership, unions need a new strategy. Further, unless unions adopt an aggressive political stance towards America's growing social and economic malaise, the chance of bringing the increasingly discontented new millions of clerical, professional, and technical employees as well as the working poor into the unions will rapidly disappear.

WORKERS, THE POOR, AND THE ECONOMIC POLICY DEBATE

America is not prepared for the new world economic order. The current economic crisis is still regarded by many economists as well as a large proportion of the American people as merely a cyclical downturn that requires government action of some sort. The neo-conservatives want to "tune" the monetary system according to fluctuations in prices for commodities, gold, and the dollar; according to its leading lights, a combination of tax cuts for individuals and corporations, a smaller public sector, (excluding, of course, arms), and a tight money policy to reduce inflation will eventually lift the United States out of the mess. After two years of the Reagan administration implementing these policies, the economic outlook remains grim; most of the leading indicators showed that, at best, America could achieve a modest upturn as the cycle finally ran its course, but short of a major conventional war a new boom was out of the question, at least for some years. Of course, even the prophets of the so-called "permanent" global capitalist crisis, the Marxists, do not deny the likelihood of eventual improvement. The Marxist theory does not predict complete systemic breakdown; on the contrary, Marxists regard the crisis as merely the necessary condition for a new surge of capital accumulation. According to the theory, its length varies according to the extent of government intervention, credit policies, state investment, the type of crisis (e.g., overproduction and "realization"—difficulties in converting goods into money), and other factors.

The neo-liberals, whose most important spokespersons are financier Felix Rohatyn and economist Lester Thurow, agree with the general thrust of neo-conservative supply side economics by emphasizing the

importance of government actions to stimulate the investment they consider necessary for growth and new jobs. They agree that the old-time
religion of deficit financing, the welfare state, and high wages propelled
by militant trade union struggles is a thing of the past. They depart from
the orthodox supply siders in that they openly declare the need both for
national planning and for a new social contract in which trade unions will
be restored to full partnership with government and business. According
to *Business Week*, whose feature "The Reindustrialization of America" was
a virtual manifesto of neo-liberal policy, the key aim of planning is to
make American intermediate technology industries competitive again on
the world market.[1] In addition to targeting investment to update plants
and equipment, the neo-liberals would undertake two further programs
to integrate labor into the process: (1) Workers would be asked, through
wage and benefits concessions, to assist reindustrialization in return for
new incentive programs such as profit sharing and job security guarantees. (2) Government and business would offer new opportunities through
education and training to upgrade existing skills, jobs for technically displaced workers, and the development of an income maintenance program
in the protracted transition period ahead.

There is nothing in this broad position with which conventional liberals
can disagree except its rejection of a strong welfare state. The "restoration
of the social safety net" includes the main elements of the traditional
labor-liberal program—lengthening jobless benefits; strengthening social
security rather than dismantling it; a massive public works program to
create jobs, frankly acknowledging the government as employer of last
resort; eliminating the peonage system of "working off" the welfare check
and increasing benefits; and providing an expanded housing, education,
and health program aimed at the people left destitute by the crisis. I do
not wish to minimize the differences between those (like the neo-liberals)
who basically accept conservative fiscal policy but want national planning
for full employment through private investment, and the old New Dealers for whom the welfare state, the most mature example of national
planning possible within current political boundaries, is a permanent
social "right." The progressive wing of the Democratic Party, although
profoundly weakened by the reaction formation of the neo-liberals, still
represents the best available hope for creating "capitalism with a human
face." Senator Edward Kennedy's proposals for limited public ownership
of production facilities to modernize a national rail system, which would
result in substantial employment for displaced auto workers, metalwork-
ers and others in the northeast and midwest, is a step beyond exclusive
reliance on the market system to produce solutions to the process of
deindustrialization and economic crisis. But the overall direction of liberal policy represents, with the important exception of a commitment to
welfare, an accommodation to supply side economics. For example,

shortly after his election to New York's Governorship, Democrat Mario Cuomo wasted little time "sending a message" to major holders of state bonds (banks, insurance companies, and large private investors), that he means to balance the budget by 1984 and that fiscal conservatism will remain the hallmark of his administration as it was for his Democratic predecessor.

The concept of the partnership, not planning, dominates both liberal and neo-liberal policy alternatives to Reaganomics. As Michael Harrington has wisely asserted, the question is not whether we shall enter a phase of national planning but for whom and how planning will be undertaken. Contrary to the claims of supply siders, the first years of the Reagan administration demonstrate that the interventionist state is still the dominant mode of governance. The tax reforms enacted by Congress in 1981 were redistributive in reverse, transferring billions of dollars from the poor to the rich. State and local taxation has followed the prescription that what is good for business is good for the community, with some of the losses in federal aid being made up by increased sales and other excise taxes. In many places, the income losses sustained by tax initiatives limiting real estate levies, became permanent even for commercial and industrial property. Monetarism entails considerable state manipulation of the money supply to achieve higher levels of private business investment. Reagan frankly stated that stemming inflation through budget cuts and high interest rates for consumer spending produces unemployment. The early phase of the current crisis was artificially deepened by the intervention of the administration. Unemployment has proven one effective means of reducing prices and as the President has often admitted, we cannot have full employment, a balanced budget, *and* lower prices. Of course, he is perfectly correct, but an astronomical military budget contradicts and undermines his anti-inflation program.

Within the progressive wing two variants may be distinguished: the old welfare staters who accept the consensual perspective that high levels of military spending are necessary on cold war grounds (even if the level is somewhat lower than Reagan's), but insist on the restoration of the safety net package even at the risk of some inflation; and the "radicals" who have in various ways taken account of the fact that the crisis exhibits features consistent with the pattern of postwar declines in industrial production and employment such as occurred in 1954, 1958, 1960–61, and 1971. Some radicals do not dispute the objective of reindustrializing America, the central objective of the neo-liberal program. For some left economists like Raford Boddy and James Crotty, the underlying foundation for the economic crisis has been overexpansion. Continuous growth results in tight labor markets. Wages went up and productivity declined because workers were not willing during the boom to change work rules or tolerate technological change to improve output. As labor costs rose and pro-

ductivity stagnated, profits were squeezed. Capital's way out of this
dilemma was to stimulate a recession.[2]

Taking his cue from this analysis, David Gordon has proposed new
measures to increase worker productivity by means of providing incentives beyond wage increases. According to Gordon, reindustrialization
can be achieved by bringing workers into the picture, particularly worker
ownership or at least co-management of leading industries currently faced
with sharpened competition and eventual extinction. The convergence of
Gordon's program with the orientation of neo-liberals is striking, even if
the analytic basis of his program differs from that of economists such as
Thurow who would stress the need for cutting taxes and thus trimming
the welfare state to free investment for planned reindustrialization. However, as Barry Bluestone and Bennett Harrison have argued, "The rise of
international competition and the increase in the velocity of capital mobility make the entire panoply of liberal policies ineffective, unaffordable
and ultimately unproductive."[3] Measures oriented to increasing worker
productivity, even if accompanied by partnership concepts of the Left or
on the Right, will emulate the Japanese model of modern paternalism
which was imported (in the 1920's) from the United States in the first
place. A genuine radical alternative must reject the frank neo-liberal
admiration for the achievements of the postwar Japanese economy, because the Japanese system brings strong pressure for conformity "that can
easily restrict dissent and stifle individualism."[4] Further, the Japanese
system of job guarantees, an important element in neo-liberal reindustrialization proposals, "only work[s] in a 'dual economy'." Some firms and
their workers occupy privileged economic niches and the large competitive sector of small-scale production and service are exempted from the
job security provisions, thus creating a class of "temporary" workers that
is subject to market fluctuations.

The debate on reindustrialization must focus not on productivity problems but on this depression and on the new world economic order. This is
the only basis for rebuilding the progressive alliance. The rhetoric of
"democratic reindustrialization" is a fairly imaginative but unexceptional
synthesis of the various structural reforms proposed in this country, Great
Britain, and elsewhere. These emphasize the importance of saving the
"smokestack" industries located in the United States in the industrial
heartland and the northeastern regions, by targeting government investment to such places as Youngstown's two large closed steel mills, Buffalo,
where the huge Bethlehem Steel Mill is virtually dismantled, and Detroit, where the gaunt auto plants stand like ghosts in the city's landscape
reminding its residents of better times. The Democrats' reindustrialization action is a transitional program to preserve the traditional working
class communities. The model for all proposals for "rational reindustrialization" is the British Lucas Corporate Plan,[5] developed by shop stewards

and union members in this defense plant which was suffering shutdowns because of losses in military contracts. Professional, technical, and craft workers in the plant proposed "that management shift production to 150 new product lines ranging from a new type of kidney dialysis machine to a revolutionary road rail vehicle for use in transportation in deficient third world countries."[6] Secondly, the employees proposed "new more democratic forms of task organisation on the shop floor." The British government would have been required to issue contracts to the plant, but the proposals were rejected both by the government and management on neo-conservative grounds.

The key alternatives to both Reaganomics and liberal policies of all varieties involve three different innovations:

(1) The transfer of public investment from arms to socially useful production is essential.

(2) Conversion of product lines should not require closing plants and capital flight should be restrained. Like all other features of the program, democratic reinvestment means that workers and their communities should be involved in determining what is produced and where. Consequently, federal and state legislation is needed to prohibit corporations from closing plants without prior approval, a decision that entails relocation rights for workers, restitution to communities for environmental damage and lost income, and worker/community buy-outs with federal investment assistance to upgrade the plant technology and adjust worker skills in order to make it competitive.

(3) New management arrangements at the shop floor are required to implement the concept of democratic decision making. This might mean that workers elect their managers, that technologies be introduced to conform to the aim of full employment, and pay differentials are reduced among occupations performing similar tasks. It would also encourage rotating repetitive jobs to make work more interesting, and, in the industries where computer-mediated technology prevails, reinstituting face to face interaction as a guiding principle of organizing work flow.

Productivity problems in older industries are not produced only by backward technologies and or by excessive wages. Much of the responsibility for higher costs is due to excessively large managerial staffs which result from corporate policies aimed at domination of the productive labor force. The issue of whether a bulging bureaucracy has caused high, uncompetitive "labor costs" remains untouched by all liberal and neo-liberal critiques of current corporate practices because their focus remains tied to consensual growth policies and the interests of managerial hierarchies.

In the main, trade unions have placed themselves on the liberal side of the debate. A notable exception, the Machinists, have proposed the massive conversion of arms plants in which many of their own members are employed, to production for social use. The union's analysis of the consequences of the high military budget shows that these plants are heavily capital-intensive, producing fewer jobs than the other industries, and that unproductive military expenditures contribute to economic woes. At the same time, together with the Auto Workers and other unions in basic industries, the union has supported the so-called "domestic content" bill which requires that ninety percent of product content be produced in the United States. This legislation is admittedly a departure from the free trade policies historically adopted by organized labor, but it is less xenophobic than "buy American" campaigns because it focuses on the issue of "outsourcing," which has been a major employer weapon to weaken unions and an important reason for high unemployment in some industries. It also corresponds to similar measures in effect in other countries, particularly France, Germany, and Japan, with whom U.S. corporations compete. The bill to control outsourcing recognizes the danger to workers' living standards posed by the new international division of labor and the capital flight and plant shutdowns that have accompanied it. The "Atari" Democrats of the west and southwest, the business base for neoliberalism, believe the "sunset" industries are best abandoned in favor of targeting investment towards the "sunrise" production industries such as computers, numerical controls, and robotics, and software industries such as management systems, computer programs, and financial services. The progressive unions have advanced from the traditional liberal alternative of strengthening the safety net under unemployment by moving towards political and legislative policies that stress reindustrialization, public control of some investment decisions and over the pace and type of technologically directed investment.

However, left and liberal economists, like their adversaries who have emphasized the ideological basis of their programs by silence on the subject of investment control, are similarly bereft of political and strategic reflexivity. They present themselves within the discourses of economic professionalism; their arguments are buttressed by empirical demonstration, are policy rather than politically oriented, and, although by no means "value free," are framed in the language of objectivity—the language of technocratic management rather than political intellectuals. Programs are offered to those who presumably accept the power of the argument and demonstration that underlies them. Some of the work of the labor-oriented economists is directed towards rebuilding the trade union and political left, a fraction of which, the now defunct Progressive Alliance (a 1970's coalition of trade union, consumer, feminist, and black organizations as well as the two major organizations of the democratic socialists), began to extend the boundaries of economic thinking beyond the New Deal. Yet, perhaps they feel constrained both by the conservative political environment which has persuaded most intellectuals that ideological discretion is the better part of valor, and by their own professional commitments to dispassion. The trouble with this stance is that it presumes the terrain of their opponents (the main problem is to build a better economic mousetrap) rather than comprehending that policies arise from ideological commitments and strategic perspectives. Therefore, the rest of this chapter will draw the implications of the current political and economic situation for my analysis of the historical development of the labor movement and the political alliance of which it is a part.

CLASS COMPROMISE OR CLASS STRUGGLE?

The ideological choices for the labor movement reduce to three concurrent and alternating positions:

(1) Labor can remain a pressure group within a larger social and political coalition dedicated to building the liberal state. This choice was historically validated by the specific circumstances of U.S. capitalist development, particularly the formation of a liberal fraction of capital willing to enter a social compromise with the trade unions on the basis of shared political but not economic power and the reluctance of the labor leadership themselves to organize independent political vehicles. At the same time, the long three-part partnership that guided trade union ideological commitments has not always implied that the labor movement be reduced to a pressure group, although it has frequently been forced into this position when out of power.

(2) "Trade unionism, pure and simple" has never really been an option—neither for the conservative Gompers nor the revolutionaries in the IWW. Social contract unionism is forced upon trade unions by the third stage of the capital/labor relation but not socialist or oppositional politics. On the other hand, the daily practice of many unions has corresponded to the business union principle that the goal of the movement is to sell its labor power at the highest possible price and political interventions are confined to "supporting its friends and punishing its enemies."

(3) Class struggle unionism implies the labor movement enters the opposition to capital in this long period of realignment of world markets, with partnership being reinterpreted by capital to signify labor's subordination. In all cases the ideological stance of class struggle unionism requires labor to organize a political vehicle independent of capital, through which workers' interests may be expressed. This vehicle may be a political party in which labor occupies a major position of power, or a political alliance with other social movements that uses the Democratic Party as an arena.

Workers do not choose the perspective of the opposition out of moral will, but because the alternative of political integration is effectively closed to them. My first claim is that the assumption of all liberal programs claiming that a viable economic framework exists for class compromises and partnerships has been overtaken by the new epoch marked by the domination of world market conditions over the U.S. national economy. The limits imposed by transnational investment and international competition set new constraints on collective bargaining and national economic policy which taken alone are no longer adequate to protect workers and their communities. Under these conditions, no industry or plant is sacrosanct and all of the terms of the previous social consensus that the state is obliged to provide income security for retirees and the unemployed has been seriously eroded. National capital, no less than multinational firms, has responded to the challenge posed by the new world economic order by renegotiating the terms of the social contract to protect its investments or, failing labor's agreement, has migrated to sectors of the global economy and other regions of the world offering higher profit rates. At the same time, as the last decade has shown, the fraction of capital that supported the old social contract has lost the ability to direct state policy. The new corporate consensus is that lacking a way out of the crisis, capital's best strategy is to weaken worker resistance by threats of migration, punitive measures such as actual migration when workers refuse to budge, and a massive assault on the welfare state.

The major debates within liberal capitalist circles center on arms policy rather than economic alternatives. A considerable fraction, led by the Rockefeller interests but also including important intellectuals aligned with the historic cold war position such as George Kennan and Cyrus Vance, have opposed Reagan's nuclear arsenal buildup on both strategic and economic grounds. Together with growing popular opposition to the administration's massive arms budget, its intention to deploy nuclear missiles in Europe, and its general antipathy to arms control agreements with the Soviet Union, this fraction has played an enormously important role in the recent upsurge of the peace movement, contributing both materially and politically to its recent successes.

One of the effects of the foreign policy splits within the "higher circles" has been to open a wedge for others concerned with new directions in economic policy. To be sure, cutting the military budget may not strengthen either the welfare state or public investment in conversion for social use and there is no evidence that these capitalist interests are more progressive than the neo-liberals. In the main, they favor the main direction of supply side welfare policy, although they may differ on the ideological trappings Reagan has placed on his fiscal and monetary program.

There is no doubt that the traditional liberal fractions of capital are trying to reconstruct class compromise on a new program of labor sacrifice and that a large segment of labor's progressive as well as centrist leadership is attracted to this project precisely because it is more expedient than any strategy that threatens to further isolate them socially and politically. Given the deepening crisis in the labor movement itself, particularly its diminishing weight among the work force and especially in the most dynamic sectors of the economy, many unions are naturally seeking allies among the neo-liberals as well as the New Dealers. Since trade union leadership has traditionally been ideologically integrated into consensual approaches to national political and social relations, the main task for a strategy which proposes that labor turn to class struggle unionism is to specify the conditions that would make it possible. I have already stressed the centrality of a major organizing effort among the working poor, administrative workers, and those engaged in knowledge and machine production of the new scientifically based technologies. A commitment by the labor movement to extend its social and economic base would entail making alliances with new social movements with whom the majority of trade unions have had either hostile relations in the past or have only recently made tactical coalitions. The importance of these movements, particularly the women's movement and those among racial and national minorities, is demonstrated by the fact that the major trade union organizing successes of the 1960's and the 1970's were almost entirely concentrated among these groups. As I have argued, when unions allied themselves with the social aspirations of blacks and women as well as fighting for their economic demands, the labor movement took on a dynamic quality; it lost its exclusively bureaucratic and conservative appearance of the 1950's and became, in part, a social movement rather than a business organization.

Nevertheless, in the 1960's and early 1970's many unions were able to integrate organizing among these new groups with a progressive version of the political ideology of corporativism. Now, when the old alliances are crumbling, ideological pragmatism cannot be sustained. Organizing takes on the character of a social mission because it challenges the policy of most large corporations to forge new arrangements based upon a coercive model of labor relations among non-union employees. The intervention of unions would require them to invent a language and a program that acknowledges that this is the era of the *zero sum game.* Among the working poor, the discourses of exploitation and liberation would dominate their rhetoric of mobilization; consistent battle for amnesty for the millions of new immigrants and traditional union members would require confronting large corporate groups such as agribusiness which want a restrictive policy in order to maintain labor's subordination. Similarly, the struggle against sweatshop and child labor, which in the early decades of the twentieth century gained support among enlightened fractions of the professional middle classes and liberal capital, may no longer be a popular cause in times of economic contraction. On the other hand, unions must confront the liberals with their recent indifference to these issues. If they mount a significant challenge to the sweated conditions of the underground economy, unions might win active support among some of these groups. Further, a union alliance with the new national minorities from Asia and Latin America will certainly raise serious issues among those in the labor movement who remain antipathetic to the foreign-born on protectionist grounds. Unless a broad-scale effort is made to reverse the traditional anti-foreign bias among many rank and file workers and secondary union leaders, the Garment Workers and others interested in organizing the working poor and enacting legislation to protect their political and economic rights, will remain frustrated.

Among administrative employees and scientific and technological occupations in advanced sectors, unions would invoke the relatively suppressed symbols of self-management and work floor democracy as well as traditional job security and salary concerns. The ideology of self-management and co-management is not compatible with the terms of the old social contract which recognized the employer's domination of the work organization, investment decisions, and direction of the labor force. Neo-liberal advocates of a new social contract have not offered to break management's grip over these decisions, merely to provide richer incentives for worker collaboration. The fight for self-management is not only a necessary program for organizing, it is an important element of a new class-oriented unionism because the gain for employees would be a power loss for top management. Unions would have to consult with those possessing the knowledge of the specific mode of work organization in these sectors in order to make any progress at all. But such a step would entail reflexive reexamination of trade union practices that still cede management's rights on the shop floor in conventional industries as well. This task is particularly urgent precisely because many "intermediate technology" workplaces are undergoing substantial transition that parallels the more advanced sectors.

David Noble has shown that the selection of numerical controls (N/C) technology to automate machine tools was conditioned by "massive" air force support for N/C over alternatives such as record playbacks that would have preserved the skill of the traditional machinist in the labor process. N/C transfers control over the machine tool from the machinists to programmers familiar with mathematics and complex computer languages. Introducing N/C into this industry, especially the standardization of a complex language rather than alternative simpler languages, meant that many smaller shops which had traditionally been important producers of machine tools and parts have been gradually squeezed out of business because only those with access to "large computers and mathematically sophisticated programmers" can compete for business, much of which emanates from the military. Noble contends that N/C enhanced management's authority over the labor process in the machine tool industry in which craft labor maintained considerable power until the 1970's. However, he points out that N/C does not resolve the problem of control because close machine tolerances require careful attention by the operator who may still determine the pacing of the feed rate of the tape despite management's effort to "keep the operators out of the planning process." N/C operators contend that their skills are downgraded by the transfer of design function to the programmers and argue that the new technology is not necessarily more efficient when measured by product quality but merely enhances managerial authority.[7]

The traditional stance of unions has been to "go along" with technological advances because they accept the notion that progress is inevitable and the major issue concerning changes in the work process is whether they will share in the benefits of increased efficiency. The problem with the current pace of automation in production sectors is that workers are losing control on the shop floor because labor has had no program to gain a larger voice in determining the pace and direction of technologically oriented investment. Unions traditionally do not offer analyses of the forms of technological transformation but confine themselves to dealing with its effects on employment and wage levels. This strategy made some sense in the era of American global dominance when workers, with difficulty at times, were able to get other jobs. In times when entire crafts and conventional skills are being destroyed, unions are being challenged to develop policies that may arrest displacement, to intervene in investment/technical decisions concerning their members' jobs, and to demand training priority for their own members for the new occupations that displace them. Management argues that the new international division of labor constitutes an imperative that the old technologies be replaced or the plant dies. Unions would demand education rights for their members as well as the power to modify investment in order to protect traditional jobs and skills. Noble's description of alternative technological choices, particularly the possibility of inventing simpler languages adequate to smaller computers would make training a less complex and economically prohibitive matter. Unions would be obliged to challenge management's technology of control on the shop floor by insisting on the operator's prerogative to set the pace of the machine, and on the inclusion of the union operators in the planning process.

The 1982 Machinist Union's Scientists and Engineers conference began to address the many issues associated with technology control. The most important recommendation it made was that the union establish technology control committees at the local and district levels that would be integrated with the plant bargaining committee. These committees would be charged with developing a "technology control program" as a bargaining issue. Adopting some of the more advanced European models, particularly those of Scandinavian countries, the conference urged contract language be developed to protect Machinists' members through *advance notice and mandatory consultation* between management and the union "prior to company decision to implement or install new technology equipment or systems." This proposal approximates the standard Steel agreement's Section 2A which for many years constituted the heart of the union's protection of work rules and the traditional labor process. It was precisely this section of the contract that became the leading issue in the 1959, 116-day steelworkers' strike and its removal a linchpin of the Experimental National Agreement of 1971 when the union, in order to cooperate with reindustrialization of the industry, relaxed its historic controls over the introduction of new technology. As history has demonstrated, this premature and massive concession to management proved fruitless and has resulted in disaster for steelworkers.

The truly innovative proposals made by the Machinists union's scientific and technical group are: (1) the demand that "union have a thorough knowledge of and voice in the design of the systems and include the shop floor workers in the loop;" (2) that management proposals for new technology "be presented to the union in language easily understood by all persons without special knowledge of the technology concerned;" (3) the right to monitor control room and control center operations; (4) "that retraining and job classifications for workers displaced or transferred by new technology be agreed upon *before* the company is locked into purchase;" and (5) that "disputes over the introduction of or use and misuse of New Technology is a strikeable issue."

The union has also proposed a technology bill of rights which would amend the National Labor Relations Act and other labor regulatory legislation to embody full employment principles, share the fruits of new technology between management and workers, institute a tax on employers using robotics, and provide broad rights for workers and their unions to participate in decisions concerning the introduction of new technology.

The Machinists' program embodies the major features of a democratic workers-control perspective on technological transformation. Their approach is both relevant to shop floor negotiations and new national legislation, that is, it combines collective bargaining with political struggle. Unfortunately, the Machinists are perhaps the only union prepared to discuss, much less undertake, a program whose fundamental assumption is a frontal assault on management's unilateral power over investment decisions. It also specifies some concrete steps to contest corporate authority.

When unions in intermediate production sectors concern themselves with issues of management and control they will be confronted with the fact that class struggle is brought out in the open and the necessity of developing arms' length relationships with employers with whom they negotiate. If they are forced to grant concessions in order to preserve jobs, they would demand a large measure of control over investment, the quality of technological change, market decisions, and shop floor management. In its early negotiation over concessions with the General Motors Corporation the UAW sought to rescind the unilateral right of management to lay off workers due to market conditions. Employers would be obliged to extend income maintenance programs for unemployed workers beyond the one-year limit of current contractual agreements. Unlike the penchant of the Steelworkers leaders to conclude long-term no-strike agreements with the industry, any concessions would be of short duration. The labor movement would refuse to give up the strike weapon and would incorporate reverse corporate concessions into the agreement when market conditions improved.

The position which argues that there is no basis for renegotiating union contracts in times of severe economic crisis forgets that workers themselves are not always prepared to fight when capital migration is the likely result, especially when there are no alternatives on the horizon because conservative state policy has removed the safety net. On the other hand, unions must renounce the one-way street since one concession leads to another under conditions of more or less permanent depression in some industries. At the same time the crisis in the older "lemon" industries opens the door to union/community collaboration to save plants and local economies by innovations such as worker buyouts and the formation of community investment corporations which assume ownership under a system of worker self-management. However, as Staughton Lynd has recently argued, such ownership transfers would not be feasible unless government investment is provided for such activities as modernization. But if the federal government were committed to a democratic public investment policy and a broad program of reconstructing the deteriorated infra-structure such as roads, rails, communications, and water systems in major urban and rural areas suffering severe economic distress, community and worker-run industries could produce basic materials for these products for social use.

A transitional program of structural reforms such as saving low and intermediate technology industries is in serious conflict with those who advocate abandoning the industrial heartlands and consumer industry-based northeast regions by focusing public policy exclusively on making Americans a "world class" industrial power through high technology investments.[8]

Even if the "smokestack" policies are not *sufficient* to address current economic realities they are *necessary* from another point of view. Traditional centers of union, black, and feminist strength, especially the large metropolitan areas of the northeast and midwest, are important to pre-

serve for building progressive political, social, and cultural power, con-
tradicting the strategy that argues America needs to enter the nuclear and
computer age with both feet and that the lemon industries are a drag on
investment. It is not that neo-liberal analysis has no merit; indeed, just as
the Socialist government in France has placed high priority on development in advanced technological sectors, so a progressive United
States government would have no choice but to move in similar directions. However, the French model does not leave the private sector free
to control the investment program; the government has control of steering mechanisms such as the banking system, has tripled the pure research
and development budget in its first two years in office, has strengthened
the social safety net for workers who have been rendered unemployed by
the world economic crisis, and has preserved the state commitment to
strong education, health, and pension programs. These policies have produced some pressure on prices and weakened the value of the franc in
world money markets. And it must be admitted that some retrenchment
has occurred from its original and bold program. Yet the social base of the
socialist movement has supported the overall direction of the program
even though it is widely interpreted as an attack on private sector corporations for whom the tax burden and the nationalization of advanced
technology industries remain anathema.

Naturally, ideological politics are an intrinsic part of the European
social environment. With few exceptions, notably in the less advanced
countries such as Italy, the labor movement harbors few illusions that a
left-wing policy will gain the support of any considerable capitalist fraction in times of severe contraction. The politics of redistribution are the
foundation of labor and democratic socialist programs in Scandinavia and
Southern Europe where socialist governments have recently assumed
power. This does not imply a revolutionary transfer of power; European
socialism is still constrained by the capitalist world market, but there is no
question of making workers pay most of the costs of the crisis because the
ideology and program of socialist political power are pro-labor.

The labor movement is not socially powerful enough in the United
States to constitute a new political party of its own. But its considerable
social weight, despite losses, makes possible the prospect of what I shall
call a *new political bloc,* consisting of an alliance between the trade unions
and other social and political forces that are *objectively* aligned in opposition to the dominant neo-liberal and conservative fractions of capital. The
formation of the new bloc presupposes that: (1) Labor adopts the ideological perspective of class struggle or, at the minimum, recognizes that it
has been forced by historical conditions into opposition to the multinational corporations and the conservative fraction of national capital. (2)
Labor adopts a radically new program for dealing with popular needs
which diverges from the main drift of the liberal policy while incorporat-

ing some aspects of it. The basis of the new program would be democratic control over both investment and management in both traditional and advanced sectors. (3) Labor builds a new partnership with the new social movements—with women, national, and racial minorities; with the environmental and ecology movements that have challenged investment priorities on social rather than economic grounds, arguing that the destruction of the natural world is an unacceptable price to pay for economic growth and consumptions gains; with the hard pressed middle classes, the small manufacturers, shopkeepers, those in retail and wholesale trades, and independent professionals; and with the peace movement which has begun to challenge not only the arms budget and U.S. nuclear arsenals but social priorities as well.

The question of whether a "breakaway" fraction of big capital will join such a bloc cannot be answered in advance. The perspectives for class politics in America have frequently been thwarted by the ability of liberal corporatism to oppose its own short-term interests by forging partnerships with social reformers and the labor movement. Such a fraction may emerge as the new politics gains strength in order to forestall a transfer of power from which it would be excluded.

When I speak of women, racial, and national minority movements, and some elements of the middle classes in the large cities, I do not exclude the specific issue struggles that are the political and social forms within which movements of class, race, and sex express themselves. For example, welfare rights organizations are both labor movements and movements for human rights. Similarly, workers often join neighborhood-based struggles for better housing, and the middle strata have formed the backbone of the ecology and peace movements. Thus the organization forms taken by single issue movements often hide the fact that they are socially constituted along class, race, and sex lines. The task for a strategy of building a political bloc out of the multiplicity of forms is not only to find a common program of action, but to identify the social forces likely to compose the political vehicles.

Such an alliance or bloc will not succeed if it insists on the subordination of women's issues, ecology concerns, or race issues to a narrow economic focus. The bloc would be multilayered—it would be constituted by its differences as much as its agreements. The various participants would be obliged to negotiate the grounds upon which mutual collaboration can be developed.

(1) Even if it is evident that women have become among the most important new constituents of the trade unions, it does not follow that the labor leadership is prepared to offer explicit support to feminist demands such as abortion rights, or to conduct a determined struggle for changing the double burden suffered by working women by fighting for child care as a bargaining demand. These questions must become the subject for

dialogue if a long-term alliance is to be successfully developed between unions and the women's movement. The time has plainly passed when women will subordinate their autonomous demands to an economic program even in times of crisis. Of course, there are outspoken advocates of such subordination within the women's movement, but these are in the minority. In short, while unions played an important part in behalf of the recent struggle to pass an Equal Rights Amendment to the Constitution, this economic measure does not subsume social issues.

(2) The two major issues posed by the environmental and ecological movements are of a different order:

(a) Campaigns by such organizations as the Sierra Club and the League for Conservation Voters (it opposes the program of the Reagan administration to sell public land for energy exploration and production) have received support from a number of trade unions. But when movements oppose the development plans of the nuclear industry and propose (on ecological grounds) alternative energy development such as solar and wind energy for both home heating and industrial use, many construction unions, faced with long-term unemployment, have joined with the industry to lobby for permission to expand reactor production despite the safety and health hazards. Of course, not all unions have sided with the construction trades and nuclear industry. The labor-backed Citizens Labor Energy Coalition (CLEC) brought together unions such as Machinists, Auto Workers, State, County, and Municipal Employees with anti-corporate energy activists and ecologists to oppose nuclear development and other environmentally unsound energy programs. But there is little chance of bringing a united labor movement into the various environmental coalitions; just as unions have taken different sides on race and sex issues, so we can expect only a fraction of unions to support alliances with ecologists.

(b) Many critics of both environmental policy and the past expansionist economic policies have challenged the idea of the primacy of macroeconomic growth politics for resolving problems such as unemployment, poverty, and reindustrialization. From the New Deal to our own times, the central thrust of both liberal and neo-conservative economic policy has been to stimulate investment by either monetary manipulation or pump priming fiscal policies. In turn, renewed private investment was regarded as the best way to achieve full employment. For example, tax policy was understood by Keynesian and conservative economists and business groups as a part of growth strategies; they understood progressive taxation that favored low and middle income groups as a means to stimulate mass consumption rather than as a redistributive mechanism, although to some extent it served both functions. In turn, reducing business taxes has been justified by the general criteria of "trickle down" economics. Macroeconomic planners remain indifferent to such issues as the quality of life, the usefulness of product lines, or the deleterious effects of some kinds of investment compared to others. As Keynes wryly remarked somewhere, pump priming mechanisms are not concerned with whether workers dig holes, make destructive weapons, or engage in socially useful production—the whole point is to change the propensities of both investors and consumers by means of government intervention.

Some economists and social theorists who accept the ecological perspective which insists that the problem of the deteriorating quality of life as well as the dangers to the relationships between society and external nature demand a new attitude to economic growth have proposed the idea of "no-growth" economics. For most Americans, renouncing expansion implies renunciation of social mobility, personal happiness, and other aspects of the American dream. To pose the issue as economic growth against "no growth" is, in my view, counter to the objective of building a new political bloc. Some of those who would sound the alarm of uncontrolled investment have tended to abstract their concerns from the concrete aspirations of most Americans and therefore have foreclosed the chance of posing a serious challenge to the macroeconomic prescription for solving the crisis.

Growth has become a metaphor for progress and economic expansion a displacement of the quest for happiness. When puritanical appeals emanating from ecological "realists" urge Americans to abandon consumerism as an indefensible narcissism, they are performing an important unintended repressive function on behalf of the prevailing economic and political order. This position becomes even more egregious in the context of race and sex inequality, mass unemployment, and poverty. My position recognizes the validity of the arguments of those like Alan Wolfe who have argued that growth as an ideological imposition on the discourses of American politics has performed a repressive function in preventing social contradictions from becoming a public issue.[9] Moreover, the idea that an expanded pie is the key to progress has deeply mystified workers' consciousness of their own class position, or, to be more exact, has powerfully influenced the choice made by unions to enter a partnership with capital rather than engage in class struggle.

The degree to which the frontier and its successors have become entwined with the constitution of American ideology and have been formative of unconscious and conscious "needs," makes it unlikely that critics of the macrogrowth ideology will be heard unless progressives invent an alternative language for social and economic progress that incorporates the aspiration for psychological growth, empowerment, and self-management. In effect, a progressive discourse of expansion would combine the constituents of democratic control with the project of making economic policy consistent with an ecological conception of a better quality of life. This position is far from critics of industrial society who believe "small is beautiful," or those like Christopher Lasch and Jean Elshtain who would apply an anti-individualist ethic to social policy. A new politics would be obliged to argue that happiness is a political and social right, but that the dominant policies are linked to a false conception of growth that is opposed to personal development, community solidarity, and collective empowerment.

(3) Twenty-five years ago the civil rights movement succeeded in capturing America's imagination by penetrating the deeply felt aspirations shared by most Americans for freedom and equality. The movement won the support of most major unions, but, as in other segments of American life, was greeted with hostility by a substantial minority in the labor movement. When blacks and activists demanded "affirmative action" hiring, as well as upgrading programs in skilled trades and occupations in construction, media, health, and education, many trade unionists and professionals complained about "reverse discrimination" that barred whites from equal opportunity. For some unions black hiring demands were perceived as threats to job security in an increasingly uncertain labor market. A third group was just plain racist, arguing that blacks were incapable of performing certain tasks and unable to learn. When genetic issues were not raised, the spurious theories of social disorganization were invoked to thwart black aspirations. In the late 1960's women entered the historical stage with similar demands and found the same resistance both among employers and some unions who claimed that they were either physically or intellectually incapable of performing such jobs as firefighter, police officer, or manager.

(4) At the same time, as I have noted earlier, the peace movement poses one of the most difficult problems from the perspective of labor's relation to capital and the state because it has challenged the underlying logic of the permanent war economy. For many unions, including the dovish Machinists and the more conservative Steelworkers, foreign and military policy questions are bread and butter issues for their members. Although defense production employs fewer workers in proportion to capital investment than ever before because of the advanced character of military technologies, millions of union members, their families, and the communities in which the plants are located are, in effect, dependent on continuous military contracts to sustain their livelihoods. This economic fact of life has made many union leaders militant supporters of a strong defense establishment or, alternatively, reluctant to take public disarmament positions either because they fear political reprisals in their home locals or because they genuinely believe that the peace movement will hurt their members economically. Under these conditions it is remarkable that President William Winpinsinger of the Machinists has become a staunch advocate of bilateral negotiations to achieve arms control and eventual disarmament. Apart from the Machinists, the small independent

Electrical Workers Union and some UAW officials, few unions in defense industries have been willing to bite the hand that feeds them.

However, the economic reasons for labor's reticence on peace and disarmament are not sufficient to account for the generally pro-defense military position of the AFL-CIO. Many unionists sincerely believe the doctrine according to which there exists a threat of Soviet military aggression against the United States and Western Europe. Their support of Reagan's defense policy, although recently tempered by his excessive military budget under adverse economic conditions, is a continuation of a long tradition of collaboration between the American labor movement and U.S. foreign policy. Labor accepts cold war assumptions with more vehemence than any other major institutions of American society, in the first place because it is coherent with the historical legacy of the corporativist partnership since the First World War, secondly because powerful blocs of Eastern European immigrants have influenced labor's view of the Soviet Union, and finally because the internal struggle for political and ideological supremacy between anti-communists and the so-called left wing has colored labor's international perspectives. During the years immediately preceding his death in 1969, UAW President Walter Reuther began to significantly alter his own position, owing in a large measure to the influence of the anti-Vietnam war movement. Together with other progressive unionists, Reuther mounted an ideological attack on the virulent anti-communism of AFL-CIO chief George Meany. Reuther took his union out of the CIO in 1967 because of these and other disagreements while others, like Jerry Wurf of AFSCME and the Clothing Workers leaders, maintained their opposition to the close collaboration between the Federation, the State Department, and other responsible U.S. agencies in the conduct of U.S. foreign policy. Meany and his successor, Lane Kirkland, began to slowly dissociate themselves from the Reagan policy of supporting "authoritarian" regimes in the Third World that resisted social revolution, but AFL-CIO policy has not moved too far from its counterinsurgent anti-communism of the postwar period.

Today there is no consensus among AFL-CIO unions on international affairs. The UAW has gone so far as to enter discussions with auto workers unions in France and Italy that share similar problems with multinational corporations, despite their communist leadership. Similarly, the AFSCME had widened its contacts with union groups abroad with whom it does not share ideological agreement. These initiatives are still fairly rare in the American labor movement, but they indicate a tendency towards political independence in some unions with respect to AFL-CIO foreign policy that was virtually out of the question before 1965.

Trade unionists will not find solace in the unilateralist disarmament positions of many peace groups. The progressive wing of the labor movement is likely to continue to support the idea that the United States needs a strong military defense against international aggression. But it has already shown its interest in joining coalitions with peace groups on limited issues such as the nuclear freeze initiative which during the 1982 elections was approved by voters in nine states and many local communities. In many nuclear freeze campaigns, notably in California and Wisconsin, trade union officials from major unions and state and local labor councils differed from AFL-CIO policy by actively supporting the ballot initiatives. Second, a growing number of Federation affiliates have approved resolutions opposing the ballooning military budget, a task made considerably easier by the Reagan administration's perceived anti-labor stance on economic issues. In addition, the AFL-CIO has expressed reservations about the size of the budget for the first time in its history, a sign that the combined pressure of economic crisis and the growing role of the peace movement in American politics has made inroads among the more moderate and conservative unions.

However, it would be a mistake to place too much stock in mild AFL-CIO criticism of the military budget. International issues in the internal politics of the labor movement still divides left from right more than any other until now. The majority of unions are solidly on the right, not only on the arms budget but also on related issues such as the Middle East and attitudes towards the revolutionary movements in Latin America and U.S. policy in Western Europe. The only broad consensus within organized labor is support for the Polish Solidarity movement and opposition to the Soviet invasion of Afghanistan.

These experiences suggest that just as fractions of capital have joined in past progressive coalitions, the labor movement cannot be united in a single bloc. The working class is organized in dual labor markets according to job hierarchies, and the sexual and racial divisions of labor. Workers in different sectors enjoy differential access to job security, upgrading, income, and other measures of economic well-being; the uneven development of the labor movement corresponds to the uneven development of different sections of the economy. Moreover, unions have different ideological, political, and organizational traditions that condition their social receptivity. For example, the socialist tradition of the Machinists Union has mediated, to some degree, the ideological complexion of its leadership was well as its craft traditions which historically placed it in opposition to black and unskilled workers. The transformation of the union from a fairly typical craft organization to a mass industrial union in the 1940's helped bring it closer to the socially responsive CIO traditions, especially because its most direct competitors were two of the more democratic unions, the Auto Workers and the Electrical, Radio and Machine Workers. For these reasons it is not enough to specify the economic context of unionism when determining their political and ideological directions. The new political bloc will attract only a fraction of organized labor while others will remain fixed in the old politics for some time.

POLITICAL STRATEGIES

In the aftermath of the 1980 presidential election the AFL-CIO was constrained to formally abandon its official nonpartisan stance. In conformity with its practice of allying itself with the Democratic Party, the Federation declared that it intended to intervene in determining the next Democratic candidate in 1984 and that its executive council might make an endorsement before the spring primaries that year. AFL-CIO leaders were undoubtedly reluctant to become so openly partisan, but they had good reasons for reversing their traditional policy of informal alliance.

Since 1936 union leaders had been closely consulted by the party leadership on matters of the platform as well as selection of the presidential candidate. As I have argued, organized labor had been part of a leadership coalition that *constituted* the Democratic Party, not merely a junior partner. Until the mid-1960's the party was composed of four major groups: (1) the professionals who controlled its formal machinery, many of whom were leaders of big city political machines which enjoyed continuity between elected officials; (2) the liberal professionals who composed the key cadre of mass constituencies allied to the party, such as blacks and women, the Americans for Democratic Action, the NAACP (the leading civil rights organization until the 1960's), and the American Civil Liberties Union; (3) "representatives" of the liberal fraction of capital historically connected to the party, who were often Wall Street investment banking heads such as Herbert Lehman and Averell Harriman, or major regional capitalists like Joseph Kennedy from Boston, the Marshall Field family in Chicago, and an important group of Southern industrialists like Luther Hodges whose ties to the party had different roots than the corporate liberals; and (4) the trade union leaders. The trade union leaders who participated in the internal life of the party were by no means representative of more than a majority fraction of the labor movement and organized workers. Nevertheless, they were constituted as representations of the working class interest per se, which meant that labor functioned both as a pressure group for particular union interests and as the spokesperson for a broader constituency than its own membership.

The party convention was the major decision-making body between presidential elections. But although the Democrats relished floor fights because they rarely reached a consensus before any convention after Roosevelt, key labor leaders were frequently consulted as to whether a particular presidential hopeful was "acceptable" to them. The trade unions had virtual veto power over the Democratic candidate, but except at the local level where union leaders were free to support various "acceptable" candidates in accordance with regional and ethnic preferences, the national labor leaders never played their hand before the convention, preferring to lobby their favorites in private.

The preferential primary, which had force in only a minority of states until the 1960's, changed the old method of selection. Union leaders suddenly found themselves out of power within the party, not because they were not integrated into its apparatus, but because the apparatus was itself in the process of challenge from the outside. Eugene McCarthy never really had a chance for the Democratic nomination in 1968, but his strong anti-war candidacy against the insiders' favorite, Hubert Humphrey, encouraged George McGovern to try again four years later and he won. The top leaders of the AFL-CIO who favored Henry Jackson of Washington or stood reluctantly behind Humphrey found themselves outmaneuvered and defeated by a group of political amateurs headed by a grass roots movement of middle strata anti-war activists and a minority of union leaders who broke from the AFL-CIO's officially neutral position.

In 1976, the pattern set by McGovern was repeated by Jimmy Carter who emerged from nowhere (amply financed by large multinational contributions) to take the primaries and the convention by storm. Of course, organized labor made its peace with Carter well before the general election and supplied its resources of money and personnel to assist in his victory. But the pattern of consultation had temporarily been broken; unless labor was prepared to enter the primaries supporting its own candidate rather than one that is drawn from a larger list of acceptable aspirants, it would be condemned to following decisions made by others.

Whether the AFL-CIO leadership succeeds in persuading its executive council to become an overt political player in the Democratic primary, the announcement made in 1981 by the new Democratic National Chairman, Charles Mannatt, that power has returned to the professionals also signified the reemergence of the leadership coalition including labor. Fifteen AFL-CIO leaders have become members of the National Committee and will play a role in the selection process, even if it means that international unions will become the vehicle for labor's primary participation rather than the official Federation.

The most distressing feature of labor's new political strategy is that the most powerful wing of the Democratic Party is now the neo-liberal fraction. Its major intellectuals, Thurow, Amitai Etzioni, and Leonard Silk (economic columnist for *The New York Times*) have successfully shifted the entire political debate within the coalition to the right. In order to defeat Reagan a substantial group of labor leaders are prepared to go along with the "moderate" program of a reduced welfare state, balanced budgets, and national corporativist type planning (read worker sacrifices) to stimulate investments. In 1983, the leading neo-liberal candidates,

Senators Gary Hart of Colorado and John Glenn of Ohio, as well as the centrist former vice president, Walter Mondale, articulated the basic principles of the neo-liberal strategy for the economic crisis. Until 1982, their leading antagonist was Ted Kennedy, an almost classic proponent of the liberal old time religion; Kennedy's problems were not confined to controversies about his personal conduct but to the political perception that his position is somewhat arcane. These factors combined to force his decision not to enter the race for Democratic nomination. Welfare liberalism is simply inadequate to the present situation. It is based on economic policies that stress growth at the expense of ecological and structural considerations, and its political appeal is confined to restoring the social safety net, a position that gains widespread support among blacks, low wage industrial workers, and a large fraction of women but seems oblivious to the central problems associated with the new world economic order and the division of labor. To be sure, congressional liberals like Kennedy have slowly incorporated some of the most advanced concepts offered by progressives in the social movements, but these are not coherently integrated into a new approach to national economic and social planning; they are not oriented to redistributive justice except for the most economically disadvantaged groups.

Whatever the outcome of particular elections, I must distinguish two issues—creating a vehicle for a new political bloc, and the program on which that bloc will be formed.

The trade unions, major women's organizations such as the National Organization of Women and the Women's Political Caucus, the environmental groups, the peace movement and, to a lesser extent, the civil rights movement and a variety of locally based "citizens action" organizations engaged in diverse struggles such as housing, urban, and economic redevelopment politics, and energy organizing have each determined that their issue-based nonpartisan orientation requires substantial revision. Prompted by the conservative takeover of the Republican Party, these movements have been forced into greater partisanship in order to make the Democrats responsive to their demands.

Proponents of an independent "third" or labor party have traditionally argued that the Democrats are structurally incapable of embracing a genuinely progressive program. The Democratic platform, no matter how liberal, is invariably vitiated, they argue, by the congressional party, a measurably more conservative series of economic and ideological blocs than the convention. Therefore, to attempt to reform the party from within so that it can reflect the aspirations of its working class, blacks, women's constituencies, and its middle class base is to condemn the incipient progressive movement to frustration and defeat. Those holding these critical views typically invoke the European working class movement as an example worth emulating. They point to mass labor and socialist parties in all other advanced capitalist countries, including Canada where the New Democratic Party, formed in the 1960's, has been able to gather some twenty percent of the vote in federal elections, and has frequently captured political power in some Western Canadian provinces.

In the United States, a labor party formation is made difficult by legal factors, principally the absence of a parliamentary system and restrictive state laws making it difficult for third parties to gain ballot status. The American situation is complicated by the coalition character of the two major parties whose talent for integrating their potential opposition was generated by the specific circumstances of U.S. capitalist development discussed earlier. Nevertheless, the major reason there has not been a successful labor or socialist electoral vehicle at the national level is because the majority of the labor movement has never considered itself global opponents of capital. Instead it has been ideologically, if not always politically, integrated into the prevailing system. At the same time, it would be a serious error to assume that its participation within the Democratic Party has been marked by unrelieved subordination. Since the defeat of the Socialist Party as a serious challenger to the two major parties the Democrats were the American equivalent of European Social Democracy.

I do not wish to minimize the essential differences between the European mass *independent* socialist and workers parties and the Democratic Party in the United States where the labor movement has since 1966 (when the coalition began to unravel) played an increasingly subordinate role in a party that was never entirely its own. Yet the traditional left analysis which is content to brand the Democrats as "one of the two parties of finance capital" leads to a dead end. It ignores the incontrovertible fact that for most of this century workers, blacks, and a major fraction of professionals and other members of the middle strata have regarded the Democratic Party as their own.

There is, moreover, a second similarity between the Democratic Party and many European socialist parties which many radicals overlook: both have tended to be controlled by professional politicos. In the early years of the century the parties of socialism in western Europe were marked by mass participation in their affairs. But the trend since the end of the Second World War has been towards increasing professionalization of the party cadre and a growing reliance on the parliamentary party for leadership. This pattern has been reproduced in the United States. During the early years of the New Deal, the Democratic Party was dynamized by infusions of rank and file union leaders, groups from the black community and ethnic minorities from eastern and southern Europe. But with the breakup of cohesive concentrations of large-scale industry in the big cities (which lead to the decline of industrial unions and the traditional neighborhoods), the participation of workers in electoral affairs has been radically reduced. In the 1960's and early 1970's fractions of the "new class" of professional and technical employees entered the party's liberal wing and for a time edged the professional politicians from leadership in many states and in the national party. This struggle was especially facilitated by the reform of the primary system which allowed the insurgents to take control over the nomination of candidates away from the regular party organizations. Using the primary, any individual organized grouping could field candidates of their own. The two-election system in the United States favored liberal and left intervention in the Democratic Party during the rise of the civil rights and anti-war movements, and for a time the parties became a field of battle. However, today the old professional politicians seem to be succeeding in recapturing the party, especially in the face of the growing weakness of the labor movement on one hand and of the activists of the mass movements of the progressive middle strata minorities on the other.

Even so, the fact is that the primary system in the United States has made party structures much weaker than those of western Europe. The current efforts to resuscitate the Democratic political machine may succeed at the national level, if the "leadership" coalition composed of professional politicians, top union officials, and the leaders of the civil rights and women's national organization holds together around a program of limited welfare and social rights measures. In this scenario, the party would revert to its older style, in which the apparatus is administered by professionals who share power with the leaders representing large constituencies and that fraction of capital which is prepared to recognize the effectiveness of "left" corporatism.

The trouble with this strategy, as I have shown, is that there are substantial ideological and economic barriers to achieving even the modest defensive program of saving the remnants of the New Deal. Moreover, the tendencies of neo-liberal and liberal politicians to downplay or capitulate on social issues such as sexual rights, death penalty legislation, and other measures designed to strengthen democratic freedoms, has weakened the alliance that can save the welfare state's achievements. Finally, the macrogrowth ideology of mainstream Democrats has meant that they have been obliged to softpedal environmental issues, especially nuclear power and ecologically regressive growth of extractive industries. However desirable an independent political party that would become the vehicle of an emerging progressive alliance, the success of this strategy depends on resolving the ideological and programmatic issues facing the potential new partners. As I have argued, the first condition for achieving a new political vehicle is to conduct a determined struggle to free the labor movement of its reliance on the strategy of corporativism, that is, its dependence on the liberals and neo-liberals and its hesitancy to create a new partnership of opposition to the prevailing political culture, and its own traditions of contract unionism.

The first step in this long process is to make conscious the fact that the new and dynamic section of the labor movement is already constituted out of the mass constituencies of the new social movements. In this context the alliance would merely be the political form of an emerging integration at the grass roots. Since questions of leadership do not follow automatically from social and cultural changes, they must be addressed both separately and in relation to these changes. My argument is that labor's leadership is lagging behind the actual transition in the composition of the labor movement that is already underway. With major exceptions, the labor movement's policies presuppose conditions that no longer exist: a profile of the rank and file members as relatively prosperous, skilled and unskilled workers in a monopoly production sector industry or in construction and transportation trades which no longer describes the emerging majority. The old working class, embattled by capital flight, technological change and economic crisis, remains an important segment of the labor movement. But the new majority is a complex of relatively low wage public employees, workers in the retail and wholesale trades, and professionals whose fairly high incomes have not purchased a large measure of either job security or dignity on the job.

The unexpected is more characteristic of today's labor movement than ever before. For example, thirty years ago, the idea that baseball and football players would mount picket lines and stay on strike as long as steelworkers was far from anyone's predictions, least of all the athletes' themselves. But the integration of sports, the media, and the banks have produced a revolution of rising athlete expectations. Despite high incomes, professional athletes have a short productive career; any player lasting more than five years in the big leagues considers himself lucky. If injuries do not permanently consign him to the sidelines, the fierce competition for the tiny number of top slots will. More degrading than even the risk of permanent injury or failure, players were subject to veritable peonage. Although they were free to quit the game, they were slaves to the owners during their working careers. They were sold like property and, even if their pay was high compared to other workers, they could not switch teams if they received a better offer.

One of the most stunning developments in the labor movement over the past decade has been the explosion of organizing among professionals in the glamor industries. As television income has lined team owners' pockets, most players with few exceptions remained tied to short-term contracts in which there was no shared income provision. The complete transformation of professional sports into a business and the growing "class" awareness of players has produced not only a number of new players' unions but a new set of demands. In the two-month long 1982 football players' strike, one of the most hotly contested issues was the players' demand for a share in television income. Just as the baseball players had broken the famous "reserve" clause which had kept players in blatant bondage a decade earlier, the football players introduced a new dimension in glamor unionism. Even though they did not win this demand at the 1982 negotiations, the principle that workers are entitled to a share of technological benefits is likely to be among the key union demands of the future.

The new unionism would break down the barriers of traditional class distinctions enforced by statute, custom, and employer insistence that professionals and managerial employees remained tied to capital. This means that it would address explicitly the issues of domination and subordination at the workplace and in the political arena and would be obliged to formulate its economic and social demands under the single rubric of *self-management,* a framework that contains the fundamental ideological banner of redistributive justice, not only of economic resources but also of social and political power.

This framework is bound neither to the past in which the working class was more or less narrowly defined against intermediate as well as ruling classes, nor to the traditional working class politics. Thus, neither the concept of the specific *labor* party nor the old Gompers inspired partnership makes sense. The key link between actually existing organized labor and the new social movements including professionals will not be made until trade unions make conscious the dilemma of their old strategy and aggressively seek offensive alliances that put labor's program to deal with the crisis in opposition to those of the neo-liberals and the conservatives.

A PROGRAM FOR THE NEW PROGRESSIVE ALLIANCE

1. At the transitional level, labor and the social movements would make common cause with the Democratic Party liberals to restore and conceptually expand the safety net now being dismantled by the Reagan administration whose policies in this regard are treated with passive but benign acquiescence by neo-liberal "moderates" of both parties. Among the most important features of the program are:

   A. Raise federal standards for unemployment insurance to two years' coverage from the current six months and increase the minimum amount to half a worker's pay with no maximums. This is essentially the AFL-CIO program which, unfortunately, has not received the broad support it deserves.

   B. Amend the Wage and Hour Act by reducing the forty-hour week to thirty hours. This is an historic demand of the progressive wing of the

trade union movement made to ameliorate the catastrophe of technological change more than economic crisis. Clearly, it should be a major
bargaining demand in those industries with substantial technological
displacement but has not been advanced for the same reasons that have
caused labor's retreats in recent years. Nevertheless, a shorter work-
week is an integral part of an offensive program to shift the burden of the
crisis from workers to employers and would help reduce unemployment.

C. Permit no cuts in Social Security. This has been the singular success of
the liberal wing of the Democratic Party in the late 1970's and 1980's,
principally because organized labor has been joined by a powerful organization of senior citizens who are today the most politicized movement in the country. A sizable portion of the senior citizens activist core
was recruited from among retired trade unionists.[10]

D. Major jobs program. The "rebuilding America" proposals of the Machinists Union included more than the liberals have traditionally bargained
for. Not only do they call for massive public works but also for conver-
sions of abandoned or underutilized plants which could be retooled to
produce goods for social use rather than war materials or goods for which
the plant is no longer competitive. Such a jobs program would also
incorporate the principle of government as employer of last resort. This
commitment would entail expanding social sector institutions such as
schools as well as job training and health care, especially if the alliance
pressed for the enactment of a national health program that went beyond medical care for the aged.

E. Government investment funds would be made available for worker buy-
outs and community ownership schemes to save plants abandoned by
capital flight. The alliance would support the Kennedy Bill for the renovation of mass transit through government owned and worker managed
production facilities.

F. Immediate passage of the Equal Rights Amendment and renewed enforcement of affirmative action hiring in all Jobs and Training programs,
especially in the construction industry where the hiring of blacks and
women has remained miniscule throughout the 1970's and early 1980's
even in those regions where unions and employers made some efforts to
alter hiring practices. The importance of the anti-discrimination programs is especially great now that both parties have agreed to enact
some legislation aimed at rebuilding the eroded infrastructures of urban
and rural areas. Unless labor joins the civil rights and women's movements in a determined effort to make sure that increasing employment
opportunities are shared with women and minorities, the effect of a new
public works program can be to sharpen the discriminatory employment
patterns that have contributed to the perpetuation of considerable black
poverty even in prosperous times.

Such programs as the domestic content bill must be strongly pushed by
the progressive alliance.[11] At the same time, labor and other social movements need renewed focus on a national retraining program directed to

displaced workers. This program should be financed out of general funds but should also be linked to legislation that provides guaranteed income as well as training allowances for workers impacted adversely not only by foreign competition as in current legislation, but also by technological change as provided in the Machinists' Technological Bill of Rights.

The basic ideological orientation of all these short-term measures must be anti-militarist and redistributive. In the first place, the relative strength of the European welfare state is demonstrably due as much to the fact that most of these countries have been free of the crushing burden of unproductive arms expenditures since the end of the Second World War as to the power of their labor movements to enforce its provisions. The current transition in American labor's position on the arms buildup opens up new opportunities for political debate in the coming decade. Cutting the military budget is a major source of revenue but would still require a new source of general revenue to alleviate the American worker of the burden of the economic crisis and the world realignment.

2. The progressive alliance would have to make arguments that showed the benefits to private corporations of public facilities such as roads, water, communications, transportation, and sanitation. These corporations should be required to pay the costs of these services since roads and mass transit facilities bring workers to and from the job, most water is consumed by industry, and sanitation, except for private households, is engaged in cleaning the waste products of commercial and industrial firms.

3. One of the major features of any industrial society is the need for a literate labor force. Increasing knowledge of mathematics and reading and writing are the basic skills without which industry cannot reproduce, much less expand. Corporations have joined the neo-conservative attack against public education as a boondoggle for unproductive professionals. They have countered in the past decade by stepping up their "contributions" to private universities such as MIT, Columbia, and other Ivy League institutions which have more or less openly declared their alliance with business. These universities train middle and top managers and the leading scientific and technological professionals whose labor is necessary for resuming capital accumulation. Consistent with a historical arrangement, the commanding heights of multinational corporations have insisted that the costs of training technical, service, and manual workers remains the responsibility of the public sector but have been increasingly reluctant to share the social costs. Given the fiscal crisis of local governments, raising corporate taxes and taxes on high personal incomes is the only means by which federal funds can be raised to assure that public elementary, secondary, and post-secondary schools are able, even in theory, to provide the basic education workers need to become active

workers, much less have opportunities to enter skilled and professional ranks.

4. America needs national legislation that limits the ability of capital to migrate at will within the United States and to other parts of the world. Tax policy should be directed to providing penalties for such arbitrary migration. Alternatively, federal tax incentives should be retained for corporations that agree to recapitalize existing facilities and provide retraining for existing workers. The extent of penalties would have to be sufficient to constitute a deterrent to migrate.

Neither the program for restoring the social safety net nor a tax policy that reverses new tendencies by shifting the burden of taxes back to the corporations is beyond the scope of liberal ideology. In some respects it would propose a new program for rebuilding America along the lines of the old New Deal, but would differ in three major respects: although it would recognize defense needs, it would renounce both militarism and the old Keynesian penchant for deficit financing because it would raise revenues from a class-based tax policy.

The boundaries of a progressive/liberal coalition are the issues of what I have called zero sum, redistribution, anti-corporate politics. Here, as I have argued previously in this book, one can expect only a fraction of capital, its political allies, and its intellectuals to join a new political bloc if the progressives succeed in imposing their social and intellectual weight on discourses about economic policy. If the social movements remain internally fragmented and organizationally weak, the likely result will be a piecemeal incorporation of elements of this program into a new corporativist consensus, the liberality of which depends entirely on the relationship of political forces instead of the rationality of the proposals. The boundary on the left remains the question of whether labor will break from its exclusive concern with short-term economic reforms to join with movements seeking a different type of redistributive justice, the extension of "democratic vistas" to include sexual, ecological, and racial freedom whose parameters include, but are not confined by, economic criteria. The fundamental theoretical question here is the difference between economic definitions and social criteria for freedom. The importance of the workplace-based concerns with democratizing the workplace by sharing authority in the labor process over investment decisions, merger agreements, and product selection is their interaction with movements concerned with women's autonomy; liberating nature from what Herbert Marcuse has called instrumental rationality in which the external world is regarded as no more than raw material for exploitation by the production machine; and black freedom—in addition to its struggle for economic opportunity and social equality, the black freedom movement has raised the serious issue concerning racism as a form of cultural and social domination.

Beyond the transitional program is a program to end the domination of nature by society, women by men, blacks by whites, and labor by capital. These questions are already on the agenda of new social movements in many parts of the world including our own, although they are not contained by demands embodied in transitional proposals such as public control over investment, a class-based tax policy, and a broad social welfare state. They are concerned with the old dream of the whole person and recognize that economic, social, and cultural questions are part of a wider vision of ending social domination in all aspects of social relations.

It is no longer a question of an external alliance between labor and other movements; the cultural and political successes of the new movements have already produced a new ideological *sensibility* within broad fractions of the labor movement which includes, but is not dominated by, the old fraction working class that still adheres to an (attenuated) kind of class-based social unionism. In practice, the new demands have expressed themselves in the program of *The Green Party* in Germany, an independent party of feminists, ecologists, and youth which has captured five percent of the vote and has shaped the program of the left wing of the Social Democratic Party which also adopted much of the transitional economic program discussed here. In France, the program of the ruling Socialist party has adopted a New Deal-type safety net policy with the important addition of nationalization of investment mechanisms and research and development activities. The left wing of the British Labour Party is committed to the main tenets of a program that embraces the concept of the political bloc discussed here and has succeeded in persuading a fraction of the trade union movement to join it; and, of course, much of the Machinists' program on technology is borrowed from that of Scandinavian labor whose political vehicle, the Social Democratic Party, is really an alliance between the unions and social movements concerned with issues of domination. The left-sponsored referendum in Sweden that would have suspended nuclear power development went down to defeat at the polls but succeeded in gaining substantial electoral support.

Although it is premature to expect any major section of the Democratic Party, including most of organized labor, to support an economic and social platform that would begin to raise new historic demands, these ideas are already in circulation, mostly framed as democratically controlled reindustrialization programs:

1. Traditionally labor and progressive movements in Europe have not been content to support nationalization of sick industries such as steel, coal, and autos in order to forestall mass unemployment and industrial collapse. "Lemon socialism" has been sharply criticized in recent years because it simply reproduces the historical tendency for the capital to cut its losses by socializing those investment sectors that are unprofitable. Such was the case in the United States with the recent nationalization of

the rail system and earlier with nationalization of private power development in rural areas during the Depression that gave rise to the
Tennessee Valley Authority, Metropolitan Transit systems, and other enterprises abandoned by risk capital.

The French have taken a different path by nationalizing some technologically advanced sectors as well as completing the bank nationalization
begun earlier. Although a system of genuine self-management, co-
management, or workers' control has not been instituted, these moves
represent a departure from lemon socialism worth emulating in the
United States. Public control over investment through tax policy, regulation, and nationalization are particularly urgent if the threat posed by
capital strikes (which is really what capital flight is) to redistributive
policies is to be averted. Critics of proposals for structural reforms for the
economy have reminded social innovators that the most likely result of
any serious effort to control investment would be accelerated capital migration, nonproductive saving, and a fierce political counterattack by
large corporations which over the past several years have mobilized themselves for more direct intervention in the political process than ever
before. They point out (rightly) that control over investment by the state
entails nationalization because capital's political and economic resistance
would be effective as long as investment remained exclusively a corporate
decision.

Of course, co-management of investment steering mechanisms does
not imply blanket nationalization of all businesses. For example, small
companies would actually benefit from such public programs because
credit controls would be geared to making small investment easier than
technological and other investments that could be undertaken only by
large corporations. In addition, private sector corporations prepared to
cooperate with socially useful programs would be granted consideration
in determining interest rates, government contracts, and tax policies. In
some cases, notably those industries where private investment has been
more or less permanently shifted, public corporations would be established under workers' control. These corporations would eventually revert to workers or community ownership.

2. High on a progressive agenda would be the restoration of the corporate profits tax which has been all but eliminated by the last two administrations. This would raise considerable revenue from such tax-free
corporations as the oil industry, the utilities, and others which historically
have been able to take advantage of so-called loopholes that permit tax
writeoffs for exploration and capital accretion programs. All capital growth
would be taxed.

3. Industrial development would be ecologically mediated. I refer to
more than environmental protection for such resources as water, air,
minerals, and forests which are the traditional concerns of the movement.

I want to emphasize the importance of a wider conception of ecology to include forms of social domination. For example, publicly directed investment programs would be required not only to promote a racially and sexually integrated labor force, but also to meet high standards of occupational safety and health which might preclude certain enterprises. The new health issue of stress would obviously occupy prominent consideration in advanced sectors, a criterion that might require mandatory programs of labor process transformation which embody the broad principles of autonomy, self-management, and skill development to enable task rotation.

4. As in France, the federal government should assume responsibility for directing investment in the development of natural resources, scientific discovery and technological innovation. Nationalizing these functions would not necessarily induce democratic control over research and development unless specific measures were taken to bring workers and affected citizens on policy boards charged with oversight of these activities. Even the traditional regulatory functions of the federal government, as coopted by corporations as they have in the past, provide a formal means for redress. Environmentalists, displaced workers, and professionals would be able to share information that could lead to substantial intervention in policy making if these were public sector activities.

5. The absolute right of all workers to strike would be guaranteed by law. I place this demand beyond the consensual program of a progressive liberal alliance because it is extremely controversial among many for whom public service is still not considered a labor process and for whom public workers are still civil servants.

6. A sweeping new immigration policy would be instituted which recognizes the American traditions of liberty not only for victims of political repression but also for the millions who have suffered the economic exploitation and social domination imposed by multinational policies of subjecting other countries to dependency. Labor and its allies would have a serious debate on many of these provisions. Clearly the United States cannot be the refuge for the whole underdeveloped world even if the United States and Western powers are responsible for maintaining these conditions. On the other hand, the millions of recent immigrants must be granted amnesty and a rational immigration policy removing the arbitrary authority of employers is urgently needed.

7. The progressive political bloc would be required to introduce new concepts guiding U.S. foreign economic and military policy. It would oppose U.S. support of "authoritarian" as well as "totalitarian" regimes and acknowledge the legitimacy of movements for national independence and political and social liberation, even those with which the United States disagrees. At the same time, American foreign labor policy would encourage the formation of democratic labor movements in every coun-

try, including the absolute right of workers to strike and to control their own organizations. American foreign policy would be guided by the same principles of democratic and social policy within the United States. This is not the place to discuss these issues in detail, but any analysis of the U.S. political climate since the war will immediately recognize the importance of a large-scale renovation of U.S. policy abroad which inhibits the possibility of a new politics at home.

8. In the past decade many unions, economists, and social movements have raised the question about the social uses of the vast union-administered pension and social welfare fund. More recently, some have been asked whether an American version of the Meidner plan, introduced by Swedish Social Democrats, could be applied in this country. The Meidner plan would invest these funds in industries as a means of stimulating worker control over investment decisions and workplace organization. Unions would gradually take over ownership and control of key industries as well as deploy funds for other social uses.

In the United States unions have debated whether to shift pension fund investments from private sector corporations to housing, day care, and other socially useful production and services. Current state and federal laws limit the autonomy of pension administrators in making investment decisions to profitable activities. And, of course, even where pension funds represent a major portion of capitalization of a given firm, the union has assumed little or no responsibility for taking a role in these corporations' investment programs. But, as the union struggle against J.P. Stevens shows, union power can be mobilized to force these corporations to conform to standards of economic and social justice precisely because of the close ties between brokers and investment bankers, many of whom sit on corporate boards of directors, and the unions. Today's challenge is to find the legal and social conditions to wield pension power for social uses that can protect the fiscal integrity of the funds. Unions could easily play an enormous role in a program of reindustrialization for social use and provide new services such as housing and day care to their members and other working people with these funds.

9. In the 1930's the Social Security System became a major New Deal innovation because unions and other advocates of federally financed pensions compromised by permitting the system to remain separate from the general treasury. The current crisis in social security has been produced in a large measure by the economic crisis, but more saliently by the inability of this mode of financing to keep up with demographic trends that make more Americans eligible for benefits. The coming collapse of the Social Security System has not been produced by either of these factors but by its separation from normal means of collecting funds. Labor, senior citizens, and others concerned with saving the Social Se-

curity System must fight to integrate the program in the general treasury funds. Similarly, proposals for national health care should not be made part of the Social Security System as presently organized unless this is seen as a short-term arrangement.

CONCLUSION

I have argued that the revitalization of the American labor movement depends, now as before, on its ability to forge a political alliance with new social movements. Secondly, I have shown that the conditions which prevented the trade unions and other elements of the labor movement from charting an independent political course have come to an end; today, capital's gain is the worker's loss since the economic pie can only expand if workers accept a new partnership that will result in the long-term decline of their hard won standard of living. Third, I have offered a program appropriate to a new labor strategy of political and ideological independence.

These proposals only specify the *conditions of possibility* and cannot predict that the current labor leadership or the rank and file will choose a new course. The questions remain. Are there material grounds for hope? Do the defeats of the past decade prefigure a rebirth?

Nearly twenty years ago, Andre Gorz and Serge Mallet argued that the scientific and technological revolution (call it automation, cybernation, "high" technology) contains an intrinsic contradiction; while capital has finally reached a historical stage where its dream of the elimination of most of manual labor from the process of production and reproduction is within reach, the old crafts, the semiskilled and unskilled workers have been so reduced in social power that they no longer constitute a political threat to the social system. Intellectual labor finally dominates manual labor in all advanced industrial countries. To a large extent "mechanical reproduction" has been removed to the less advanced nations but even there such technologies as robotics, numerical controls, and microprocessors have replaced unskilled labor. In the advanced countries there is a veritable army of intellectual labor at all levels of the occupational hierarchy—the technical intelligentsia as well as the millions of clerical workers and the proletarianized technical wage workers.

The various middle strata which in the age of mechanization were successfully integrated by capital as its managerial arm, also find themselves distanced from power. These occupations no longer entail significant authority at the workplace, nor are they secure signs of status, prestige, or honor. In this context, professionalism, long regarded as a conservative social ideology because its parameters separated an important stratum from the mass worker, becomes an unexpected source of social and political opposition. The new intellectual, robbed of a position near the top of the occupational hierarchy, tried in the 1960's and 1970's to regain social power by means of engaging in social movements such as ecological struggles, feminism, and professional trade unionism. Similarly, the millions of women who entered the labor force only to discover that oppression at the workplace followed subordination at home have demonstrated political and economic militancy far in advance of traditional production workers.

The source for a new "labor movement" is precisely the same as that for the victory of capital in the past two decades: having defeated the strong production unions by means of capital flight, technical innovation, and recession, the large corporations confront their own "cadre" as formidable opponents. The business journals are once again rehearsing the litany of productivity crisis, alienated labor, and political disaffection. Sociologists perceive the new revolt as "fragmentation," and the new social movements present themselves as middle class protest movements. However, another way of understanding the "consumer" or middle class is to comprehend them in terms of the new conditions that have produced mass proletarianization among the technical and professional intelligentsia. Although by no means the only forces brought into existence by the new international division of labor and its accompanying technological revolution, the various strata that constitute the "new class" are clearly the most dynamic and volatile among recently formed social groups.

The transformation of industrial capitalism into late capitalism has also produced a new proletariat within advanced capitalist countries. As we have seen, it is formed by the conjunction of immigration and migration, the "liberation" of manual labor from factories, the proliferation of masses of unemployed youth and people considered too old to work by the economic order. In an age of contraction, stagnation, and slow growth, these workers are either permanently excluded from the labor force or consigned to the subterranean niches of the underground economy and the low paid service sectors. The United States has not yet felt the full impact of the economic degradation of large portions of its basic population. Mass disaffection has not yet taken political paths, but expresses itself as social disorder, crime, and silent protests of which illiteracy, apathy, and indifference are the names affixed by mainstream social commentators and administrators. The current economic crisis has increased their number by exponential proportions. Although, thus far, no mass social movements have appeared to express their conditions and represent their interests, such quiescence is, at best, a temporary respite for those who have gained by the misery of the underclasses. Even as social scientists proclaim the anomie, the disorganization that poverty is supposed to reinforce, some straws in the wind belie these safe forecasts. The formation of a permanent sub-proletariat is as foreign to American ideology as the Depression has been to its expectations. The resurgence of concern with issues of race and ethnicity reflects both the partial setbacks suffered by the civil rights movement and broad-scale recognition by policymakers that race and class issues are social dynamite. After fifteen years during which the corporate order created a new black middle class even as the conditions of life deteriorated for the mass of racial and national minorities, we have learned that the "race issue" won't go away, especially in times of economic crisis and technological restructuring that has resulted in the profound misery of nearly all peoples of color.[1]

My contention has been that only the politicization of social protest can produce a resurgent labor movement and that the "new" labor movement must itself become a social alliance that links work and living spaces, economic, political and social struggle. These perspectives are far from the recent traditions of the actual labor movement but close to the new situation that it faces. What remains unknown is whether, after an analysis shows what *must* be done, the rank and file as well as the leadership of the contemporary trade union, civil rights, women's, and middle class "consumer" movements, possess the social imagination to see their common interest—the formation of a new political bloc that opposes the priorities of capital.

I want to enter two major caveats: (1) The broad outlines of a political/ electoral program envisioning a new political bloc within which labor will play a key role does not replace collective bargaining, since the contract remains a vital constraint on the arbitrary power of capital, as well as a powerful weapon for advancing workers' struggles for a democratic workplace. (2) The task of forging a new political bloc is difficult because it would break from the traditions not only of trade unions but also of the sectorally bound social movements. These traditions have locked all of its potential partners in positions that appear etched in stone. As we know, rational argument is only one way to effect social and political change. Ideology often hangs on long after the conditions that produced it have disappeared. Therefore, there can be no certainty that despite the force of analysis the American working class, the trade unions, will be able to break with their own traditions, many of which are inscribed in centuries of struggle.

On the other hand, there exist more hopeful new currents within organized labor than at any time since before the war. A growing number of rank and file, middle level, and top union leaders are beginning to challenge the limitations of labor's program and to seriously consider alternatives. Further, especially at the local level, the number and quality of issue-based coalitions that include trade unions, women, civil rights, environmental, and peace groups, have proliferated in the past five years. Finally, trade unionists throughout the country in conferences, union meetings, and informal discussions are debating many questions that were buried for most of the last forty years—the need for a new independent political vehicle that departs from the old liberal coalition dominates the agenda of these discussions, but there is also energy in union organizing among the older unions such as the Service Employees and some Garment Workers' locals, and some of the newer groups such as clerical workers and scientists and engineers are raising new issues labor has conventionally refused to confront.

Most hopeful of all, many trade unionists recognize that a crisis exists in the labor movement and that it has profound political and ideological dimensions. Some take refuge in building better economic mousetraps, but many others are engaged in the difficult and often frustrating process of rethinking. It is to these dedicated, radical, and militant bearers of the new workers' political culture that this book has been dedicated.

NOTES

INTRODUCTION

1. Phillip Foner, *History of the Labor Movement in the United States*, 4 vols. (New York: International Publishers, 1954–67).
2. Selig Perlman, *The Theory of the Labor Movement* (New York: Augustus Kelley, 1928, 1970).
3. Jeremy Brecher, *Strike!* (New York: Straight Arrow Books, 1972).
4. James Green, *World of the Worker* (New York: Hill & Wang, 1980).
5. Before the passage of the Wagner Act, the question of state economic intervention had long been resolved among leading factions of business. If they had refused the state's role in directing investment, it was due to the relatively buoyant economy that prevailed after the Civil War until the late 1920's. The depth of the crisis resolved that issue painfully, but the last remnant of the nineteenth century liberal ideology was the notion of the free labor market which in practice meant implaccable opposition to labor unions.

CHAPTER 1

1. Rudolph Hilferding, *Finance Capital* (London: Routledge & Kegan Paul, 1981), p. 351.
2. Samuel Gompers, *Seventy Years of Life and Labor,* 2 vols. (New York: E.P. Dutton & Co., 1925).
3. Ibid., vol. 2, chap. 36.
4. Ibid.
5. Jesse S. Robinson, *The Amalgamated Association of Iron, Steel and Tin Workers* (Baltimore: Johns Hopkins University Press, 1920), p. 21.
6. Victoria de Grazia, *The Culture of Consent* (New York and Cambridge, London: Cambridge University Press, 1981).
7. C. Wright Mills, *The New Men of Power* (New York: Oxford University Press, 1948), p. 223.

CHAPTER 2

1. Christian Palloix, "The Labor Process: From Fordism to Neo-fordism," in *Labor Process and Class Strategies*, CSE pamphlet, no. 1 (1976).
2. David Montgomery, *Workers Control in America* (London: Cambridge University Press, 1979).
3. Herbert Gutman, *Work, Culture and Society* (New York: Vintage Books, 1977).
4. Samuel Gompers, *Seventy Years of Life and Labor,* 2 vols. (New York: E.P. Dutton & Co., 1925), vol. 1, p. 244.
5. Of course Lewis was the best example of this change, but he was followed by a

large number of AFL leaders, including Dave Beck of the Teamsters, Al Hayes of the Machinists, Harry Van Arsdale of the Electrical Workers and many others.

CHAPTER 3

1. Arthur Goldberg, *AFL-CIO: Labor United* (New York: McGraw Hill, 1956).
2. No comprehensive study has been made, as yet, of the fate of the eleven unions expelled from the CIO in 1949. However, with the exception of the West Coast Longshoremens and Warehousemens Union and the United Electrical Workers, all the rest have disappeared as national unions. Mine Mill and Smelter Workers were absorbed by the Steelworkers after years of intraunion rivalry; the Office and Professional Workers led their shrunken membership into District 65 or the State, County and Municipal Employees. The Food and Tobacco Workers were grabbed by the AFL Tobacco Workers in the South or joined the Longshoremen on the West Coast; the Fur and Leather Workers became a division of the Meatcutters, later to become part of the Food and Commercial Workers, but not before its top leaders were forced to resign because of their Communist Party links. The Farm Equipment Workers went into the UAW after considerable raiding which resulted in serious losses; and the Public Workers, which never enjoyed collective bargaining because its Federal government members were barred from such benefits until the 1960's, were dispersed in a number of unions such as the Teamsters and AFSCME.
3. The irony is that some of the most socially conscious unionists tend to enter these partnerships precisely because they are painfully aware of the "folly" of taking the path of opposition given the vagaries of American political culture. Often the so-called "business unionists" are among the most militant in defense of workers' gains. Unencumbered by a social vision that constrains them to grasp the big picture, the "pure and simple" leaders are more likely to conduct strikes against work rule changes such as those imposed on railroad workers over the past twenty years or the resistance offered by construction unions against the imposition of technological changes in the building industry on the East Coast. UAW Douglas Fraser, a prominent social unionist, led his union's grant of substantial wage and work rule concessions to Chrysler, Ford and General Motors corporations when they threatened to shut down plants. This act of "responsible" unionism is a sharp contrast to the resistance offered by many "business" unions.
4. For the best accounts of the fiscal crisis facing cities, see James O'Conner, *Fiscal Crisis of the State* (New York: St. Martin's Press, 1971) and William Tabb, *The Long Default: New York City and the Urban Fiscal Crisis* (New York: Monthly Review Press, 1982).
5. J. David Greenstone's *Labor in American Politics* (Chicago: University of Chicago Press, 1969) is still the only comprehensive treatment of labor political activity.
6. In the wake of the devastation of America's steel industry, the Steelworkers union has been slow to respond with alternative programs despite the loss of over 50 percent of the union's membership in basic steel. Its only response

has been to cooperate with the industry's demand for concessions or ameliorating its membership declines by mergers with other unions.

7. "The Reindustrialization of America," *Business Week,* 30 June 1980.

CHAPTER 4

1. For a classic discussion of this point, see Serge Mallet, *The New Working Class* (London: Spokesman Books, 1975).

2. That there is no intrinsic logic determining the specific demands advanced by workers in response to their loss of autonomy in the labor process is illustrated by the examples of Poland and Italy, where workers focused on the demand for self-management rather than less work. This demonstrates my argument that the *character* of workers' struggles, as distinct from their elementary existence, obeys a cultural logic that countervails the logic of capital in accordance with particular conditions. See my "The End of Political Economy," *Social Text 2* (Summer 1979), pp. 3–52.

3. For the purposes of this article, I use the term "economism" to denote the penchant of American workers and their unions to rely essentially on the strike weapon and collective bargaining to win their demands; accompanying this inclination is the tendency to eschew electoral or ideological politics. This usage differs somewhat from Lenin's characterization, in *What Is to Be Done,* of the group led by Asimov in the Russian Social Democratic Labor Party, for whom the workers' struggle at the point of production was held to be a primary avenue for revolutionary action. American economism in the labor and progressive movements assumes (a) that workers are only interested in wages and benefits or shop floor issues, (b) that politics is a foreign discourse because it implies ideological appeals, and (c) that the fate of the unions is decided by the vicissitudes of the national economy. These precepts have become a self-fulfilling prophecy in the United States.

4. As I have noted in *False Promises* (New York: McGraw-Hill, 1973), there was no debate within the CP or the Trotskyist movement concerning the relation of collective bargaining to revolution, or even the development of a political culture within the working class, on the eve of the enactment of the Wagner Act in 1935. Most of the ideological left regarded the legal guarantee of the right to form unions of the workers' choosing as an unmixed blessing.

CHAPTER 5

1. See Alan Brinkley, *Voices of Protest: Huey Long, Father Coughlin and the Great Depression* (New York: Alfred A. Knopf, 1982). This book documents the enormous influence of these right wing populist movements on the Roosevelt administration's final determination to enact major social welfare measures.

2. The two outstanding examples in this period were the Ford Motor Company and the so-called "little" steel companies led by the fiercely anti-union Tom Girdler of Republic Steel.

3. Martin Glaberman, *Wartime Strikes* (Detroit: Bewick Editions, 1980).

4. For the most detailed account of the 1946 strikes, see Jeremy Brecher, *Strike!* (New York: Straight Arrow Books, 1972).

5. Alonzo L. Hamby, *Beyond the New Deal: Harry Truman and American Liberalism* (New York: Columbia University Press, 1973), chap. 2.
6. There are few balanced treatments of the CIO split. For a generally anti-communist account, see Irving Howe and B.J. Widick, *The UAW and Walter Reuther* (New York: W.W. Norton, 1955); and Max Kampelmann, *The Communist Party and the CIO* (New York: Praeger, 1957). For pro-expelled unions' view, Len de Caux, *Labor Radical* (Boston: Beacon Press, 1972) is the account of a participant. Also, James Green, *World of the Worker* (New York: Hill & Wang, 1980 [pp. 186–209]) is generally critical of the expulsions despite his reservations about the role played by the CP during the period.
7. Hamby, *Beyond the New Deal*, p. 216. But Murray's conversion was preceded by his genuinely heroic efforts to preserve the left-center coalition. On this, see Hamby, *Beyond the New Deal*, pp. 148–49, and Green, *World of the Worker*, pp. 199–201.
8. See Stanley Aronowitz, *False Promises* (New York: McGraw-Hill, 1973), chap. 4.
9. In Great Britain, where the Labor Government took a frankly redistributive line, it achieved massive changes in welfare benefits; but in Germany and Italy the working class and its parties were defeated well into the 1960's. The conditions for the revival of world capitalism after the war entailed a considerable degree of compromise by a labor movement unable to offer a systemic alternative. The U.S. working class was prepared to fight aggressively for gains within the U.S. capitalist hegemony, but lacked the ideological traditions of the British working class in which the struggle for political gains was part of the general labor movement.
10. The 1970's working class television figure Archie Bunker is indeed a mass cultural representation of the Bunker mentality of a substantial section of the temporarily "bourgeoisified" worker of the period. Significantly, Bunker buys a tavern in the 1980's, leaving his precarious proletarian existence behind and simultaneously realizing the far horizon of manual labor's version of the American dream.
11. See Glaberman, *Wartime Strikes*.
12. The struggle for workers democracy and community self-determination has consistently been misnamed "populism" by liberals and radicals alike. The American populist tradition is a movement of small business and is historically rooted in agricultural communities. The council movement and labor anarchism are urban movements. Their call for forms of popular control over the workplace and the neighborhood are at the same time alternative strategies to the traditional Marxist emphasis on seizing state power as the first step toward social transformation.
13. The paper was published in 1963 as a discussion document for debate within the organization on the question of moving beyond campus organizing to ghetto and slum communities.
14. C. Wright Mills, *The New Men of Power* (New York: Oxford University Press, 1948), p. 223.
15. This is not to deny that the production of chips, control robots, etc., entails the employment of considerable manual labor. The issue is the degree of

subordination of the manual laborer to knowledge, whose principal personifications are managerial and technical intelligentsia.

16. The specificity of the relations of production contains of course a structural and an historical moment: the former is the position occupied by various types of labor with respect to the question of ownership and control: the latter is the development of class struggles, which alter the relations of domination within the framework of capitalist production relations. The degree to which class struggles are inscribed in the historical character of relations of production we may designate, following Sartre, the practico-inert. It appears a facticity, its history rubbed out. Cultural life—the community formation without which sustained struggles at the economic and political levels are unlikely if not unthinkable—becomes then the precondition for class struggle.

17. See Aronowitz, *False Promises*, chap. 3.

CHAPTER 6

1. This indifference was not always the case. Between 1940 and 1950 several CIO unions, notably the Office and Professional Workers, The Federation of Architects, Technicians and Engineers that later merged with UOPWA, and the Public Workers, succeeded in organizing bank employees, professionals and many clerical workers in the private sector. At one time just before the CIO split the UOPWA had 7000 bank and other financial services employees under contract with more than a dozen banks. These were all lost during the split. See Mark McColloch, "White Collar Unionism," *Science and Society,* Winter 1982–83.

2. *Handbook of Labor Organizations,* U.S. Department of Labor, 1980.

3. However, these fears were not mere fantasies in the early decades of the twentieth century when textile unionism encountered frequent employer use of black labor to replace striking white workers in the mills.

4. David J. Garrow, *The FBI and Martin Luther King Jr.* (New York: W.W. Norton Co., 1981), p. 189.

5. Ibid., p. 213–16.

6. In a conversation with the author.

7. Susan Reverby, "Work Hierarchies in the Health Industry," in *Health-PAC Bulletin,* 1977.

8. Although, in 1982 half of physicians' assistants were women.

9. American preeminence in machine production is now seriously under attack by French, German, and Japanese competitors, but the technological lead enjoyed by the United States is difficult to overcome in all sectors and there are reasons to assert that the alignment of world production of capital goods, chiefly electronically based control equipment linked to cybernetics, will find the United States in a strong position for some time to come.

10. "Race Against Time: Automation of the Office," *Working Women* (Cleveland, 1980), p. 5.

11. Shoshana Zuboff, "New Worlds of Computer Mediated Work," *Harvard Business Review,* Sept.–Oct. 1982, p. 144.

12. Joan M. Greenbaum, *In the Name of Efficiency* (Philadelphia: Temple University Press, 1979), pp. 64–65.
13. Serge Mallet, *The New Working Class* (London: Spokesman Books, 1975), pp. 2–3.
14. Phillip Kraft, *Programmers and Managers: The Routinization of Computer Programming in the United States* (New York: Heidelberg Science Library Springer-Verlag, 1977), quoted in Greenbaum, *In the Name of Efficiency*, p. 17.
15. This is not the place to rehearse the ambiguous legacy of AFT involvement in educational issues. Suffice it to say here that the union has been caught in the contradiction between its own craft union character and its social traditions. On the one hand, it takes an active interest in broad matters of educational policy beyond the immediate employment concerns of its members. On the other, it has frequently posed its parochial interests against those of parents who have demanded greater voice in the administration of schools, particularly over curriculum and teacher selection. The union has sided with the traditional education bureaucracy, civil service law and local governments which it perceives as more sympathetic than community control advocates to its particular interests.
16. Clive Jenkins and Barrie Sherman, *White Collar Unionism: The Rebellious Salariat* (London: Routledge & Kegan Paul, 1979).

CHAPTER 7

1. *Business Week*, 30 June 1980.
2. Raford Boddy and James Croddy, "Class Conflict and Macro-policy: The Political Business Cycle," *Review of Radical Political Economics*, Spring 1975.
3. Barry Bluestone and Bennett Harrison, *The Deindustrialization of America* (New York: Basic Books, 1982), p. 208.
4. Ibid., p. 218.
5. See especially Mike Cooley, "The Lucas Aerospace Plan," *Architect or Bee* (London: CSE Books, 1979).
6. Bluestone and Harrison, *The Deindustrialization of America*, p. 250.
7. David Noble, "Before the Fact: Social Choice in Machine Design," in Andrew Zimbalist, ed., *Case Studies in the Labor Process* (New York: Monthly Review Press, 1979).
8. The major problem with an economic policy oriented exclusively to high technology investment is illustrated by the Atari corporation's March 1983 decision to remove its 1700 worker California plant overseas, claiming "high labor costs." See "High Technology Jobs Going Overseas as U.S. Costs Rise," *New York Times*, 19 March 1983.
9. Alan Wolfe, *America's Impasse* (New York: Pantheon, 1981).
10. However, in Spring 1983 Congress accepted the recommendations of a bipartisan commission appointed by President Reagan to reform the social security system that gradually erodes such gains as retirement at age 65, indexing benefits to price rises and folds federal employees into the system rather than permitting them to retain a more lucrative private benefit plan.
11. The domestic content bill has two principal opponents: multinational corpora-

tions for whom free trade simply means the power to shift capital at will when "labor costs" or other production expenses are considered too high or when unions come knocking at the door; and some on the left who insist that the bill inhibits a trade policy that might benefit the Third World. The main problem with the latter view is that it remains insensitive to the use of free trade arguments to put world labor in competition with itself. Although domestic content legislation is no substitute for a genuine international labor movement, its provision would constitute a substantial deterrent to capital flight.

CONCLUSION

1. In recent years, liberal and conservative political science has declared the decline of race as a political issue. The ink was barely dry from this pronouncement when America's second city, Chicago, experienced the most racially motivated election in recent history, in which a progressive black congressperson Harold Washington faced his defeated primary opponent Jane Byrne and a Republican, both of whom hoped to benefit from the racial issue.

INDEX